Education for a Free Society

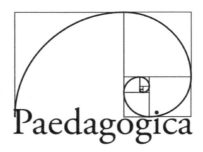

Paedagogica

Sebastian Engelmann, Norm Friesen and Karsten Kenklies
General Editors

Vol. 3

Education for a Free Society

Paul Feyerabend and the Pedagogy of Irritation

Karsten Kenklies and Sebastian Engelmann, Editors

PETER LANG
New York · Berlin · Bruxelles · Chennai · Lausanne · Oxford

Library of Congress Control Number: 2024931430

Bibliographic information published by the Deutsche Nationalbibliothek.
The German National Library lists this publication in the German
National Bibliography; detailed bibliographic data is available
on the Internet at http://dnb.d-nb.de.

Cover design by Peter Lang Group AG

ISBN 9781636676975 (hardback)
ISBN 9781636676944 (paperback)
ISBN 9781636676951 (ebook)
ISBN 9781636676968 (epub)
DOI 10.3726/b21660

© 2024 Peter Lang Group AG, Lausanne
Published by Peter Lang Publishing Inc., New York, USA
info@peterlang.com - www.peterlang.com

This book is dedicated to Olaf Breidbach (1957–2014), whose generous teaching illuminated worlds and minds. *Ex Ienā lux.*

Contents

Acknowledgements

The editors wish to thank not only our authors whose unwavering faith and assistance carried us through the whole process of preparing this publication, but also Grazia Borrini-Feyerabend, who offered support and help with this project from its very beginning in 2021 to its conclusion in 2024. Special thanks are also due to Louis Waterman-Evans, Matteo Collodel, Mike Stuart, Susann Hofbauer, Clemens Bach, and Piotr Zamojski, all for varied but indispensably supportive contributions in moving this project forward.

Part I: Feyerabend and the Pedagogy of Irritation: An Introduction

KARSTEN KENKLIES AND SEBASTIAN ENGELMANN

> Feyerabend, the Salvador Dali of academic philosophy, and currently the worst enemy of science
> Theocharis and Psimopoulos (1987, p. 596)

> Paul Feyerabend was a free spirit – irreverent, brilliant, outrageous, life-enhancing, unreliable and, for most who knew him, a lovable individual.
> Watkins (1994)

He was the *enfant terrible* of Philosophy, or more specifically: of the Philosophy of Science – Paul Feyerabend. It might not be an exaggeration to state that Feyerabend was one of the most influential forces that changed the Philosophy of Science in the second half of the twentieth century. He contributed to that seminal colloquium in London 1965, which – even though it was chaired by the more traditional Karl R. Popper – represented a new, historically and sociologically informed way of doing Philosophy of Science in discussing the ideas of Thomas S. Kuhn. Feyerabend, whose contribution is presented in *Criticism and the Growth of Knowledge* (Lakatos & Musgrave, 1970) arguably offered one of the highlights of that meeting in comparing modern science to organised crime. Based on his intimate knowledge of the history of the sciences and of the contemporary state of especially physics, his background in philosophy, and his genuine interest in the arts, Feyerabend never missed an opportunity to challenge prevalent views of the sciences and philosophy. Even though his seemingly anarchistic views often outraged the established circles of academia, it is, at least partially, to his credit that our understanding of the sciences and philosophy, of their proceedings and their influence in society, are viewed with a much more critical eye.

Born in 1924 in Vienna, Feyerabend was drafted into the German army in 1942, where he rose to the rank of Lieutenant. A battle injury received in 1945 would cause him health problems for the rest of his life. After the war, Feyerabend went to Thuringia to take on a job in the small town of Apolda and to study singing and stage-management in Weimar. Here he joined the 'Cultural Association for the Democratic Reform of Germany'. He then returned to Vienna to study history and sociology but soon became dissatisfied and therefore transferred to physics. Here he met the physicist Felix Ehrenhaft, whose scientific practice would influence his later views on the nature of science. Changing his subject again – this time to philosophy – he submitted his final thesis on observation sentences. Meeting him for the first time in 1948 at the international summer seminar of the Austrian College Society in Alpbach, Feyerabend became a follower of Karl Popper – a fellowship that he would later renounce in strong words. While in Vienna, Feyerabend became the leader of the 'Kraft Circle', a student philosophy club centred around Viktor Kraft, a former member of the Vienna Circle, who was his dissertation supervisor. It was also during this time that Feyerabend met Ludwig Wittgenstein, who visited the Kraft Circle to give a talk, and Bertolt Brecht. An invitation to come to Cambridge for further studies under Wittgenstein was accepted. Unfortunately, Wittgenstein died before Feyerabend arrived in Cambridge, and so he went to London instead to study with Popper; he remained, however, very closely connected to Wittgenstein and would proceed to publish on his philosophy. Although Popper applied for an extension of Feyerabend's scholarship, he decided to return to Vienna, while also declining an offer to become Popper's research assistant. Instead, he became the assistant of Arthur Pap in Vienna. After his first academic appointment at the University of Bristol, Feyerabend accepted a visiting researcher position at the University of California in Berkeley in 1958, which was turned into a permanent position just one year later. In Berkeley, Feyerabend gradually increased the intellectual distance to Popper, so that in 1970, not only *Consolations for the Specialist* was published, in which he attacked Popper from the perspective of Thomas S. Kuhn (*The Structure of Scientific Revolutions*, 1962/1970[2]), but also the essay version of 'Against Method: Outline of an Anarchistic Theory of Knowledge', in which he introduced for the first time his idea of an *epistemological anarchism*. After the plans to write a volume of *For and Against Method* together with Imre Lakatos had to be abandoned (Lakatos unfortunately died), Feyerabend published 1975 with *Against Method* his first book. He spent the following years defending the anarchistic epistemology and methodological plurality outlined here against his critics – attempts that culminated 1978 in the publication of *Science in a Free Society*, where he not only outlined his defence but also extended his argument into the political realm. The coming years saw a plethora of publications in which Feyerabend expanded and clarified his position, for example, through inclusion of reflections on the relation of the sciences and arts. In 1988, a second, revised edition of *Against Method* appeared. In 1989, after marrying Grazia Borrini, the couple left for Italy and Switzerland, and Feyerabend officially resigned from Berkeley in 1990. In between, he held several positions at different universities: University College London (1967–1970), the London School of Economics (1967), the FU Berlin (1968), Yale University (1969), the University of Auckland (1972, 1975), the University of Sussex (1974), the ETH Zurich (1980–1990); he presented lecture series at Stanford University (1967), the University of Kassel (1977) and the University of Trento (1992).

In 1993, Feyerabend developed an inoperable brain tumour, and was hospitalised. Paul Feyerabend died in Genolier, Canton Vaud, Switzerland, on 11 February 1994. Posthumously, three more books were published: *Killing Time: The Autobiography of Paul Feyerabend* (1995), *Conquest of Abundance* (1999), and *Naturphilosophie* (2009). *Against Method* was most recently republished in 2010, accompanied by a preface written by Canadian philosopher of science Ian Hacking who calls the book 'the Woodstock of Philosophy'. Feyerabend, one can take away from this, is as present as ever and people still engage with his work.

Feyerabend's broad interest in cultural affairs touched, of course, questions about education and about the ways people are educated (or: indoctrinated) into scientific beliefs and worldviews. He famously argued that education is only then true education if its teaching includes a backdoor through which one is able to leave behind exactly those teachings. He was always appalled by the way in which sciences and philosophy are taught as indisputable truths, as facts rather than as imperfect, questionable theories or, even better, as practices of searching and philosophising. And he was appalled by the closed-mindedness of a scientifically grounded and philosophically defended education system, which seemed to exclude or belittle different ways of knowing and living. It is for those reasons that the editors decided for the main title for this volume: Education for a Free Society. Obviously mirroring the naming of one of Feyerabend's own publications (*Science for a Free Society*), the title expresses our conviction that freedom represents one of or maybe even the most fundamental characteristics Feyerabend demands for education in its various guises; freedom, as the opportunity and capacity of accepting or rejecting the structures, opinions, perspectives that everybody is so forcefully invited to accept and share in a society, seems to lie at the very heart of everything Feyerabend thought about and practised as education.

In contrast to what he despised as traditional teaching and educating, Feyerabend in his own educational endeavours – in his books, his university seminars, his lectures and presentations – developed and practised a pedagogy of irritation that was based mainly on three approaches: (a) the demand of a historical consciousness, (b) the inclusion of intercultural-comparative explorations, and (c) a somewhat controversial way of communicating.

Unlike so many philosophers of science before him, Feyerabend was adamant that a true description of science must rely on investigations of those who are actually involved in doing science or regarded as scientists. Not only through his personal acquaintance with some of the most remarkable scientists of his age, but especially through his vast knowledge of historic figures in the development of the sciences – of their ways of working and thinking – Feyerabend was able to present to the astonished academic world in-depth accounts of lived science that seemed very different from the usually more normative than descriptive accounts the philosophers of science presented (Gillies, 2011; Heit & Oberheim, 2016). In this way, Feyerabend was able to prove that scientists and their predecessors are and always have been a lot more idiosyncratic, implausible, irrational than often acknowledged, and that the scientific work that is done results by no means in a straight line of progress. Feyerabend therefore must be considered as one of the predecessors of Science and Technology Studies as we know them nowadays. His historical explorations were irritating in the best ways possible: by grasping science as a situated practice, they questioned the status quo and the generally accepted narratives regarding the development and the nature of the sciences and, in doing so, he opened up the space for a much more honest and adequate understanding – and appreciation! – of one of the ways in which (at least some) humans attempted and still attempt to make sense of the world in which they live – an understanding that would, for example, also include awareness of the diverse aberrations that irritated and still irritate the development of scientific thought (as Queiroz & Garcia in this volume argue).

However, this irritation through engaging in diachronic comparison, that is, historical research, was not the only way Feyerabend chose to create moments of what can be seen as enlightening alienation (Kenklies, 2022). Also through synchronic comparisons, that is, intercultural encounters and social-anthropological research, he was able to irritate and question generally accepted truths and convictions (Donyavi & Moghaddam, 2016; Preston, 1998). Feyerabend's explorations of different cultures did not only show that scientific thinking as it has developed over centuries in 'the West' (ignoring for a moment the Occidentalism ingrained in such a notion) was just one way of many to build a relation of knowledge with the world in which we live, but they also proved that there is no convincing reason to regard the scientific approach to world and life as the single-most successful one – given that concepts like *success, truth* and *happiness* are embedded into and are part of an individual culture and, as such, hardly evaluable from outside this very culture. Based on such insights, Feyerabend proposed a form of pluralism that remained a challenge not only for epistemological or ethical but also educational theory and practice – as Garcia in this volume is able to show. And it also meant that individual approaches to world-building and meaning-making should be taken much more seriously than in previous practices of (especially science) education. The discussions of Essex in this volume give a lively example of such considerations.

Based especially on his experiences in Berkeley, Feyerabend's own pedagogical practice became nothing less than irritating and controversial at times. He

> began to teach deliberately unorthodox material – such as the history of witch-craft – and to directly and provocatively challenge some of the major tenets of modern societies, such as its faith in the rationality of science. Such critical pedagogy soon expanded to include 'guest lecturers', such as astrologers, witches and warlocks, and members of the Gay Liberation Front and the left-wing pacifist Students for a Democratic Society – all this against the backdrop of the civil rights and gay liberation movements […]. (Kidd, 2013, p. 411)

Feyerabend's view of the educator as performer (see papers of Frimberger and Shaw in this volume) made him a rather special university tutor and, if his invented dialogues (e.g. Feyerabend, 1991) are even only a vague representation of his style of communicating, then talking to him must sometimes have been a real adventure. And challenge. His lectures certainly represented a departure from the usual – and he is fondly remembered for his theatricality – and for the irritation caused:

> As can be imagined, these lectures were very enjoyable indeed, but I could not help wondering whether Feyerabend really believed what he said. Feyerabend never used formal or mathematical logic, but he had a brilliant command of informal logic and argument. I suspect that he must have learnt his skills in argument, at least in part, from Popper. This skill in argument, combined with enormous historical erudition, meant that Feyerabend was always able to defend his position against objections. But did he really believe that in say 1640, the theory of witchcraft was better confirmed by empirical evidence and rational argument than Galileo's science; or that Copernicanism triumphed over the Ptolemaic theory just because its advocates were more skilful propagandists? Did he believe these things, or was he just saying them to create a stir, and make himself well-known for his outrageous views? There was something very

enigmatic about Feyerabend, and I was never sure what he really did believe. (Gillies, 2011, p. 13)

Unlike many other lecturers, Feyerabend was teaching to induce reflection – not necessarily to transmit knowledge (although he used his extensive knowledge in history, philosophy, arts, anthropology, etc. to build his lines of argument) but to enable a dialogue (maybe in the form Robertson/Prajapati/ Chen are presenting in their paper); for him, it was of marginal importance to create a school of followers and believers. And remaining – maybe frustratingly – hazy and seemingly insincere was (and still is) an irritating but nevertheless brilliant way of detracting unwanted sycophants.

This educational side of Paul Feyerabend has yet to receive the appreciation it deserves: despite occasional papers on Feyerabend touching on the subject, there is not yet a single monograph or edited volume that is devoted to Feyerabend's Philosophy of Educational Theory and Practice. His reflections touch on a wide range of pedagogical issues, from questions around the shape of educational theories & educational research (see the chapter of Kenklies in the present volume) or the role the sciences play or should play in education to the discussion around educational aims and methods for which he proposed a unique and very much enlightening approach that connects him closely to Continental European discussions around *Bildung* in its broadest sense.

This volume will address the lacuna with regard to Feyerabend's pedagogy. It will explore at least some of the different educational perspectives to which Feyerabend's thoughts make a highly original and creative contribution. In each section, different scholars from across the globe will present and discuss the ways in which Feyerabend challenges prevalent convictions and enriches future discussions.

After this introduction, *Bernhard Hemetsberger* begins the first section of this volume – *Irritations: Paul Feyerabend in Education Studies* – with his reflections on the absence of an extended reception of Feyerabend in the existing research literature on education. His appearances in educational discussions are so sparse – and more often than not consist in a mere name check – that *Hemetsberger* feels justified to speak of him as a *theoretical bystander*. Not being content to just state such a fact, the author also presents some reflections on the possible reasons of Feyerabend's scarce presence before then exploring the different facets and educational perspectives, under which a discussion of Feyerabend's ideas and theories would be of great importance and inspiration. And it is one of those perspectives, which is then explored in the following chapter by *Karsten Kenklies*: the problem of theoretical concepts in Education Studies. Such a discussion is made more complex by the fact that there are indeed different traditions of Education Studies – traditions, which seem to have produced a variety of approaches in relation to educational theorising. In exploring those different approaches and the inspiration each could draw from Feyerabend's musings on theoretical concepts and language in general, *Kenklies* shows that such discussions are indispensable as they constitute the foundation for educational theorising in general.

The second section – *Inclusions: Feyerabend and Science Pedagogy* – is devoted to arguably the most obvious field within education for which Feyerabend has provided very important and relevant inspirations: science education. *Jane Essex* initiates in her chapter those explorations with a hitherto undiscussed connection between Feyerabend's views on science and scientific practices, the ways in which they are taught and/or presented, and the efforts around a science education that is (much more) inclusive of those pupils and students who in the usual approaches to science education are either seriously disadvantaged or even left out completely. *Essex* shows that Feyerabend's descriptions and expectations of scientific thinking are much better suited to ideas of inclusive education and pedagogy than the understandings of science, its theories and practices, that usually underpin the contemporary approaches to science education. After this chapter has shown that the definition of science itself has fundamental implications for the way it is taught and presented, the next chapter of *Deivide Garcia da Silva Oliveira* continues with a similar discussion. This text explores the pervasive influence of a uniform and monist perspective on science education and the associated problems it creates, such as indoctrination and disinterest of students in science (crisis in science teaching). Drawing on Feyerabend's pluralist philosophy, it challenges the assumption that rationality, objectivity, and truth exclusively belong to the scientific tradition. The aim is to advocate for a pluralist understanding of science, arguing that epistemic values are not confined to one tradition. The paper proposes a nuanced approach to science education, emphasizing critical thinking, proficiency ('game approach') to foster pluralist science education. The game approach claims that it is possible in daily practice to teach science without aiming to change people's system of beliefs. The chapter shows that there are an alternative to uniform science education, and it offers a path towards a more inclusive and enriching educational experience when using the Feyerabend's concept of proficiency. Expanding on the more practical aspects addressed in the previous chapter, *Lília Ferreira Souza Queiroz*, together with *Deivide Garcia da Silva Oliveira*, explores in the following chapter the question of the general content of science teaching. Contrary to what usually is presented in a science curriculum, she argues with the support of Feyerabend for the inclusion of errors and aberrations when teaching (about) science. Expanding teaching in this way could, so the argument goes, sensitise for the preliminary nature of scientific 'truths' and, maybe counter-intuitively, raise the acceptance of scientific explanations in light of the contemporary increase in anti-intellectual and/or anti-scientific sentiment: instead of an unwavering presentation of science as a collection of undeniable truths – an endeavour destined to failure in a complex modern world – it would be the inclusion of knowledge around scientific struggles and imperfections, that is, of episodes of the meandering history of science, that could build trust and faith in scientific worldviews.

The third section – *Performances: Feyerabend and Pedagogical Practice* – is devoted to more general discussions and explorations of Feyerabend's pedagogical practice. *Katja Frimberger* opens the section with a chapter which explores the theatrical aspects of Feyerabend's work and its relationship to the concept of theatre as introduced by Bertolt Brecht. Feyerabend became intimately acquainted with theatre during his stay in Apolda and especially in Weimar, where he studied theatre while taking classes in harmony, piano, singing, enunciation, and Italian. At Weimar's *Nationaltheater*, he regularly attended performances. As Frimberger shows, those influences and, especially Brecht's idea of a transformative theatre, had a significant influence on the development of Feyerabend's ideas around the relation of the arts and sciences in the process of the generation of knowledge. In the next chapter, *Jamie Shaw* discusses Feyerabend's views on the relation of education and intellectual maturity. Always worried about the ways in which so-called 'intellectuals' tend to erect a hegemony of (their very own idea of) rationality & culturality, Feyerabend – according to Shaw – developed not only a (more pluralist) theory of science but also an educational practice as university lecturer that was meant to serve as counter-point to such universalist endeavours while it attempted to respond to what Kant formulated as the foundational question of modern education: How can freedom be cultivated through – or being kept alive despite the existence of – educational influence? The last chapter of this section – written as a collaboration of *Nicola Robertson, Vijayita Prajapati*, and *Yueling Chen* – does not so much *talk about* Feyerabend's pedagogy, but endeavours to *represent it* in one of its major manifestations: as an intellectual exploration in the form of a dialogue. Addressing one of the fundamental pedagogical questions for Feyerabend – the question of the relation of world, individual freedom, and education – the authors succeed not only in highlighting the different positions and perspectives necessarily involved in such a discussion, but they achieve this through employing a method Feyerabend himself used to present his views. Emulating his method, the chapter shows the inspirational potential of this kind of writing (and discussing).

It is our hope that our readers will be inspired to follow those (or other) pedagogical trails to continue what we have started in the previous chapters: a journey to discover the various ways in which Paul Feyerabend has contributed and can still contribute to the pedagogical discussions of our time.

References

Donyavi, M., & Moghaddam Heydari, G. (2016). The impact of anthropology on Feyerabend's ontology, epistemology and methodology. *Philosophy of Science*, 6(11), 37–52.

Feyerabend, P. (1991). *Three dialogues on knowledge*. Blackwell.

Gillies, D. (2011). *Lakatos, Popper, and Feyerabend: Some personal reminiscences*. Paper delivered to the University College London, 28 February 2011. http://www.ucl.ac.uk/sts/staff/gillies/gillies_2011_lakatos_popper_feyerabend.pdf

Heit, H., & Oberheim, E. (2016). Paul Feyerabend: An historical philosopher of nature. In P. Feyerabend (Ed.), *Philosophy of nature* (pp. vii–xxvii). Polity.

Kenklies, K. (2022). Alienation: The foundation of transformative education. *Journal of Philosophy of Education*, 56(4), 577–592. https://doi.org/10.1111/1467-9752.12703

Kidd, I. J. (2013). Feyerabend on science and education. *Journal of Philosophy of Education*, 47(3), 407–422. https://doi.org/10.1111/1467-9752.12009

Lakatos, I., & Musgrave, A. (Eds.). (1970). *Criticism and the growth of knowledge: Proceedings of the international colloquium in the philosophy of science, London, 1965*. Cambridge University Press. https://doi.org/10.1017/CBO9781139171434

Preston, J. (1998). Science as supermarket: 'Post-modern' themes in Paul Feyerabend's later philosophy of science. *Studies in History and Philosophy of Science, Part A*, 29(3), 425–447. https://doi.org/10.1016/s0039-3681(98)00015-6

Theocharis, T., & Psimopoulos, M. (1987). Where science has gone wrong. *Nature*, 329, 595–598. https://doi.org/10.1038/329595a0

Watkins, J. (1994). Obituary. *Independent*, 4 March 1994 (Online). https://www.independent.co.uk/news/people/obituary-professor-paul-feyerabend-1426902.html

Part II: Irritations: Paul Feyerabend in Education Studies

Theoretical Bystander? Paul Feyerabend's Reception in Publications on Education

BERNHARD HEMETSBERGER

Vienna in the 1920s, the birthplace of Paul Feyerabend and Helmut Qualtinger, must have been a miserable but stimulating city. These circumstances provoked a search for uncommon scientific and cultural ideas and expressions (e.g. Vienna Circle, Viennese Modernism, Second Viennese School [of atonal music]). Both teenagers felt that literature, theatre and music could help to individually handle interwar and later war problems as well as issues of growing up in breaking with traditional *petit bourgeois* sentiments and their personal war involvements (Feyerabend, 1980, pp. 214–241, especially footnote 109, 1995, pp. 25–35; Wendt, 2003). However, their liberating struggles only came with alienation and resistance; thus, Feyerabend's philosophical and Qualtinger's comedic careers took time to settle, or they flourished abroad. If they ever aimed at (domestic) acceptance or defined the value of their work via popularity, the satirist Qualtinger was maybe proven right that '[i]n Vienna you first 've to die, before they celebrate you. But then you're living long' (Der Spiegel, 1986). Obviously, both are included in some or another contemporary historical survey or memory of Austria's post-war period, especially when their birth or death anniversaries are approaching. It so comes that in 2024 Paul Feyerabend's centennial will bear new books and anthologies, assessing his influences on various fields and disciplines. Qualtinger's name already decorates a Viennese council housing block since 1998 to posthumously celebrate his 70th birthday.

Even though a Plutarchian *bioi paralleloi* (parallel biographies) would be alluring, showing striking biographical similarities and opening a historical understanding of the twentieth century, this chapter focuses on Paul Feyerabend's reception in publications on education. This is seemingly a comparable arbitrary question as mentioning Qualtinger in the same breath with

Feyerabend. After all, the latter is predominantly classified as a philosopher,[1] even a classic there (Döring, 1998, p. 7), but is rarely seen as an educator or theoretical source for the foundations of education, although some references are detectable (e.g. Thompson, 2018; Wolfmeyer, 2017, p. 328). These dispersed references should be systematized in the following, to overlook the presence of Paul Feyerabend in publications on education as otherwise the claim of his absence or presence misses an empirical base. In order to leave prejudiced bubbles of Feyerabend's weight in education theory, I will map the references by using bibliometric approaches (Ball, 2014; Goldie et al., 2014). Aware of problems this access contains (Flaatten, 2015; Hauschke, 2019), and what Feyerabend (1975, p. 43) thought about 'this appearance of success', I will present my findings in the first section (I). In the following – section two (II) – I try to offer interpretations to the meagre results found. While additional thoughts and questions (III) close the chapter, indicating hints to the inspiration Feyerabend could bear for today's educational theory.

1. Wanted: Paul Feyerabend – Dead or Alive?

There are various possibilities to get an impression of how researchers and their work disseminated, were referenced, processed or conquered. The history of ideas (e.g. Zumhof, 2021), network analysis (e.g. Ball & Junemann, 2012) or bibliometrics (e.g. Ball, 2014) are currently well-known and flourishing sectors in scientific research. Is the moment of origin giving birth to later on influential thoughts of significance or should network analysis probably show that 'echo chambers' give the impression of important ideas, one should better have heard of (Goldie et al., 2014)? Albeit, Paul Feyerabend is, at least for students of philosophical programs, already a familiar name (see Döring, 1998). His overall presence in scientific publications is remarkable indeed, but not outstanding. In order to get an overview on this rating and on referencing Paul Feyerabend in scientific publications in any field, one could consult two major sources providing easily accessible databases.[2] JSTOR and Taylor & Francis (T&F) provide data through metadata, n-grams, and word counts for most articles and book chapters, and for all research reports and pamphlets available for download on

---

1 I am very grateful to my friend and philosopher of law, Jakob E. Gaigg, for his key questions, hints and ideas by which this chapter was enriched.
2 Scopus and Web of Science were used as comparative databases and showed similar results, requiring paid membership though. JSTOR and T&F should allow critical readers of this chapter to recheck my data on a free basis. These databases cover predominantly English, besides Spanish, German and publications written in other languages.

their homepages (JSTOR 2022). Until 2020, JSTOR counts 6,441 hits for the name Paul Feyerabend, compared to 1,233 via T&F. To avoid double counts, the numbers remain separated, but they already offer a first glimpse to Feyerabend references. A closer investigation of these numbers shows that the respective education sections of JSTOR name 289 references to Feyerabend, which are 4 % of all references. Similarly, T&F reveals 10 % of all Feyerabend references to education, which are 134 hits. A visualisation (see Graph 1) helps to evaluate the ratios.

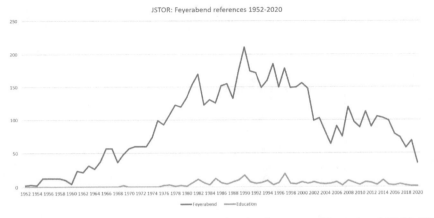

JSTOR: Feyerabend references 1952-2020

Graph 1: Overall references and education-related references to Feyerabend 1952–2020 covered by JSTOR

The section categorisation of 'education' with JSTOR and T&F was, besides a list of covered journals, not specified. Therefore, the criteria used to categorise the respective journals to the 'education' section remain blurred. However, journal lists are easily available on the homepages; counting 177 with JSTOR and 274 with T&F. These are the first limitations of the empirical analysis; however, the graph shows rising and declining periods of referencing Feyerabend. In all fields covered by the databases, a normal distribution appears, starting with Feyerabend entering the world of academia and publishing in the 1950s to the end of 2020. From the 1970s to the first decade of the new millennium Feyerabend was – in his league – intensively quoted or mentioned in disciplines and fields covered by JSTOR with an all-time high of 211 in 1990. For both graph lines a decrease during the last years is recorded, while Feyerabend *grosso modo* is no main reference point in any field, compared with Karl Popper (20,248 in all fields and 888 in education; JSTOR), Thomas Kuhn (55,114/ 3,583 JSTOR) or Michel Foucault (63,631/3,042 T&F), for example.

Publications assigned to education by JSTOR and T&F never surpassed the level of 19 mentions of Paul Feyerabend in a year. The outstanding years were

1990 with 17 and 1997 with 19 mentions. T&F lists 7 mentions in 1991 and 6 in 2008 as years of most intensive referencing. Why these years surpassed, if only marginally, others would call for a closer investigation of topics covered in these years in educational publications. A textual analysis would compensate these empirical shortcomings and offer insight to referenced texts by Feyerabend in educational publications. It is possible though, to point out which texts of Feyerabend were most prominently used when dealing with educational questions (see Graphs 2 and 3).

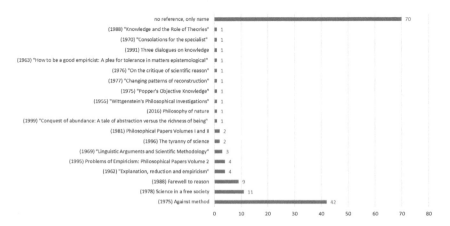

Graph 2: T&F covers 134 references to Feyerabend in education-related publications, using the listed pieces

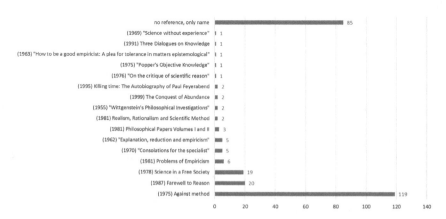

Graph 3: JSTOR covers 256 references to Feyerabend in education-related publications, using the listed pieces

JSTOR covers 256 hits for Paul Feyerabend in their education section. In 85 cases only the name appears, without any reference to one of his publications. Predominantly, Feyerabend is not named as a single person either, but in combination, as *trio infernal*, with Popper and Kuhn, sometimes also together with Lakatos. Some mentions are reviews of a publication or introductions to an issue and therefore show a different structure. In total, 171 educational publications remain where Feyerabend is referenced, either with multiple publications used or with one single reference. *Against Method* was clearly employed as the main reference point. 119 mentions are by far beyond *Farewell to Reason* (20) and *Science in a Free Society* (19). Way behind in this list are *Problems of Empiricism* (6), 'Consolations for the Specialist' (5), and 'Explanation, Reduction and Empiricism' (5).

For T&F 134 hits in the education section were counted. Again, a considerable number of 70 publications only refer to Paul Feyerabend as a name, without revealing a source. As for the data of JSTOR, this has nothing to say about the intensity and depth of using Paul Feyerabend. 64 publications remain, referencing the author of interest with publications. A similar picture as with JSTOR appears. In the first place, *Against Method* is referenced 42 times. Again, followed by *Science in a Free Society* (11) and *Farewell to Reason* (9), 'Explanation, Reduction and Empiricism' (4) and *Problems of Empiricism* (4) are mentioned. 'Linguistic Arguments and Scientific Methodology' (3) replaces 'Consolations for the Specialist' from JSTOR's ranking. So, what can we possibly conclude with these findings? Is Paul Feyerabend, with a special consideration of the field of education, dead or alive as a reference point?

2. *Interrogation: Paul Feyerabend's Plea – an Interpretation*

To claim Feyerabend's irrelevance in publications on education would be exaggerated. However, Feyerabend was only received scarcely in publications on questions of education (see, e.g. Geelan, 2001, 2006; Kidd, 2013, 2016). Also, my limited data analysis supports the hitherto unchecked opinion of some literature that Feyerabend is to be considered a *theoretical bystander* when it comes to theories, systems or foundations of education published during the last seventy years. His meagre presence – my *first* interpretation – does not mean complete absence or invisibility of Feyerabend in publications on education though, but places him at the sideline. A brighter general visibility is dated back to a period during 1970 and 2010, with a peak in 1990. A possible connection to the publication of *Against Method* and *Science in a Free Society* during the late 1970s and *Farewell to Reason* at the end of the 1980s seems plausible. They provoked loud and harsh criticism (Preston,

1997), Feyerabend himself perpetuated with likewise reactions (see, e.g. Feyerabend, 1976, p. 45, footnote 6,[3] 1980, chapter 7, appendix). In educational publications only in 1990 and 1997 a higher frequency of references is observable, which might be connected to these discussions.

Therefore, the *second* interpretation seeks for a possible answer as to why Feyerabend was overall hardly referenced in educational publications. At crucial points of his arguments in *Against Method* (1975, e.g. pp. 52–53) and *Science in a Free Society* (1980, e.g. p. 71, pp. 77–78, p. 93, p. 116, footnote 4, chapter 11) Feyerabend concludes that education, school systems and teachings are suppressive, confining and inhibiting in their current shape. These two publications were predominantly referenced in educational publications, as they probably provoked responses or processing. It seems, without digging into these referencing publications on a textual level, that the deficit diagnosis of Feyerabend opened up a possibility for these referencing texts to claim changes and reforms in education and schooling, as well as to express dissatisfaction with scientific approaches to educational phenomena as, for example, Richard Rorty (1988, p. 23, 1989) did. These public educational reform claims, constantly looming and detectable (Hemetsberger, 2022), however, were most loudly stated during the 1960s to the 1980s and Feyerabend may therefore have missed earlier and more 'fertile ground' (Koselleck, 1959, p. 86) for this sort of critique. This could be an explanation why Feyerabend was never really intensively processed – positively recognised, productively affiliated or negatively refused – in educational publications; he was for educational debates 'late to the show' (which was not his intention to participate in, to be fair). Moreover, the decline of references in publications on education to Feyerabend up to the present day may find an explanation here as well.

However, offering a *third* interpretative comment, if Feyerabend was referenced, he was as often indicated only by name as *Against Method*, which is about 160 times adding up data from JSTOR and T&F. This number indicates that Feyerabend was probably likewise used as a 'brand' or even 'catchy person' under the assumption that readers will get the link as verifiable text passages were referenced. The observation that in many cases Feyerabend was named in a row with colleagues, when only the name is outlined, also allows for a different interpretation: named in line with Popper and Kuhn seems to marginalise Feyerabend (in education as well as other fields), being placed third in this line, or refers to conceptual differences. While Popper is famous for his doctrine of falsification, Kuhn is referenced very often for his idea of scientific revolutions, which both offer interpretations to explain change in

---

3 Interestingly, this footnote is not included in the original English edition of 1975 at p. 28.

scientific paradigms, where Feyerabend (e.g. 1970) counterposed his claim of *anything goes*. This anarchistic approach should explain and enable progress that in any way anybody is free to choose (Feyerabend, 1976, pp. 44–45). Critics and many educators being used to directive approaches, found this idea too chaotic or imprecise (Feyerabend, 1980, appendix). The need of explanation, regarding the numerous misinterpretations of this concept (addressed by Feyerabend, 1980, p. 150, chapter 7), may have affected his position as little persuasive reference.

It seems, *fourth* interpretation, there is no systematic positioning of Feyerabend in publications on education or in educational dictionaries, which draw more extensively on Popper or Kuhn. Some study textbooks (e.g. Hutterer, 2008, pp. 205–206) include Feyerabend however – probably also because of local reasons at the University of Vienna – only to conclude that his concept of *anything goes* offers no more than consolation to deeply specialised and scientifically constrained educational researchers. Besides these interpretations, educational texts referencing Feyerabend may lack citations themselves, creating inspiration for fellow researchers or 'echo chambers' (Goldie et al., 2014) to increase references to his works. Another assumption for Feyerabend's marginal reception in this field could be his own casual mode of 'including a backdoor through which one is able to leave', without any aspiration to convince or build a body of students and followers (Feyerabend, 1995, pp. 121–126) spreading and promoting his ideas.

This does not mean that Paul Feyerabend is in any case irrelevant for educational thinking. He wrote in fragments about education himself, which is not significantly referenced though, whereas education is a central axis of his ideas (see above). *Fifth* interpretation, Feyerabend's awareness of the problem of teaching and education probably did not meet the *zeitgeist* of a majority of educational researchers when published. They were used to decide on matter, meaning, and choice (Labaree, 2010) and not so much on the 'self-abandonment' of trained professional habitus. Even when he is rarely clear about the question of education, beyond fundamental criticism, there are paragraphs shedding light on his conception: He imagines education that would live from a rich reservoir of different points of view permitting the choice of traditions most advantageous to the individual. The teacher's task would consist of facilitating this choice, not in replacing it by some 'truth' of his own (Feyerabend, 1980, p. 235). This is important to Feyerabend (1995, p. 97) as young people 'see the world in a special way, and yet the slightest pressure can make them see it differently. A good teacher respects this instability. Unfortunately, most educators use it "to teach the truth," as they call the process of imparting their own puny ideas.' It should become clearer why he thought that teaching necessitates to 'include a backdoor through which one is able to leave'. Critics responded that neither good nor bad are addressable respectively (Feyerabend, 1980, p. 216) so, '[w]hat can we do while our criminals, their judges and henchmen, while the philosophers, poets, prophets who try to force us into their patterns, and while we, who are collaborators or victims or simply bystanders, are still in a barbaric state? The answer is obvious: with a few exceptions we shall act in a barbaric way' (Feyerabend, 1995, p. 175).

3. Judgment: Paul Feyerabend as Theoretical Bystander in Education?

It seems plausible to frame Paul Feyerabend as a theoretical bystander in the field of education, when assessing references to him. However, Feyerabend's oeuvre includes worthwhile ideas and inspirational even inviting thoughts to think about as educational researcher. As the previous sections showed, this means one has to handle prejudices and misinterpretations as well as a rarely used body of literature and ideas. Moreover, there are fundamental questions one should consider in order to link Feyerabend and educational questions.

Obviously, Feyerabend (1980, p. 33) deals with ideas of cosmology, that is, questions of fundamental structures organising life. This excludes, or at least sidelines questions of cosmogony, that is, the question of accounts of the absolute origins of matter, space and time especially ancient Greeks rated central (Gregory, 2007, p. 1). While cosmology assumes an existent order, cosmogony asks for the possible origins of orders. This difference explains Feyerabend's paleness when it comes to outline or to foster change. Feyerabend (1975, p. 24) is content with the expectation of 'catastrophic changes in the physical environment, wars, the breakdown of encompassing systems of morality, political revolutions, [that] will transform adult reaction patterns as well, including important patterns of argumentation. Such a transformation may again be an entirely natural process and the only function of a rational argument may lie in the fact that it increases the mental tension that precedes and causes the behavioral outburst.' As suppressive traditions could be, and traditions seem to be indicated by adult reaction patterns, this approach needs to wait for catastrophes and crises in order to stimulate change. Furthermore, in Feyerabend's (1980, pp. 41–43) view, it is fundamentally different if one is observer or participant of a tradition and hence interpreting something as catastrophic or not. Change is in fact inherent in traditions that one gets to know only by participation (Feyerabend, 1980, p. 116, footnote 4). Via education this change is not precipitated, as famous divergent arguments and promises explain. However, this may conceptualise education way too narrow for Feyerabend. Anyhow, education is seen as centre of power, which all traditions should equally have access to (Feyerabend, 1980, p. 72) in order to undermine supremacy of only one tradition. This is of importance, as education is one technique of conquering differing traditions by expansive and ambitious traditions, though (Feyerabend, 1980, p. 71). The position of argumentation Feyerabend inhabits is itself inevitably tied to a tradition one grew up with, was socialised into and frames the perception of life, but aims for an opening of the tradition and in a way for a superordinate instance (actually impossible within relativist thinking). We have one dichotomy here which Feyerabend leaves unanswered[4] and open for educational researchers. *How is education conceptualised, when its role is predefined by more or less stable traditions, which should be concurrently opened to tolerate various other traditions through non-conductive education?*

Given the appearance of change, education – especially institutionalised education – still bears the danger of indoctrination and hence makes individuals unfree (Feyerabend, 1980, p. 118, footnote 5). This idea stems from the false assumption, according to Feyerabend (1980, p. 18), that institutions are there to protect individuals. How education should be organised instead, besides educational institutions, in a highly specialised and differentiated society remains an open question. Richard Rorty (1989, p. 200) suggests, while sticking to institutional forms, that 'primary and secondary education will always be a matter of familiarizing the young with what their elders take to be true, whether it is true or not. It is not, and never will be, the function of lower-level education to challenge the prevailing consensus about what is true. Socialization has to come before individuation, and education for freedom cannot begin before some constraints have been imposed.' He divides pre-college and college education and introduces the idea of matureness, enabling college youth to critically get rid of knowledge, truth-claims and ideas, which were taught in elementary and secondary schools. Feyerabend (1980, p. 168, 294) applies matureness as well, when it comes to participate in a free society. Matureness is learnt with active involvement in decisions of open approaches, meaning citizens' groups, and failures as well as accomplishments – the best strategy also for education (Feyerabend, 1980, p. 165). However, the level of matureness to fully participate in a free society is not specified. While Rorty assumes to encourage pupils in advanced levels

4 Even when asked straightforwardly, Feyerabend (1980, pp. 287–289) vaguely replied to assess this on a case-to-case basis and via citizens' groups, which are by the way conceptualised as ultimately capable of arranging a common criteria of decision finding. One has to ask, where this criterion is coming from.

of schooling to reject previously learnt ideas to break free, Feyerabend prefers never to allow pupils to get in touch with predefined approaches in order to stay free. However, trial and error are only certifiable within a community (and its conception of truth), where citizens' groups would most probably recruit their members to moreover agree on certain decisions according to their shared rules and ideas. The question arises: *How is education freely socialising people or what is to be considered education besides an undirected traditionalising of young people to matureness?*

Moreover, content in educational settings would be an additional field of interest to highlight. Feyerabend (1980, pp. 193, 233) suggests to publicly control taught content which is presented only if free citizens need this information. Besides the superordinate instance of public control, which is worth questioning (see above), the idea of deciding on when and what information is needed stays unclear. The utility of information has to be decided on the purpose of free citizens and defend itself to the direction of a small, white, intellectual group of 'facists of ideas' aka scientists (Feyerabend, 1980). How to meet desires of groups eager to learn, though? 'During the days of the so-called student revolution I discussed the philosophies that had accompanied earlier revolutionary movements. [...] More black people turned up in my classes (many more, percentagewise, than are on campus today), and I was often at a loss. Should I continue feeding them the intellectual delicacies that were part of the white culture? I was a teacher, a professor even; I had accumulated information about all sorts of things and had strong opinions on a variety of topics and little respect for the leading lights of my profession. But now I felt ignorant and out of place' (Feyerabend, 1995, p. 123). The double bind of Feyerabend being a professor and choosing content stays precarious, although the audience chooses freely to participate. Even if individuals are connecting in deciding on content to be taught in citizens' groups (Feyerabend, 1980, pp. 104, 232), the mechanisms and power relations need to be considered. Feyerabend presents a way how he tried to address these problems within institutionalised university teaching:

> I gave two standard lectures, one on general philosophy, the other on the philosophy of science. I also ran a seminar in which I would invite the participants to expound their own ideas. That was not the customary way of doing things. Most of my colleagues turned seminars into means for spreading their views or the views of the school to which they belonged. [...] I preferred a more informal procedure. Some seminars were excellent, other were the pits. [...] Still, I didn't like big shots in my seminars – they always made me feel silly. They took ideas seriously while I just tried to get things over with. I hardly ever prepared my lectures; I made a few notes and expected rhetoric to carry me through. The

method had worked on my lecture trips. But filling space with noise for an entire semester was a different matter. (Feyerabend, 1995, pp. 121–122)

While Feyerabend seemingly found a way to deal with problems of teaching within his mindset and theoretical ideas, the question of quality, that is, the utility of content for free citizens participating in teachings and the question of didactical arrangements, that is, the moves to increase comprehensibility of content, beyond intuition while participating in traditions (Feyerabend, 1980, p. 116, footnote 4), remain open questions. Teaching cannot surpass a formal concatenation of various ideas without cohesion, considering the relativist accusation of exclusion against whatever positioning (Feyerabend, 1975, p. 52). Education in this pluralistic approach misses by definition an ordering and cohering instance, so, *Which content is more than noise and educative in a utilitarian sense for free citizens?*

If socialising and communalising content, as common ground, various individuals (even as members of different traditions) could rely on and find ways to communicate with each other is missing, Feyerabend nevertheless sees no mandatory potential of conflict between individuals or traditions. This thesis underlays the assumption though, that these different traditions and individuals are in any way concerned about the other and are willing to employ separate rules than the 'law of the strongest'. In this view, interactions of traditions and their results are dependent on historical circumstances and different case-by-case (Feyerabend, 1980, p. 39). It seems plausible and possible, however, that no common principle is found in these interactions to agree on (Feyerabend, 1980, p. 56) and state structures are only justifiable to guarantee free space for traditions and the possibility for coexistence (again, a superordinate instance, actually not thinkable with Feyerabend), while the idea of a pluralism of values, ideas and theories should enhance citizen's lives more than one single 'ideology' (Feyerabend, 1980, pp. 19–20). Traditions, overall, seem very much hypostatised and as unitary blocks for Feyerabend (e.g. 2005) implying constant talk at cross purposes. Several questions arise here, but a central one in our context would be: *How can different traditions meet each other or get in contact when common ground is missing, inter alia states – defined by spacial borders – and content – defined by comprehensive structures – usually provide?*

This imperfect set of questions and thoughts from an educational perspective towards the work of Paul Feyerabend may inspire further involvement of his ideas in pedagogical approaches. However, the work already done in education and building a base to start connected theoretical reflections with Paul Feyerabend is quite limited. The empirical, bibliometric approach employed in the first section showed the rare use of Feyerabend in publications on education and especially the narrow reception of his work, focusing especially on *About Method, Farewell to Reason* and *Science in a Free Society*. A broader reception of Feyerabend's publications may stimulate foundational ideas of education and to a certain extent also for society and science. However, the helped along turn of Feyerabend from a theoretical bystander to a significant voice in education may open up the question of the scientific status of education studies at universities. At least a dynamic could be initiated which Helmut Qualtinger was looking for in his work, in questioning and dissolving the obvious, the ordinary and the unnoticed, even if in all consequences this meant a total revision of conceptualising a phenomenon.

References

Ball, R. (2014). *Bibliometrie. Einfach – verständlich – nachvollziehbar*. De Gruyter.

Ball, S., & Junemann, C. (2012). *Networks, new governance and education*. Policy Press.

Der Spiegel. (1986). Nachruf Helmut Qualtinger. *Der Spiegel*, 5 October (Nr. 41). https://www.spiegel.de/politik/helmut-qualtinger-a-478a17c5-0002-0001-0000-000013519800

Döring, E. (1998). *Paul K. Feyerabend zur Einführung*. Junius.

Feyerabend, P. (1970). Consolations for the specialist. In I. Lakatos & A. Musgrave (Eds.), *Criticism and the growth of knowledge. Proceedings of the international colloquium in the philosophy of science, London, 1965* (Vol. 4, pp. 197–230). Cambridge University Press.

Feyerabend, P. (1975). *Against method. Outline of an anarchistic theory of knowledge*. NLB.

Feyerabend, P. (1976). *Wider den methodenzwang. Skizze einer anarchistischen Erkenntnistheorie*. Suhrkamp.

Feyerabend, P. (1980). *Erkenntnis für freie Menschen. Veränderte Ausgabe*. Suhrkamp.

Feyerabend, P. (1995). *Killing time. The autobiography of Paul Feyerabend*. University of Chicago Press.

Feyerabend, P. (2005). *Die Vernichtung der Vielfalt. Ein Bericht*. Passagen Verlag.

Flaatten, H. (2015). Publication footprints and pitfalls of bibliometry. *Acta Anaesthesiologica Scandinavica*, 60(2016), 3–5. https://doi.org/10.1111/aas.12655

Geelan, D. R. (2001). Feyerabend revisited: Epistemological anarchy and disciplined eclecticism in educational research. *Australian Educational Researcher*, 28(1), 129–146.

Geelan, D. R. (2006). *Undead theories. Constructivism, eclecticism and research in education*. Sense.

Goldie, D., Linick, M., Jabbar, H., & Lubienski, C. (2014). Using bibliometric and social media analyses to explore the 'echo chamber' hypothesis. *Educational Policy*, 28(2), 281–305. https://doi.org/10.1177/0895904813515330

Gregory, A. (2007). *Ancient Greek cosmogony*. Bloomsbury.

Hauschke,Ch.(2019).ProblematischeAspektebibliometrie-basierterForschungs-evaluierung. *Informationspraxis*, 5(1), 1–17. https://doi.org/10.11588/ip.2019.1.49609

Hemetsberger, B. (2022). *Schooling in crisis. Rise and fall of a German-American success story.* Peter Lang.

Hutterer, R. (2008). *Methodologischer Pluralismus. Reader zur Vorlesung.* Börsedruck.

Kidd, I. J. (2013). Feyerabend on science and education. *Journal of Philosophy of Education*, 47(3), 407–422.

Kidd, I. J. (2016). Feyerabend on politics, education, and scientific culture. *Studies in History and Philosophy of Science*, 57(2016), 121–128. http://dx.doi.org/10.1016/j.shpsa.2015.11.009

Koselleck, R. (1959). *Kritik und Krise. Ein Beitrag zur Pathogenese der bürgerlichen Welt.* Verlag Karl Alber.

Labaree, D. F. (2010). *Someone has to fail. The zero-sum game of public schooling.* Harvard University Press.

Preston, J. (1997). *Feyerabend: Philosophy, science and society.* Polity Press.

Rorty, R. (1988). *Solidarität oder Objektivität? Drei philosophische Essays.* Reclam.

Rorty, R. (1989). Education without dogma. Truth, freedom, & our universities. *Dissent*, 36(2), 198–204.

Thompson, Ch. (2018). Umstrittene Gründe. Erziehungswissenschaftliche Beiträge zur Bildung und Kritik des Wissens der Bildungsforschung. *Erziehungswissenschaft*, 56(29), 105–112. https://doi.org/10.3224/ezw.v29i1.12

Wendt, G. (2003). Qualtinger Helmut. In *Neue Deutsche Biographie* (Vol. 21, pp. 33–34). https://www.deutsche-biographie.de/pnd126870691.html#ndbcontent

Wolfmeyer, M. (2017). Anarchist epistemologies and the separation of science and state: The critique and relevance of Paul Feyerabend to educational foundations. *Educational Studies*, 53(4), 327–341. https://doi.org/10.1080/00131946.2017.1334657

Zumhof, T. (2021). Ideengeschichte. In M. Caruso, C. Groppe, K.-P. Horn, G. Kluchert, & Mietzner, U. (Eds.), *Historische Bildungsforschung. Konzepte – Methoden – Forschungsfelder* (pp. 69–78). Klinkhardt.

Limitations of Abundance? The Role of Concepts in Educational Discourse

Karsten Kenklies

What is particular about educational research is that culturally different tra-ditions of educational discourses have very different understandings of the role concepts play within theoretical musings. So it might come as a sur-prise to many German-speaking academics to discover that their Anglophone colleagues are somewhat relaxed when it comes to the definitions of even foundational terms: some, if not most, educational handbooks or textbooks may introduce certain important notions – the very notion of 'education', however, is usually taken for granted while a request for a clear definition is then greeted with either rejection, or with a rather unclear characterisation. On the other hand, Anglophone academics seem to be equally surprised to hear that Germans tend to work with very clear – but constantly contested – definitions, using them as much as criteria for in- or exclusion of theorems and whole discussions, as these precisely defined concepts function as the cornerstones upon which the cathedrals of educational theories are built.

As a result, rather different ways of theorising education emerge, and with these comes a difference in the very institutionalisation of the related academic discourses, with the field of educational research being either an independent academic discipline (as it happens with *Pädagogik* or *Erziehungswissenschaft* in the German-speaking context), or a dependent academic field with con-tributions of a variety of academic disciplines, namely psychology, sociol-ogy, philosophy, history, and others (as it happens with education studies in the UK).

While comparing such different approaches might not be too difficult, evaluating them seems rather elusive, given the absence of independent cri-teria according to which the success of theorising could be judged. This is so because evaluations of theories and evaluations of practices based on or accompanied by such theories follow criteria, which in themselves are part of those discourses. For Paul Feyerabend, such discussions lie at the heart of his lifelong interest in the shape of a Philosophy of Science. Discussing the later Philosophy of Science, Feyerabend not only draws attention to such questions but attempts to develop a justified opinion about the value of theoretical concepts for the development of a scientific understanding of the world. It is, however, peculiar to Feyerabend's explorations that he concentrates on discussions of theories and concepts in the natural sciences. Despite such an emphasis, in his oeuvre one can find musings about, for example, the relevance or irrelevance of abstract ethical concepts, and he laments the tendency of the so-called philosophers to create such abstract categories in which the variety of reality seems to disappear. This is what he refers to as *Conquest of Abundance* – the title of his posthumously published book.

At first glance, Feyerabend's stance seems to comply with the Anglophone tendency in educational discourses to be *laissez-faire* about definitions, to not emphasise the relevance of a shared understanding of foundational notions, to embrace the idea of a theoretical haziness. On the other hand, one has to ask if this really is the case in light not only of Feyerabend's own approaches to discussing interpretations, but also in relation to the characteristic nature of educational discourses.

Addressing those uncertainties, this chapter will firstly explore the position Feyerabend develops in relation to the relevance of theoretical entities to then see, what contribution this may offer for the discussions around the nature of educational theorising: What are different approaches to educational theorising, and is there a specifically Feyerabendian approach to the theoretical practices representing the academic study of education?

1. Introduction: A Cultural Division – Approaches to Reflecting on Education

Recent years have seen an exponential increase of international encounters between educational academics across the globe. International research projects, attainment & assessment studies, the demand for the internationalisation of universities with regard to the teaching force and offered courses, the reality of a high student mobility and the increased mobility of academics caused by fluctuating precarities in different job markets or by demands for a stronger international profile – all this and other factors have brought forth a multiplication of academic communication about education. And with it, two effects have become visible (at least in education discourses): (1) English has been established as *lingua franca* of academic communication, forcing every

non-native speaker to not only learn English but also to translate culturally highly dependent, indigenous pedagogical notions into English (usually
with huge difficulties); and (2) a rising awareness that cultures of academic
research into education show a huge variety, caused by the differences in
self-understanding of the researchers of different cultures or nations (Whitty
& Furlong, 2017). Not only is there no internationally shared pedagogical
vocabulary, but there is also no universally accepted approach to do research
into education.[1] It is precisely the awareness of the fact that the previous sentence will probably be understood very differently in Anglophone cultures
and in those not working in the conceptual framework provided by English
notions like *education* or *schooling*, which makes international communication amongst researchers rather difficult. To use just one example: for me as
a German educationalist who has been and still is teaching and researching
in Scotland, it has been a profound and unsettling experience to see the very
different approach to education research and education understanding prevalent here. Not only do the German fundamental pedagogical notions like
Erziehung and *Bildung* have no direct equivalent in English (and *education*
no real equivalent in German), my self-understanding of what I am doing as
education researcher (as a so-called *Allgemeiner Pädagoge*) does not find a
reflection in the Anglophone world.

This difference is visible in a variety of aspects, and in an age of trans-
and interculturality, one would not need to essentialise those differences to
cultural or national differences as if there weren't different approaches and
understandings within such boundaries.[2] However, it is one specific curiosity that provided the inspiration for the explorations of this chapter: the
fact that in a German-speaking context, there is a whole sub-discipline of
the academic discipline of *Erziehungswissenschaft* ('Education Studies') that

---

1 Those claims already are difficult to make as they presuppose a shared reference of
   the notion of *education* or *educational* or *pedagogy*. It will be part of the argument
   developed here that this reference does not exist. But for now, the associative prox-
   imity of the references should allow for understanding what is meant here.
2 In fact, since the so-called *Empirical Turn* in the 1960s in Germany, *Erziehungswissenschaft* morphed more and more into a Social Science not dissimilar to the
   Anglophone approach. While taking the traditional approach and its notional framework (and the pedagogical reality formed through it) for granted, the actual discipline now embraces researchers of very different persuasion, and the discussion
   this chapter is about to present is one engaged with within the boundaries of the
   discipline. However, it should always be remembered that while I am talking about
   German and *Anglophone*, those serve solely as markers for different approaches
   (which historically have a somewhat clearer identifiable localisation) but not as essen-
   tialised cultural categories.

deals with notional questions, with definitions and relations of pedagogical notions (*Allgemeine Pädagogik* or General/Systematic Pedagogy), in which researchers of course do not agree on one single definition for the fundamental notions, while at the same time agreeing that having a precise definition is indispensable for academic discussions about the phenomenon in question. In comparison, in an Anglophone context, the very definition of *education* is often treated with general indifference, which even leads to the absence of precisely this definition in the *Oxford Dictionary of Education* (Wallace, 2015). While one side seems to obsess about precision and clarity with regard to the used notional framework, the other side seems rather flexible and disinterested in such a level of precision (and more often than not turns the question *What is education?* into *What is education for?*, seemingly assuming that either everyone already knows what *education* actually is, or that education can and should be defined solely by its religious/ economic/ social, etc. function). To reiterate, by no means do those characteristics have to be taken as defining nations, but as defining very different approaches, two traditions of doing educational research, that have emerged in different sites (also geographically) and developed in *longue durée* processes. They don't define nations, but they are entangled in different cultural contexts. These entanglements are contingent since there is no necessity in the fact that one approach developed here and the other there, but they are effective inasmuch as they leave marks. And as such, they become worthy of investigating.[3]

It is exactly on the back of those insights that the following chapter turns to Paul Feyerabend to discuss fundamentally different approaches to academic engagement with education. As will be shown in the first section, Feyerabend seems to discuss the problems and downfalls of approaches that put emphasis on precision of notions and concepts – accusing them of conquering the abundance of the world. Furthermore, it seems as if Feyerabend would indeed be criticising those who insist on precise definitions, that is, conceptual closeness, when engaging in the (also pedagogical) theorising of the world, which should employ a conceptual openness. However, things are not as clear-cut as they seem at first sight. Especially in relation to *education*, the ensuing discussions around the conceptual closeness of openness are rather complex and do not lend themselves to easy answers. To prove this, I will introduce Feyerabend's position, in order to then apply his position to pedagogical thinking while trying to take the challenge presented by

3 It is therefore more an effect of my personal intercultural encounter when the two approaches discussed here are discussed in cultural terms: such references are mere snapshots of a specific point in time, i.e. of an era that may have passed already.

Feyerabend seriously. In the last step, I will suggest what a Feyerabendian approach to pedagogical conceptualisations could look like. But before we can try to fly with such open wings, it is necessary to understand Feyerabend's apparent critique of conceptual precision and the closeness that comes with it.

2. Feyerabend's Critique of Abstraction: A Defence of Abundance

In many respects, the posthumously published *Conquest of Abundance* (1999) could be taken as a culmination of many of Feyerabend's strings of thought. Threads which he developed in publications throughout his life are woven into a multi-coloured shimmering fabric with which he hopes to show that the world is by no means as clear and monochrome as science would have it; philosophy, history, art, literature, the sciences – they all get engaged to produce an argument against the dry and grey abstractions with which, according to Feyerabend, modern science and philosophy wish to replace a world of infinite abundance.

To allow for the appreciation of this argument, Feyerabend discusses different stages of world-making.

2.1. Stages of World-Making

> Anyone who tries to make sense of a puzzling sequence of events, her or his own actions included, is forced to introduce ideas that are not in the events themselves, but put them in perspective. [...] There is no escape: understanding a subject means transforming it, lifting it out of a natural habitat and inserting it into a model or a theory or a poetic account of it. [...] Even the simple attempt to describe may throw a veil of illusion over the world. (Feyerabend, 1999, p. 12)

Understanding reality inevitably means transforming it. With this classic hermeneutic proposition Feyerabend distinguishes between two layers of 'reality': that which could be called 'crude' reality, senseless world, uncomprehended domain, and that which has been brought into the frame of human understanding through description or explanation. Of course, taking this statement seriously would mean that the uncomprehended domain itself is already part of the comprehended world: to be classified as 'incomprehensible' means to already be located within the world of comprehension – as its limit, boundary, quasi-beyond. Important here is that Feyerabend acknowledges that this act of bestowing the world with meaning is a necessary one, and that, in a somewhat paradoxical manner, 'a large part of the abundance that surrounds us here on Earth arose in the attempt to conquer abundance' (Feyerabend, 1999, p. 13). Feyerabend himself offers different

ways of expressing this ontological structure (seemingly with a preference
for the second one): (a) there is some Being as Ultimate Reality, which itself
and the conditions of its acting remain forever shrouded in darkness while
we have evidence of how this Being reacts when approached in different ways
(Feyerabend, 1999, p. 213); or (b) what he calls a 'ontological (epistemological) pluralism' in which we would have to admit that there are many different
sorts of objects and features that stand in all sorts of complex relations to
each other and of which some seem to rely entirely on human interests while
others seem a little more independent (a hierarchy which becomes the more
obscure the more we try to remove ourselves from it) (Feyerabend, 1999).

While acknowledging the existential necessity of those hermeneutic acts
of interpreting the 'out there' *as* world, Feyerabend points out that some
individuals and groups go beyond those in supplementing 'this (natural or
divine) process by conscious decisions of their own' (Feyerabend, 1999). And
it is especially in those additional acts of interpretation that he sees the danger of unnecessarily reducing the abundance that is the world as a whole to
a mere shadow of itself. He particularly accuses the early Greek philosophers
and (then) scientists of promoting such limiting approaches to the world. To
illuminate the limiting nature of their approaches, Feyerabend seems to distinguish between good and bad dualisms.

2.2. Good and Bad Dualisms

It can be said that the initial act of bestowing meaning upon the world creates a first dualism: on one side, the chaotic, incomprehensible, disordered,
and on the other side the meaningful, comprehended, somehow ordered.
Using Classic Greek notions, this dualism is the one of *chaos* (χάος) vs. *kos-
mos* (κόσμος). As stated above, Feyerabend takes this dualism to be necessary
for humans in their natural tendency to make sense of the world. In fact,
this dualism is itself already part of this process of sense-making inasmuch
it represents a cosmological, sometimes even genetic, or epistemological
description of the world that surrounds us. It is cosmological inasmuch *chaos*
(sometimes as *apeiron* (ἄπειρον)) represents the place outside of the ordered
universe. It is genetic in that it serves as the state out of which the ordered
world arises (by itself, or through a divine act of creation). It is epistemological because it is the chaotic unordered material that humans organise into the
world as they understand it.

According to Feyerabend, it is then the side of the ordered world,
the κόσμος, that has to endure the violation through the introduction of
yet another, this time bad, dualism. Not content with the primordial

differentiation between the disordered and the ordered, a certain group of people now 'introduced gross dichotomies such as real/apparent, knowledge/opinion, righteous/sinful'. Taking the idea of κόσμος even further, '[t]he early Greek philosophers and scientists especially assumed that the "real world" they had introduced in this way was simple, uniform, subjected to stable principles, and the same for all' (Feyerabend, 1999, p. 13). In this way, a new dualism disrupted the common view, which had already bestowed dazzling arrays of meaning to the world, and accused this common knowledge of being untrue and illusionary. And unlike the first dualism, in which general sense is made of the world by everyone, it is the exclusivity that has now been introduced through the second dualism – an exclusivity that apparently allows only a chosen few to understand the world as it 'really' is – which Feyerabend targets with his vitriolic and well-known critique. So it was the acceptance of many different gods and deities an act of sense-making that created a colourful and variable universe to live in in a myriad of ways, whereas the argumentative introduction of the one god, the one ἀρχή, the one first principle, through, for example, Xenophanes and Parmenides, has to be taken not as a step towards the truth, but as a movement towards paucity and blandness of understanding. Hailed as progress towards universal truth by scientists and philosophers who did not hesitate to accept such ancestral ideas as foundations for their own worldviews, it has been one of Feyerabend's general goals to attack such simplistic understandings that believe to be in possession of universally accepted criteria for making such evaluations. Instead, he would hold that worldviews remain largely incommensurable since they either evaluate each other based on only their own criteria (which is unfair), or a third worldview is introduced to provide a new set of criteria.[4]

Despite Feyerabend's unending efforts to expose common misunderstandings, particularly of the work scientists (as the hailed prophets and providers of progress through truth) are involved in, it has proven difficult to rid especially the Western academic world (and the academic traditions elsewhere, which – voluntarily or involuntarily – followed those patterns) from those deep-seated convictions about the merits and exclusivity of access to truth provided by the sciences. Feyerabend's incommensurable relativism has not yet been widely adopted as a foundation of neither the public understanding

---

4 This is a lot more difficult than it sounds, as a position has to be developed that actually is able to equally make sense of the worldviews compared – which is nearly impossible without reference to a Hegelian approach of a sublative dynamism, as Feyerabend concedes in his *Naturphilosophie* (2009); in most cases, the third worldview simply is a third worldview that happily sits next to the previous two perspectives, adding another position without truly sublating the previous two.

of the sciences nor the institutions based upon such views, for example, institutions of (Higher) education; views expressing similar thoughts, for example, Rorty (1989), have been equally contested or ignored.

There may be a myriad of reasons why Feyerabend has not had the impact his thoughts and arguments deserve. What is important here is the realisation that Feyerabend almost exclusively talked either about the sciences, that is, the natural sciences, or philosophy: one trying to make sense of the surrounding material world, the other trying to bring order into the notions with which we attempt to make sense. There is no easy way from here to evaluate what Feyerabend's thoughts could possibly mean for an academic discipline like Education Studies, for whatever the actual extent to which Education Studies is (also) a humanities field of research/academic discipline, it will need an additional effort to apply Feyerabend to the humanities (about which Feyerabend did not talk so extensively beyond occasional comments). The next section will show that this is far from simple. It will begin with a presentation of the different ways in which Education Studies has been conceptualised and organised in different cultural spheres.

3. Building of a World: Concepts and the Pedagogical Reality

It has already been stated: Neither is *education* a term that can easily be translated into other languages, nor can it be used to represent foreign notions without massive distortions. Thus, it may not come as a surprise then if *Education Studies* as the academic approach to study *education* is by no means a universal phenomenon. Therefore, the presentation of a traditionally Anglophone approach in comparison to a traditionally German approach can only be understood as an introduction of examples – and it may be the topic of a future discussion to see if they also are indeed exemplary.

Of course, it appears to be futile to assume that what will be presented here is universally shared in even the specified cultures; we will talk about tendencies and, in the end, this presentation may owe as much to the empirical investigation of those pedagogical cultures as it does to the assumed possibility to draw a systematic distinction (and in saying that, I may actually betray my intellectual background in German *Allgemeine Pädagogik* or General/Systematic Pedagogy, as it is often rather helplessly translated).

3.1. Educational Reality: Description of an Institution

To get a first impression of the Anglophone approach, it may be helpful to have a closer look at a book on education as an example. *Scottish Education* is a standard volume discussing all matters of education in Scotland. Published every 5 years, it follows the developments that shape the national educational sector; it is now in its 5th edition (Bryce et al., 2018). Analysing this volume, it becomes obvious that the notion of *education* refers almost exclusively to formal education, that is, schooling and the other forms of organised teaching and learning that precede or succeed the school period. The book overview promises explorations of Scottish Primary, Secondary, Further, & Higher Education, of the independent sector, and of politics and policies of education in Scotland. And indeed: when laypersons and academics (at least in the UK) speak of *education*, they usually refer to the institutionalised sub-system of society that is devoted to the organisation of learning. So-called *informal education* may be a topic for academic discussions, but generally its existence is a mere afterthought, and in books like the one mentioned it has no space at all. In distinction, a notion like *educational* can refer to either matters of *education* (in a broad sense), or – much more often – it refers to a process that is thought to be formative for someone whereby the formation is regarded to be positive. With notions like *educative* and *educated*, one has definitely entered a normative realm in which very concrete normative expectations have to be met whereas the relation to processes of schooling has more or less disappeared except in acknowledging those states of being as desired outcomes of schooling (Peters, 1966). While *education* (and partially *educational*) then are descriptive references to (predominantly) the school system, *educative* and *educated* are normatively loaded notions describing concrete desired states of being. So, it would make perfect sense in English to say that *education is not necessarily educative*, or that *those who suffered through education are still not educated*.

If *education* is mainly related to the institutional structures, it is not surprising that *Education Studies* is the academic investigation of these structures; its logic is then constituted by the perspectives perceived to be relevant to discuss all matters of *education*, that is, (pre-/post-) schooling. Traditionally, it was four perspectives that were seen as relevant contributors – each of them relating to a specific academic discipline: history, psychology, sociology and philosophy (Furlong & Lawn, 2011). Members of those disciplines then specialised within their disciplines on questions relating to *education* (history of ed., philosophy of ed., …). Instead of being an academic discipline in its own right, the Anglophone *Education Studies* is originally conceived as a field of research with a variety of contributing perspectives, which is provided by researchers disciplinarily bound to their original disciplines as philosophers, sociologists, historians, or psychologists (which also explains why in English, one can be a *philosopher* or *sociologist* – but not in the same way an *educationalist*).[5] Although there are discussions about the roles of those specific disciplines as apparently foundational complements, and despite the fact that other disciplines have found their way into the education research setting (e.g. data science) as well as other research fields (e.g. Gender Studies, Childhood Studies), the logic has not changed: the unity of the research object – and with it the unity of *Education Studies* as a specific field of research – is provided by the institutions (traditionally categorised as *education*) and the people engaging with them.[6] No matter how many different academic disciplines or research fields contribute to the field of education research, they are always bound together by the specific object of interest, petrified in the walls that make up a building called *school, kindergarten, university*, etc. This is very different from a traditional German *Pädagogik* and the way it generates its research object, the *Pädagogische Wirklichkeit* (pedagogical reality).

3.2. Pädagogische Wirklichkeit: *Interpretative Creation of a World*

German *Pädagogik* (and with it, *Erziehungswissenschaft*) defines its research object in a very different way. Instead of taking its starting point from institutions and their supposed function, it is built on the assumption of human relations – but not just any human relations, but those in which one person deliberately attempts to initiate, support, or guide learning or a positive transformation in another (or sometimes the very same) person (Friesen & Kenklies, 2022). Although often imagined as a relation between adults and children, this structure is not generally limited to certain age groups, genders, locations, etc. Such relations can exist in families, cultural institutions, schools, and kindergartens, and everywhere else; they exist between people of different ages or between peers; they can be long-lasting or ephemeral. The pedagogical relation is taken to be a distinct relation, a specific form of interpersonal engagement, which can be distinguished from other human relations. Its definition – e.g. '*Education* […] is the deliberate attempt to engage with the relations someone has in order to change and improve those relations; *education* is about initiating, guiding, supporting, directing of learning and (trans)formation' (Kenklies, 2020, p. 618) – constitutes a genuine realm of human activity that therefore is deemed to be a worthy object

5 It is not necessary here to get into the discussion around the difference and maybe complementary nature of Anglophone *Education Studies* and *Curriculum Studies*. Both are predominantly focused on schools.
6 There is not enough space here to discuss how this situation evolved over time.

of a genuine and independent academic discipline called *Pädagogik* (modern: *Erziehungswissenschaft*). One of its founders, J. F. Herbart, defined its research object along the lines of a logic of those kind of relations (Herbart, 1806, 1896), while according to him, pedagogical theories should develop and make use of their own genuine pedagogical notions (Herbart, 1896, p. 83). Here, the academic research into the pedagogical phenomenon is organised as academic discipline, which – organised around its fundamental notions – not only includes different perspectives (e.g. sociological, historical, psychological, philosophical, etc.) but also a branch in which the discipline reflects on itself and its fundamental notions (called *Allgemeine Pädagogik*, often translated as General/ Systematic Pedagogy).[7]

While an Anglophone *Education Studies* is composed as a field of research whose unity is generated through the assumed real-world objects instantiated by educational institutions and their inhabitants, the unity of German *Pädagogik* is guaranteed by the definition of a specific reality of human relations and the different aspects associated with those relations; while academics working in or contributing to *Education Studies* often (but not always) consider themselves to be academics of a variety of academic disciplines (whose inclusion into the department does not so much rely on a definition of the field but on obvious connections to matters relating to formal education), academics working in *Pädagogik* or *Erziehunsgwissenschaft* consider themselves to be *Pädagogen* (pedagogues) or *Erziehunsgwissenschaftler* (educationalists), and their academic discipline would stand as equal in Social Science faculties next to, for example, Sociology, Political Science, and Psychology.

On the surface, this approach to organising educational research may seem similar as the unity of the research and teaching is provided by some world-object. However, this object of interest seems to be of a different nature

---

7 With *Education Studies* organised as a field of research rather than as a genuine academic discipline, this self-reflexive branch is missing from the fabric of educational research: with no discipline existent, there is nothing that seems to demand those kinds of self-reflections. There could be, though: it is very curious that despite the fact that *Education Studies* pretends to be a field of research, one hardly finds any discussions of the actual *field character* of this field of research. What does or does not belong to the field remains undiscussed. That does not mean that there aren't boundaries (which is easy to recognise when one attempts to apply for research funding with the AHRC – the UK Arts & Humanities Research Council – which is impossible as all *education* research needs to be funded by the ESRC – the Economic & Social Research Council, which usually demands empirical research). However, there does not seem to be much discussion of the boundaries and characteristics of this field of research, which does not surprise given that all contributors belong to their own academic disciplines or fields.

and, therefore, the resulting research differs quite substantially. This will be explored in the next section.

3.3. *Objects of Investigative Desire*

What then is the difference between the objects of investigative desire? Well, on the one hand, we are quite literally looking at schools, universities, and kindergartens – researchers are looking at the institutions, the materialised buildings that represent those institutions, the spaces and its inhabitants. It could be classified as empirical in the sense that education research assumes to have found an object in the world – which often is also named through plaques, inscriptions, signs and is thus categorised through them as such an institution – which it then endeavours to investigate, explain and understand. There is not much difference here to doing research into trees or planets: all are apparently easily identifiable objects which then become the focus of attention (that things are not so simple may become clear when remembering the discussions around the stellar object called 'Pluto', which used to be categorised as 'planet', then was taken out of this category, only to be re-categorised as 'planet' quite recently). The categorisation itself is rarely questioned, and usually researchers take the categorisation that provides them with their research object for granted. Even the contributing discipline of philosophy – whose task it would be to reflect on notions – does not often engage in discussions around the classification of something as education; it does, however, engage much more with the normative discussions around the meaning of *educative* or *educational* (and through those discussions attempts to determine whether something is indeed *education*). This means, based on an apparently common agreement on what is the object of interest, discussions evolve around the way it is (how it functions), and the way it should be.

The object of interest for *Pädagogik* or *Erziehungswissenschaft* is different inasmuch it is not empirical in the same sense since it rests on a specific interpretation of human reality – an interpretation that adds interpretative characteristics to a situation which (that is the assumption) becomes more comprehensible through adding this perspective. A gesture, an addressing, a sentence or an action can (but does not have to) be classified as a *pedagogical* gesture, address, or speech act, and in doing so, it is bestowed with a certain meaning, that is, it is understood to be part of an extended attempt to improve someone's relations to something or someone (if we take for a moment this to be the definition of 'pedagogy' or 'education'). Here, it is very clearly a preceding definition of 'the pedagogical/ educational' that allows for 'recognising' education or pedagogy 'out there in the world', whereby this act of 'recognising' is actually an act of interpreting something as a specifically *pedagogical / educational* situation (and the question regarding the aim or reason for adding such an interpretative layer arises; see below). So, unlike the apparently simply 'found' objects like schools, universities, kindergartens, the object of *Pädagogik* or *Erziehunsgwissenschaft* is constructed through interpreting the world with the help of definitions provided by the very same academic discipline (within which it is the aforementioned branch of *Allgemeine Pädagogik* that provides those definitions[8] and that continues to discuss those definitive concepts that underpin pedagogical/ educational academic discourse and that allow for the provision of a pedagogical reality as research object through adding this pedagogico-interpretative layer to the 'normal' human reality).[9]

It would take us too far away were we to discuss why those two approaches are so different, and it would need a lot more historical research to clarify those developments. Whereas the Anglophone approach seems to be closely related to a somewhat pragmatist approach in its descriptive side (those institutions are clearly existent – there are buildings called *schools*, with plaques showing their names as *schools* – and now the simple task is to investigate those existing objects) and, closely related, to ordinary language philosophy in its normative approach (traditionally, Philosophy of Education would centre around explorations of the usage of the words *educated* or *educational*), it may seem that the German approach is much more heavily related to idealist philosophy, which focuses on subjects and their *Geist*, that is, the ways they make sense of and hereby shape the reality. One could argue (without

---

8 Its relation to Comparative Pedagogy and Historical Pedagogy are manifold and too complex to be explored here in brevity.

9 It is worth mentioning, that in recent years, the development within German *Pädagogik* or *Erziehunsgwissenschaft* has meant that the here as Anglophone presented approach has gained traction, and with it the same kind of nearly empirical underpinning of the discipline. More often than in previous eras, it is now the case that researchers act as general Social Scientists who engage with the investigation of traditionally as pedagogical/ educational classified contexts (schools, families, youth clubs, kindergartens, etc.) without asking or questioning those categorisations anymore. The pedagogical/ educational reality is then taken for granted – and taken as an object of interest like trees or planets – and investigated as such. That this then is indeed *pedagogical/ educational* research can be justified solely through the persistence of traditional classifications in discourses – but not through the conscious interpretation of a situation as a genuine pedagogical/ educational situation. And intercultural dialogues – forever haunted by the dominance of English as academic *lingua franca* – are then based on such shared unconscious acceptance of the same contexts, institutions, buildings as indeed educational contexts, institutions, buildings.

this being explored further here) that the former is more closely related to empiricist approaches of researching nature, whereas the latter is more closely related to hermeneutic approaches of researching human culture.

The question then arises, how Feyerabend's reflections relate to both approaches to doing research into 'education'. This will be explored in the following section.

4. Different Worlds, or What would an Abundant Pedagogical Theory look like?

The previous discussions hopefully have shown that the puzzlement that inspired this paper cannot easily be solved by stating that one approach to education research is better than the other. Rather, it seems that they have to be treated as almost incommensurable, to use yet another concept made famous by P. Feyerabend and T. Kuhn who seemingly independently introduced it at the same time to the discussions around scientific theories[10] (Feyerabend 1962, 1975). As both approaches construct their object of research very differently (notwithstanding all the decidedly non-reflected translational habits that without hesitation translate notions from one language into another), the ensuing theories create very different pedagogical or educational worlds (and already this assertion does not make much sense as it has to assume that what is now referred to as *educational* is a correct or at least close enough translation of German words like *Erziehung* or *Bildung* – which has to remain in question). It may already be far too negligent to gather those together under a shared banner of *pedagogy* (e.g. in asserting something like: 'Pedagogical notions cannot easily be translated from one language into another.') as that would assume that it is clear enough that all those notions can indeed be associated with at least the *pedagogical* realm (which again is doubtful, given the lack of clear meaning of the English notion of *pedagogy* despite, of course, the shared etymological history of the English *pedagogy* and the German

---

10 In his later work, Feyerabend seems to distance himself from earlier ideas of incommensurability inasmuch he now assumes cultures and discourses to be a lot closer than previously stated. Taking states of trans- and interculturality, i.e. cultural amalgamations, more serious than before, Feyerabend (1994) seems to reject the idea that cultures are isolated from each other strongly enough to be or become incommensurable. And indeed, the present chapter may serve as proof: Despite the fact that pedagogical notions are not really translatable from one language into another, it still can (and has to) be assumed that members of both approaches described here do understand this text. This only is possible if we assume that pedagogical cultures are indeed not completely incommensurable.

Pädagogik) – an association that then could serve as a third perspective to comparatively relate both approaches. So, either one then accepts that there is a fundamental incommensurability of approaches and related theories, or one takes advantage of the haziness of *pedagogy* and *Pädagogik* and simply assumes a third position, from which all can be related and from which it may make sense to declare discussions to be at least related enough to be presented under one analytical roof. The fact that – despite all misunderstandings and frustrating communication breakdowns – there seems to be at least some degree of understanding within intercultural discussions can probably be taken as justification to subscribe to the second view – albeit without now expecting that there could indeed be an external position from which both approaches could not only be linked together but also evaluated against some external standard that would then demand the adaption of one approach against the other.[11]

For the question at hand here, it then follows that Feyerabend's contribution to educational thinking may be understood differently depending on the approach one is taking to educational research. Therefore, the question cannot be, whether or not Feyerabend would agree with a more lenient way of using definitions (also including the absence of any notional definition) as it seems to be the case in many apparently *educational* debates still ongoing in the Anglosphere, or if he would support the idea that a definition is needed to identify the object of interest in the first place as seems to be the German way. Instead, the question is: what does Feyerabend say about each of the approaches separately? The following will present at least some initial thoughts responding to this challenge.

4.1. *Feyerabendian* Education Studies

Within the perspective of *Education Studies*, one has to remember that notions like *education* and *educational/educative* may not actually follow the

---

11 There is, of course, the interesting notion of *learning* (or in German: *Lernen*) that seems to provide some link between approaches. However, on closer view, this remains rather difficult. Not only is the notion of *learning* itself difficult as its meaning is curtailed to ex-post references (it cannot really refer to an ongoing process if it does not wish to be completely speculative), nor does at least the German *Lernen* qualify as a sufficient condition which, if fulfilled, testifies to the presence of educational/ pedagogical processes: Whereas the processes resulting in *Lernen* may actually happen continuously, it is only those which are intended that belong to the pedagogical realm; mere changes (no matter how desired or welcome) do not necessarily count as either *Erziehung* or *Bildung*. As has been seen above: intentionality or intendedness is a fundamental characteristic of German pedagogical notions.

same logic; although they are etymologically related, they sometimes seem to be differentiated according to their normative content. While with *education*, people usually refer to the institutionalised system of formalised teaching and learning (an example was given above), *educational/educative* are usually normatively loaded terms referring to a welcomed and desired change of a person or result of a personal transformation. However, the distinction is not so entirely sharp, as *education* is also usually understood as comprehensively positive, with a classification of something as *bad education* then taken to be a reference to violations of what seems to be the 'natural' essence of *education* (in this sense, it also counts as a negative evaluation to state that something does not qualify as *education*).[12]

Taking seriously for now the (only analytical) distinction between *education* (referring to the formal education system) and *educative* (referring to either a specific desired state of being or a process seemingly contributing to achieving such a specific desired state of being), it would then be obvious that all the standards that Feyerabend develops for the sciences were also valid for *Education Studies* as the field in which *education* is described and analysed: *education* then is a research object not dissimilar to the objects of the natural world as it is studied by, for example, physicists or biologists. Features like incommensurability of theories, epistemic or methodological pluralism and historicity, notional openness and ambiguity, and a relativity of relevance – which, according to Feyerabend, characterise all natural sciences in themselves and in relation to non-scientific epistemologies – would then also be features of *Education Studies* and its attempts to describe or explain *education* and *educational processes*. *Education Studies* would need to acknowledge the diversity of phenomena included in what is called *education* without limiting or curtailing this abundance through insisting on using some fixed universal notions which tend to hide the individuality and particularity of whatever is described. So, while the object of interest is as easily

---

12 Just as a side note: Such a notion of *education* cannot be used to describe institutions, processes, states outwith the normative framework within which the very notion of education is formulated. The inherent normative content of this notion would not allow for it to be used as a purely descriptive notion for (synchronically or diachronically) different cultures. While for example it seems very unproblematic to refer to the *Erziehung* in the Third German Reich (since *Erziehung* is in itself a neutral term that is used to structurally describe a certain way in which people relate to each other), it should be impossible to talk about the *education* in the Third German Reich, given that *education* is an inherently positive notion that does usually not allow for it to be used to denote processes whose ethical value is doubtful. The fact that this often gets ignored within Anglophone discussions is an expression of a lack of hermeneutic and methodological awareness.

identifiable as a table or a tree, the notions for describing and explaining this object must not be fixed or exclusive (Feyerabend, 1999, p. 252ff.). Moreover, the general criterion of *success* (or *truth*) of *Education Studies* would then also be an ethical criterion, as Feyerabend insists is the case for the sciences (Feyerabend, 1999, p. 242ff.): *Education Studies* – just like physics, biology, chemistry, etc. – has found the *truth* only if it produces theories that help people to live a free and happy life (Feyerabend, 1970, p. 210); it is *successful* if it can guarantee the 'mental and physical well-being' (Feyerabend, 1999, p. 212) of those believing in it. However, it has to be remembered that the interpretation of those ethical notions – *happiness, well-being, freedom* – then depends entirely on the people engaging with them; there are no universally accepted definitions of those notions.

This also means that the normative side of *Education Studies*, for example, in its interest of discussing the values inscribed in notions like *educative*, has to accept an ethical relativism: whatever goals are set for *education*, whatever ethical theory is introduced by the *Philosophers of Education* to formulate and justify the moral framework within which *education* has to proceed as a process and has to comply with as a result, whatever therefore is set to be the meaning of notions like *educative* – those will ever only be valid (if at all) for the individual society within which those morals are formulated. More likely will be that those morals will only be accepted by some within one society, and every ethical theory that pretends to be valid for a whole society, a whole culture, a whole nation – or even for the whole of humankind – has to be rejected immediately as completely preposterous, along with all its allegedly universal norms, criterions, values – and along with them, the standards of rationality embraced by the philosophers, who equally have to accept that they are just one group of people within one culture, society, state, who formulate moral norms and values. Neither is there only one philosophy (of education), nor is it only philosophy (of education) that is allowed to formulate moral/ethical standards for *education* and *educational/educative processes*: for Feyerabend, those moralities are expressions of traditions as much as results of civic negotiations within a people (Feyerabend, 1999, p. 263).

4.2. *Feyerabendian* Erziehungswissenschaft

Unlike the research object of *Education Studies*, the object of interest of *Erziehungswissenschaft* is decidedly dissimilar to a table or a tree inasmuch it is consciously constructed through the usage of a more or less clear (albeit debated) definition of the *pedagogical* in the first place – a definition that is then used to interpret specific aspects of human reality as *pedagogical reality*.

In this sense, the *pedagogical/educational realm* is an additional layer of interpretation – added to an already existing comprehensive layer of meaning that we could call *human (or social) reality*. Without this supplementary interpretation of *human (or social) reality*, there would be no *pedagogical reality*; the *pedagogical reality* is in its shape, scope, extension entirely dependent on the notions used to interpret *human (or social) reality as pedagogical reality*. Especially in light of the fact that this second-order interpretation depends on a notion of assumed intendedness – an assumption that always is very clearly a speculation used to explain certain acts of human behaviour – *pedagogical reality* in *Erziehungswissenschaft* is of an empirical precarity that is seemingly unknown to the Anglophone *Education Studies*.[13] Consciously based on an assumption of intention, *Pädagogik* remains an important (and in a German culture seemingly unavoidable) but nevertheless highly tentative speculation about the world and its inhabitants.

So, while the Anglophone approach presupposes an easily recognisable object of research (declaring some buildings and institutions to be locations of *education*), the German approach cannot rely on such fundamental categorisations and, for such locations and institutions, definitions of the *pedagogical/educational*, of *Erziehung* and *Bildung*, are at the same time too wide and too narrow to be able to synonymise them with the locations and institutions. *Lernen* (learning) may actually happen there, but not all *Lernen* (learning) is also 'education' or 'pedagogy' given that not all learning is intended, and that learning does not only happen in schools, for example. And, of course, much more happens in a school than just 'education' or 'pedagogy': floors are wiped, lightbulbs are changed, toilets get cleaned, lunch is eaten, etc. So, what indeed is *educational* or *pedagogical* in a German context rests wholly on the definition at hand and the act of interpreting *human (or social) reality* with the use of these categories. For this to be strong, these definitions and concepts have to be reasonably clear,

13 This empirical precarity persists even in light of those positions that assume the ontological robustness of *pedagogical reality*, i.e. positions that take the entanglement in pedagogical relations to be a part of human nature (anthropology) or even the structure of being (ontology). Although such a position does have to assume that there is indeed a *pedagogical reality*, it cannot escape the difficulty of recognising this reality in the very moment of a concrete situation. Knowing that, in general, there must be a pedagogical reality, does not help in deciding whether or not it shows itself in particular in this very moment. This decision will always be an elusive and speculative act of interpretation of a given situation, and although this is made possible by generally assuming an ontological/anthropological potential, the assumption itself is not sufficient to undoubtedly interpret a concrete situation as an instance of *pedagogical reality*.

precise and applicable. So, while in *Education Studies*, concepts used to describe a pre-identified object of research can be almost fluid and variable (since they do not seem to affect the existence of the very object of research), in *Erziehungswissenschaft* one needs a clear concept of the notions used to reveal the object of research in the first place. Here, Feyerabend's call for an openness of categories to describe the world of *education* (i.e. a school or university) as a reality of abundance, has to fall flat in light of the necessity to initially establish the object of research to be able to do research at all; that what is talked about isn't simply there, waiting for its richness to be grasped and described through an ever-changing myriad of notions and concepts; that what is talked about has to be brought into the world first by the researchers before they can then dissect, analyse, describe in detail what they have introduced at the beginning. And as already stated above: the institutionalised character of self-reflecting about the ways in which a *pedagogical reality* is brought into life turns *Erziehungswissenschaft* into an independent academic discipline that reflects on itself and on its own processes of generating a research object (comparable to the ongoing attempts of sociologists to define their discipline-foundational notion *society*, or the biologists' aspirations to introduce a definition of *life* that defines their disciplinary scope). In doing so, it embraces itself as a hermeneutically spiralling discipline that consciously accepts (historically offered) fundamental *pedagogical* concepts, while constantly reflecting on them to possibly adjust those notions in the light of their power to establish a *pedagogical reality* as a second-order interpretation of *human (or social) reality*. In this sense, *Erziehungswissenschaft* is closer to what Feyerabend describes as a mythological act of making sense (Feyerabend, 1999, p. 9), in which gods and deities are 'added' (as agential forces) to trees and rivers to give them a deeper meaning than what is visible 'on surface'. However, what distinguishes *Erziehungswissenschaft* from such mythologising is the fact that not only it is conscious of those hermeneutic structures, but it also endeavours to use academically shared, precise and clear concepts to create the *pedagogical reality* that it is determined to analyse. There is little space for conceptual fluidity or haziness here because 'thought changes looks', as Feyerabend remarks (Feyerabend, 1999, p. 84). Different fundamental *educational* and *pedagogical* definitions and concepts produce a different *educational* or *pedagogical world*, and communication or discussion would become futile as all involved parties would essentially talk about different things.

Keeping this fundamental difference in mind, it is still relevant to remember that Feyerabend's expectations of sciences and theories apply here as well. The plurality is now within the discipline which, in its self-reflections, tries to establish a stable and unchanging set of notions, while acknowledging that this discussion will continue while different notions, definitions and theories are existent and used throughout the discipline; and while such a stable uniform theory or set of definitions and concepts might never come to light, there still seems to be a commonly shared conceptual denominator that allows for the discipline to be self-aware as an independent academic discipline. Ethical plurality is present as well within the disciplinary discussions around values and goals, and the battle rages on about an (at least socially) shared ethics that would allow for the formulation of an ethical minimum that guides all (contemporary) *educational* efforts (without becoming part of the very definition of '*education*': they merely allow for distinguishing between *good* or *bad*, *accepted* or *rejected* '*education*'). Last, it needs to be remembered that the mere existence of a *pedagogical reality* in the described sense has to be taken not as a necessary but a contingent way of interpreting the world: adding an interpretative layer to *human (or social) reality* in the form of a *pedagogical reality* needs to be justified in light of the question whether or not the 'resulting world is pleasant to live in, and [whether] the gains of manipulations more than compensate for the losses entailed by the removal of the [simple social] layers' (Feyerabend, 1999, p. 12). Such justifications are not easy to come by, but they need to and might be found through anthropological reflections about the ways in which we narratively create our self-identities (Kenklies, 2016).

5. An Abundant Pedagogy?

At the beginning, it was asked: Do we need clear and precise categories, concepts and definitions when doing research into '*education*'? Although this chapter presented this question in the context of an intercultural encounter, and formulated an answer in reference to different cultural discourses, the question is undoubtedly relevant beyond such culturally adopted positions: how much clarity and precision is of advantage; how much fluidity do we need to allow for the endeavour to be successful? Or, to avoid a hasty positioning here: how much fluidity is advantageous, and how much clarity and precision do we need to accept when discussing '*education*' (or anything else in the world)? Feyerabend himself seems undecided:

> The tendencies exist side by side with each other [...] The situation certainly is complex – but what is the balance? I don't think there exists a satisfying answer to this question. (Feyerabend, 1999, p. 261)

Indeed, maybe there is no general answer to such a question and, following Feyerabend, we might assume that there are different answers responding to different situations, different locations, different times – and different people.

However, there is a tendency in Feyerabend that does indeed suggest a certain preference. For this to become visible, we have to remember that the two tendencies described here were loosely described as a more empiricist *contra* a more idealist approach: while one takes *education* to be represented in certain objects (like buildings and institutions and policy papers), the other generates '*education*' by attributing certain formative intentions underlying specific acts of human behaviour; one takes the object of interest to be out there in the world – an almost natural entity, in need of an analysing description, the other consciously speculates its object of interest into existence, taking it to be a product of human intellectual-interpretative creativity.

From what has been discussed above, it should be clear that Feyerabend would not be satisfied with simply presupposing certain empirical facts or objects which, despite their necessity in analysing interpretations, are taken for granted in their existence – leaving merely the analyses as up for discussion; he would regard all the objects of a specific reality to be results of interpretative acts of meaning-making, that is, as results of human endeavours to understand the world. As such, they are not sacrosanct but should be scrutinised. Therefore, an approach to *Education Studies* that simply assumes *education* to be those concrete empirical objects that can now be analysed in what then is educational research fails to see how those objects themselves are effects of interpretations, which to critically analyse should also be within the remit of such research. An approach that takes '*education*' to be the result of such a creative interpretation in the first place is therefore much closer to what Feyerabend has in mind as academic research and reflexivity, especially when the interpretative framework that generates the object of research is itself scrutinised in reflections specifically devoted to such acts of self-reflexivity.

Such a view on Feyerabend's preferences may also simply be the result of this author's own embeddedness in this kind of tradition. Feyerabend himself states surprisingly little about the nature of the humanities (except some excursions in *Farewell to Reason* (1987)), and hermeneutics (and its awareness of the dialectics of historicity and systematicity) does not seem to play a huge role in his thinking. However, it may not be too far-fetched to assume that such a hermeneutical understanding of academic research (also into *education*) – without its traditional overtones of some aspired fusion of horizons – is much closer to his intellectual world than an almost empiricist approach would be; and his celebration of Hegel in *Conquest of Abundance* may also serve as a powerful indication for certain preferences, as indeed: 'Thought changes looks.'

References

Bruce, T. K. G., Humes, W. M., Gillies, D., Kennedy, A., Bryce, T., Davidson, J., Gillies, D., Hamilton, T., Head, G., Humes, W., Kennedy, A., & Smith, I. (Eds.). (2018). *Scottish education* (5th ed.). EUP.

Feyerabend, P. (1962). Explanation, reduction and empiricism. In H. Feigl & G. Maxwell (Ed.), *Scientific explanation, space, and time* (Minnesota Studies in the Philosophy of Science, Vol. III, pp. 28–97). University of Minneapolis Press.

Feyerabend, P. (1970). Consolations for the specialist. In I. Lakatos & A. Musgrave (Eds.), *Criticism and the growth of knowledge* (pp. 197–231). Cambridge University Press.

Feyerabend, P. (1975). *Against method. Outline of an anarchistic theory of knowledge.* New Left Books.

Feyerabend, P. (1987). *Farewell to reason.* Verso.

Feyerabend, P. (1994). Potentially every culture is all cultures. *Common Knowledge, 3*, 16–22.

Feyerabend, P. (1999). *Conquest of abundance: A tale of abstraction versus the richness of being* (B. Terpstra, Ed.). University of Chicago Press.

Feyerabend, P. (2009). *Naturphilosophie.* Suhrkamp.

Friesen, N., & Kenklies, K. (2022). Continental pedagogy & curriculum. In R. Tierney, F. Rizvi & K. Ercikan (Eds.), *International encyclopedia of education* (4th ed., Vol. VII, pp. 245-255). Elsevier.

Furlong, J., & Lawn, M. (Eds.). (2011). *Disciplines of education. Their role in the future of education research.* Routledge.

Herbart, J. F. (1806). *Allgemeine Pädagogik aus dem Zweck der Erziehung abgeleitet.* Röwer.

Herbart, J. F. (1896). *The science of education.* D.C. Heath & Co. Publishers.

Kenklies, K. (2016). Grauzonen. Pädagogik als Queer-Wissenschaft. In K. Kenklies & M. Waldmann (Eds.), *Queer Pädagogik: Annäherungen an ein Forschungsfeld* (pp. 203–220). Klinkhardt.

Kenklies, K. (2020). Dōgen's time and the flow of otiosity – exiting the educational rat race. *Journal of Philosophy of Education, 54*(3), 617–630.

Peters, R. S. (1966). *Ethics and education.* George Allen & Unwin.

Rorty, R. (1989). Education without dogmas: Truth, freedom, and our universities. *Dissent* (Spring), 198–204.

Wallace, S. (2015). *A dictionary of education* (2nd ed.). Oxford University Press.

Whitty, G., & Furlong, J. (Eds.). (2017). *Knowledge and the study of education. An international exploration.* Symposium Books.

Part III: Inclusions: Feyerabend and
Science Pedagogy

Feyerabend, the Ally of Alternative Approaches to Science and Champion of Inclusive Science Education

JANE ESSEX

1. Introduction

Although Feyerabend is often viewed by scientists, and science educators as a 'contrarian' who took pleasure in ridiculing the scientific establishment and its work, this chapter will suggest that, rather than being casually provocative, it was prescient in its approach. Authentic critique of the group of disciplines that co-exist under the collective title of science is often limited to methodological divergence or the practical consequences of their work, rather than considering its socio-political underpinnings or educational responsibilities (Erduran & Dagher, 2014). Science education, meanwhile, exists as a sometimes uneasy amalgam of three Victorian subjects forced together by policymakers and school management imperatives. At best, it offers a very attenuated version of professional science, at worst it excludes large numbers if pupils from meaningful engagement. It is provided as a precursor to professional science since current policy offers little on other functions of science in society. For this reason, science education struggles to respond to modern expectations of the enactment of equality and inclusion (Campaign for Science and Engineering, 2014). Into this domain of partisan purposes of science and traditions of elitism, Feyerabend brings some very fundamental questions that invite some deeply uncomfortable responses for science educators.

2. What Is the Relationship Between Science Education and the Practice of Science?

Much of the political and economic privilege afforded science arises from its potential to enhance economic growth and to further militaristic aims. The same importance has been attached to science education, though the link between school pupils experimenting with household materials and political or economic domination must be considered tenuous at best. Nevertheless, school science education benefits from the assumption that a link exists. This is the legacy of both nineteenth-century policymakers who persuaded the authorities that science was an essential part of education and a testimony to the socio-political forces arising from two world wars in the twentieth century. Both of these influences combined to afford science and science education an exceptionally high status (Jenkins, 2013). In order to understand how fallacious such assumptions are, and to de-bunk the mythical status afforded science, we need to ask, 'What is real science (meaning science that is done in academic or commercial settings)?' and 'What is the relationship between real science and school science?'

An analysis of cutting-edge science topics in the news or a consideration of philosophers of science, such as Popper and Kuhn, shows that real science is continually building up new knowledge and revising previous assumptions. It uses provisional models to describe and explain phenomena and these models are also subject to iterative cycles of review and revision in the light of experimental evidence. However, these exploratory and tentative qualities of scientific knowledge creation are utterly absent from school science. The curriculum is externally imposed, sequential in delivery and permitting little iteration (Villanueva et al., 2012). The content is fixed and cannot be substantially changed by teachers, let alone pupils. If a previously accepted 'truth' is questioned by a pupil, it is seen as a challenge to a teacher's authority rather than the opening up of an interesting new line of enquiry. Meanwhile experiments are seen as 'cookbook' style recipes rather than genuine investigations of unknown phenomena. The gulf between curriculum subject and the discipline of science in professional settings has become huge. It therefore seems deeply questionable to assign the same political and economic significance to school science, even as a precursor for future professionals, and professional science. Recognition of the inconsistency in the prevalent rhetoric, in the way that Feyerabend's writing leads us to do, should pave the way for a radical review of both the current curriculum and associated pedagogy.

3. How Curriculum Steals Science's Soul

Although science may well be, as its Greek etymology suggests, a way of knowing it is a way that has become highly constrained by the pressures to achieve desired outcomes, notably economic and military dominance, and, in order to serve performative drivers, ease of assessment. One consequence is that substantive knowledge has become the dominant way of knowing in school science and it is the way of knowing that is valued. Gatekeeper assessments, such as school leaving exams in science, focus on substantive knowledge, requiring successful pupils to know the chosen key concepts in science and to be able to verbalise them in the required format. This presents two major barriers to the inclusion agenda, one practical and one philosophical. At a practical level, neuro-diverse pupils struggle to recall vast quantities of substantive knowledge and so under-perform in science assessments relative to the general level of attainment in science lessons (Villanueva et al., 2012). However, related to this, and possibly contributing to this situation, is the subordination of personal knowledge to the demands of the assessments.

Science education has come to accept widely the benefits of constructivist approaches to meeting learning outcomes, as evidence has been presented showing them to facilitate active engagement with the subject matter and facilitate the making of meaning by individual pupils (Driver, 1989). However, the assumption is that they are working to piece together an understanding that corresponds to the substantive 'truth' and this is what they will then be able to set out in assessments. Little is written about what alternative responses a teacher could mount when they piece together an alternative conception, other than the vague idea that further interventions will correct the erroneous idea. Polonyi (1958) suggests that personal knowledge, that is, the knowledge we have constructed in such a way as to be meaningful and significant to ourselves, represents far more than an intellectual quest for objective truth. He posits that it also represents a personal commitment to the knowledge in a way that an assessment of substantive knowledge cannot possibly capture. The silencing of self that characterises science generally, and school science assessments especially, is especially problematic for learners whose ways of generating knowledge may be very different from those of the majority. In effect, they may perceive that their genuine efforts to engage with knowledge creation are not valid or valued. A not-infrequent example of this is how teachers view pupils who bring a different type of knowledge to that which is required to meet curriculum and assessment expectations is the extensive knowledge that children on the autistic spectrum may have on a topic of interest to them. Although the knowledge may be extensive and accurate, it is frequently considered to be a nuisance rather than an asset. Whilst focusing learning and assessment on procedural knowledge may provide a partial bridge between declarative and personal knowledge, by considering the ways in which the knowledge is created and by capturing the link between what an individual does and the derived concepts. However, this still privileges received content above novel ideas generated by the individual learner, however well they demonstrate the processes of science in so doing. In this way, both the content and pedagogy of school science are exclusionary.

Conversely, if science could support the growth of process knowledge and personal knowledge, the discipline may indeed earn its place at 'the curriculum high table' (Osborne & Dillon, 2008). Feyerabend understood the purpose of education to be far more than an induction into the 'norms' of discipline but as a process by which learners were helped to develop a critically informed position on prevalent orthodoxies (Kidd, 2013). This position foregrounds the purpose of creating future citizens, rather than future science professionals. Such a process would require a re-positioning of the substantive knowledge that the subject yields. However, it could facilitate the development of diverse new approaches to teaching and learning about the natural world. Likewise, Feyerabend's advocacy of pluralistic approaches to understanding would legitimise different forms of science, including those which are accessible to diverse learners, and which are not necessarily the same as the science needed for future professional scientists. In practice it would mean that authentic knowledge creation by learners could be valued as offering alternative ways of knowing, such as is described in Table 1. At the same time, this notion that science as encompasses diverse approaches to knowledge generation should ignite a fresh debate about the true purposes of science for the different stakeholders and could make it possible for us to acknowledge that school science does not need to function only as the preparation of future professional scientists, as happens now. This debate could admit some of the areas considered by Feyerabend (1975), such as astrology, which are usually dismissed by the science community. Moreover, it would transform outdated and deeply non-inclusive views of what science is and, by extension, who can and should do it.

A final consideration is the feasibility of this shift. Lest science educators worry that these changes could resemble a 'free for all' in the name of science. I would point out that this alternative emphasis has been seen in many countries that adopt what is termed the 'Didaktik' model of teaching. This notion, whose purposes align with those identified by Feyerabend, contrasts with the curriculum-driven model of teaching (Werler & Tahirsylaj, 2022) that has been critiqued above. Work in this area by Klafki (1995) further supports

Feyerabend's suggestion that science should not have an elevated status relative to other disciplines but that education should be evaluated according to how well it helps a learner to achieve self-determination and critical maturity. Science in its various guises can undoubtedly make an important, though far from unique, contribution to such aims.

Table 1. An example of authentic knowledge creation beyond curriculum requirements

When I was a teacher, I had a group of low-attaining pupils, most of whom had some diagnosed disability or special need. As part of their science course, they were required to plan and execute a scientific investigation for assessment purposes. I asked them to investigate the factors that affected the rate of reaction between magnesium metal and dilute acid. Having taught them the theory about what changes rates of chemical reactions, I expected them (with some support) to identify a factor they could investigate. Other pupils in the class opted to explore the effect of the temperature of the acid upon the rate of reaction or the dilution of the acid. However, I was utterly taken aback when I asked two pupils what they were investigating and they said they were looking at the effect of the size of the beaker. I looked at their results and saw that they had tried dissolving the same amount of magnesium each time, in the same concentration of acid and always at room temperature. So, methodologically correct according to the principles of scientific investigation. They then repeated the experiments in front of me and I observed what they had already noticed. When the experiment was run in 150 ml beaker, then a 250 ml beaker and, finally a 400 ml beaker, the metal reacted more quickly each time. I was genuinely puzzled. We sat together and talked about what could be happening and their questions made me think that the diameter of the beaker might be affecting the way in which the product of the reaction was dispersed. Had they been studying science at pre-university level, we would have called it entropy. As it was, they called it 'stuff dissolving and moving away faster, so more new stuff could form'. I was really impressed and, even now, call this finding 'Emily's law' in their honour. (Field notes)

4. The Current State of Science Education

The general expectation is that science education is available (and commonly compulsory) up to the earliest age at which young people may leave school. However, it is far from universally well-received by learners, regardless of its perceived strategic significance. Once it is no longer compulsory, the majority of pupils drop science, especially physics, and here the data shows a disproportionate shift away from science by certain groups of learners. The characteristics of those who are under-represented in science in the post-compulsory phase of education and thence the STEM (science, technology, engineering and mathematics) workforce are people of colour, those from disadvantaged backgrounds and those with disabilities (CaSE, 2014). Lest we imagine that this situation is an unfortunate and unintended consequence of school practice, it is worth recalling that Young (1972) berated science for its systematic segregation of pupils into three groups, which he terms pure scientists, applied scientists and failures.

However, by far the greater educational injustice is to those who are educated outside mainstream provision and who very often do not receive any science education at all. Those in specialist schools intended for those with 'special needs', disabilities, or presenting very challenging behaviours, frequently have no regular science lessons, or no science lessons whatsoever. Likewise, they commonly have no access to a specialist science teacher, even though their place of education might adjoin the main school where there are, and must be, science teachers and labs. A number of these learners enjoy science, if it is taught in a way that makes it accessible, and many are actively enthusiastic about opportunities to do science (Essex, 2018, 2020). This structural discrepancy can be accounted by several factors, including the legacy of 'special' education upon which current practice rests (Pritchard, 1963). These practices, in turn, are based upon models of disability which focus on correcting deficiency and meeting basic needs, rather than capacities, entitlements and those experiences that make life meaningful (Runswick-Cole & Hodge, 2009). However, one of the key factors in perpetuating this inequality is science itself.

The science curriculum is elitist in the cognitive demands it makes (Essex, 2018), and although the mechanisms of delivery have been subject to substantial research and much policy manipulation, the core of the curriculum content has been remarkably constant. The version of science that is portrayed in the curriculum, focuses on scientific knowledge that has been widely accepted in the scientific community having been subjected to repeated verification over many decades. This content is then presented as unassailable body of knowledge, to which pupils can add nothing but their acquiescence in stark contrast to those (commonly more popular subjects) Arts and Humanities subjects associated with 'interpretation teaching' (Barnes, 1976). This notion of communicating a fixed body of knowledge is so embedded into the culture of science education that, even at a point at which classrooms were generally being organised around the principles of constructivism, science teachers were observed still to adhere strongly to the imparting of 'facts' in what was termed 'transmission teaching' (Barnes, 1976).

The content-heavy nature of the curriculum is sustained by several intersecting mechanisms. Firstly, a content-heavy curriculum is readily assessed and so serves the performativity culture of present-day education in the UK. Teacher performance is measured by their pupils' ability to recall knowledge for high-stakes assessments, and an agreed body of knowledge makes for efficient assessment processes which do not rely heavily on teacher judgement (Apple, 2004; Ball, 2003). If, by contrast, the curriculum was to consider current controversies to which science could make a contribution but in which a consensus of opinion has not been established, assessment would be much more difficult to regulate and standardise. The second consideration ensuring that science education is resistant to radical reform relates to the practical management of change. Curriculum conservation avoids change that teachers often find difficult to handle on top of their already intense workload and ensures that the assessment 'enemy' is a known quantity. Finally, the financial burden of changing the curriculum, in terms of lab resources and printed resources, is a consideration that restrains change (Apple, 2004).

A third set of factors relates to what has been termed the science 'pipeline', the notion that school science is, first and foremost, the preparation of future science professionals (Chapman, 1991). Biesta (2020), defines three purposes of education namely subjectification (learning to see oneself as having agency, in the case of science to view oneself as a future scientist), socialisation (being inducted into a culture, in science this means being able to act and think in an accepted scientific manner, or to understand the 'nature of science') and qualification (acquiring the knowledge and skills needed for a role, such as being a professional scientist). Various initiatives have emerged in science education that variously correspond to the purposes of socialisation and subjectification, but historical analysis shows that qualification, in Biesta's sense of the term, is the unwavering focus of science education over the last hundred years (Jenkins, 2013). The consequence of this is that science has consummately failed to achieve the aspiration of 'science for all' (Reid & Hodson, 1987) and has, instead, excluded many who might benefit from the wider benefits of science education. Such benefits include learning more about how science works and its impact on society, and thus developing scientifically literate citizens, or for the development of transferable skills or simply for enjoyment (Essex, 2020). This account should not be seen as implying that science is simply operating a form of disciplinary Darwinism, in which learners fit to engage with science are able to do so, whilst those not 'adapted' to the harsh environment of formal abstract thinking, and the requirement to memorise huge amounts of facts are lost to the discipline.

It is evident that science education, with its promise of economic, political and military gains (Bybee, 1997), is a high-stakes subject. Its status lends itself to commodification in a neo-liberal climate that has permeated education in the UK since the 1970s. Science enjoys a uniquely privileged status as a gatekeeper qualification to prestigious university courses, such as medicine, dentistry, pharmacy and veterinary science. Schools frequently use their track record in getting pupils the level of science qualifications needed for entry to these undergraduate routes as a marketing tool with which to attract parental/ care provider 'custom' in the form of enrolment of their children to the school. This inhibits pressures for curriculum reform lest the academic chances of these highly attaining pupils be harmed. Notably these tend to be the pupils who cope well the traditional exams that test the ability to memorise and recall large amounts of content. This 'gatekeeper' role of science also means that teachers are reluctant to accept diverse learners onto science courses leading to pre-universities assessment qualifications, lest they damage the chances of the highfliers.

The current format of the science curriculum deters many learners because they feel alienated by it. For example, many young women who are judged academically capable of doing so, choose not to pursue physical sciences because they think it will be too hard for them; they think that only very clever people succeed and doubt their capacity to do so (Cassidy et al., 2018). The outdated and elitist curriculum instils a fear of failure and contributes to the under-representation of some groups in science. This exclusionary pressure is exemplified by a pupil with learning difficulties asked about his experiences of assisting at a stand at a science fair reported, *'Although I am not smart enough to explain science to the visitors, I asked my teacher to include me as a member. .... I helped my teacher. I carried boxes and spread water on the ground ....'* Park et al. (2019, p. 11). If we taught a different version of science, such pupils would not doubt their ability to contribute meaningfully and successfully.

Having considered the ways in which science has maintained its seat 'at the curriculum high table' (Osborne & Dillon, 2008) and how it has excluded many learners from the benefits of studying that extend beyond those of becoming a future scientist, Feyerabend's critique of science appears to have justification. The following sections will consider the distinct ways in which Feyerabend's work brings a much-needed focus to the systemic injustices of science education and the many casualties of its resistance to fundamental reform. The analysis will view his position through the lens of pupils who are commonly excluded from, or remove themselves from, science education. Through this analysis, the reader is invited to consider that his is a philosophy whose time has very much come, and whose insight guides us towards a more pluralistic, and hence more genuinely meaningful view of science, that is needed now more than ever.

5. *Challenging the Elevated Status of One Partial Version of a Subject*

Feyerabend was critical of the exceptional privilege afforded to science as a discipline (Feyerabend, 2011), and against such partisan treatment of one area of human endeavour. Indeed, he believed that society should be protected from undue influence by science in the same way that society is protected from political extremism. The suggestion that science requires active policing is in stark contrast to much of the rhetoric about science which protests its objectivity and beneficence (Chapman, 1991). His objection was largely based on the assumption that way in which scientific knowledge was generated was inherently superior, which will be considered separately. He also objected (Feyerabend, 1975) to the exaggerated claims that were made for science, such as, 'science is successful', as myths that were perpetuated by the scientific community in order to maintain their hegemonic position. However, it was also a more general unease about the assumption that one subject merited so much more consideration and resource than others. He expressed it thus,

> Scientists have more money, more authority, more sex appeal than they deserve. The most stupid procedures and the laughable results are surrounded by an aura of excellence. It is time to cut them down in size, and to give them a more modest position in society. (Feyerabend, 1975, p. 304)

If this 'special status' were to be revoked, science as a curriculum subject could no longer exert its exceptional power within educational institutions and, simultaneously, its 'reach' to currently excluded, or discouraged, learners could be extended. For pupils in mainstream schools, studying science, especially physical science would appear less of a risk, whilst in special education far more non-specialist teachers might feel confident to teach it than currently do (Essex, 2020). It would also reduce the status inequalities of teachers as experts and pupils as ignoramuses, enable science to re-position its pedagogical approach to one of co-enquiry and to come closer to the aspirations of earlier science educators, as a mechanism for imparting a liberal education (Jenkins, 2013).

Whilst Feyerabend's challenge to science's status was certainly contrary to the spirit of his day, it was not unique nor was it without precedent. The Victorian scientist Thomas Huxley thought it *'was nothing but trained and organized common sense, differing from the latter only as a veteran may differ from a raw recruit'* (Huxley, 1905, p. 45). However, Feyerabend's willingness to challenge the supremacy of science is noteworthy because it was expressed at a time when the power of technology had been seen on an unprecedented scale in the aftermath of World War 2. At the time, there was a renewed interest in science education as the means to produce specialists whose work could directly enable nations to achieve economic and military supremacy. Such beliefs found expression in the notion of the 'Sputnik Curriculum' (Bybee, 1997). The question of whether enhanced science education inevitably gives rise to commercial and military power remains unanswered, but it has certainly formed the basis for strong rhetorical argument in defence of science education (Chapman, 1991).

6. *Against (a Single Prescribed) Method*

Although the title of Feyerabend's (1975) book, *Against Method*, could be seen, especially by the scientific community, as an exhortation for a *laissez-faire* approach to methodology, it can be viewed as a call for methodological pluralism. This is entirely in keeping with the fact that science is far from a homogenous subject, but rather a group of disciplines that share some aspects of their approach but are, in other ways, quite disparate (Erduran & Dagher, 2014). Beyond the absurdity of discussing a single methodology for a heterogeneous set of subjects, reliance on 'the (sic) scientific method' is both outdated and harmful. Feyerabend acknowledged this in his move away from an earlier exposition of 'critical rationalism' (Popper, 1972) to active criticism of it. Rather, he describes science as being anarchistic, implying that it lacks organisation or control. This may seem counter-intuitive since the practice of science is regulated, and funding considerations prevent many scientists from pursuing 'blue skies' projects. Nevertheless, his notion that science comprises far more than simply following an algorithm to generate empirical data seems even more pertinent now than it was when he published.

One reason for this is that, as he stated in his 1969 article, *Science Without Experience*, science no longer relies purely on empirical observations, for instance, in the field of theoretical physics. As digital technologies gain the capacity to simulate events, it is conceivable that they will grow ever more capable of simulating purely theoretical events. Moreover, the history of science is littered with examples of people whose thinking was shaped by events and experiences beyond experimental data. Feyerabend cited the story of the Copernican revolution, which gave us the heliocentric model of our solar system, as one such success story in which the scientific method was not followed and would actually have impeded the progress of knowledge (Feyerabend, 1987).

Crucially for inclusion, the reliance on a common framework of scientific method denies the many other mechanisms for advancing scientific knowledge, including induction, intuition and random chance observations. Walpert (1994) describes science as 'tentative' and 'exploratory', rather than adhering to any prescribed method, and it is precisely these qualities that could facilitate contributions from diverse sources and experiences, generating multiple interpretations. The openness that Feyerabend and Walpert describe is exactly contrary to the expectation of formulaic experimental work, driven by a single theoretical framework. A related problem with the deductive reasoning associated with 'the' scientific method is that it renders observations theory-laden, and so potentially biased. The issue of the discrepancy between observation and reality, which is commonly experienced, is another limitation of scientific working and something that Feyerabend raised in his last, unfinished work (2001). This recognition is especially pertinent for those whose life experiences or capacity for sensory processing is very different to the majority of pupils.

One of Feyerabend's most powerful contributions to a more open and inclusive practice of science is his denial of the complete explanatory power of scientific knowledge. He does this by challenging the notion of falsification (Feyerabend, 1975) which says that scientific theories lose their acceptance once there is any evidence to refute them. He suggested that this might lead people to suppose that every theory has been tested to its limit. In reality, Feyerabend posits that no theory can ever fit all observations perfectly and that they should be recognised as useful 'best fit' approximations rather than universally applicable descriptions. By suggesting that scientific knowledge is imperfect, though doubtless very helpful in understanding the world, he undermines the uniquely privileged position it has come to occupy and admits of the possibility of other ways of knowing (Feyerabend, 1975).

In all these ways, Feyerabend's advocacy of scientific pluralism offers a very modern approach to science education for all. Whilst zealous adherence to deductive methods is deeply exclusionary, his support for other ways of knowing offers a precious opportunity to make science much more accommodating of diverse learners. Research indicates that over two-thirds of young people will not be able to carry out deductive thinking reliably at 16 years of age (Adey & Shayer, 1993). This then precludes many people who could benefit from science for the wider educational purposes of socialisation and subjectification (Biesta, 2020). To illustrate this exclusionary pressures in operation, and whether it is justified in terms of the threat to developing scientific understanding, consider the two following examples.

Today, as part of the 'Explosions' topic, class a) made 'fizzy rockets', using effervescent Vitamin C tablets in the pots for blood sugar testing strips. I videoed them trying to get their pot to fly the furthest. I was interested to see that, even though they are the highest-attaining group of students, they didn't plan their rockets, but set them off and then afterwards analysed the results to reach their conclusion. They discovered, by trial and error that there is a maximum number of tablets, after which the rocket won't fly any further. (Field notes)

The other aspect of his rejection of a dominant method was its humanitarian basis. He expressed compassion for learners, talking about '*the killing of nature and of "primitive" cultures with never a thought spent on those thus deprived of meaning for their lives*' (Feyerabend, 1987, p. 62). Now, Feyerabend seems to have been prescient in highlighting the way that the predominant form of science has actively excluded other ways of doing science and being scientific, what would now be termed 'epistemic injustice' (Fricker, 2002). *This consideration* is even more relevant now, in a world of increased social and economic polarisation, profound social inequalities and racist violence. As we face a climate catastrophe, we are beginning to understand the true value of insights, gained inductively over many generations, into how our planet works (Aikenhead, 2001).

The representation of science as a homogeneous practice, only open to educated and wealthy powerful white men, made it a powerful tool for oppression and exploitation, as Feyerabend (1978) recognised. The 'fathers' (sic) of modern science' frequently perpetrated racism that was based on very positivistic views of human diversity and Feyerabend recognised the capacity of science to be racist and oppressive in other ways as well (1987). Their toxic legacy is now being actively countered by anti-racist and de-colonising educational initiatives. Finally, policy drivers for inclusion are starting to open up such alternative presentations of science as will enable learners with learning difficulties a meaningful experience of science (Essex, 2020). All these initiatives have the power to prevent science education '*turning wonderful young people into colorless and self-righteous copies of their teachers*' (Feyerabend, 1987, p. 309).

7. *Valuing Knowledge in Line with Societal Needs*

Alongside his rejection of science's superiority, Feyerabend (1978) called for a more sympathetic response to different forms of knowledge and culture. In part this is about achieving a more rounded critique of academic disciplines but also to make the focus of education more about the development of mature citizens, rather than walking textbooks. His support for pluridisciplinary education opens up different approaches to science, as discussed in the preceding section. Beyond that, he suggests that knowledge should be valued according to its ability to address real issues and the extent to which it makes life meaningful. This view does not exclude science from his definition of what is valuable, but does require it to be something other than abstract generalisations. His expressed a strong dislike of the peremptory dismissal of viewpoints that are seen as unscientific by virtue of lacking an underpinning rational explanation that can be corroborated by experimental evidence. Amongst such targets of contempt he considers the examples of homeopathy or astrology. He regarded these as valuable, according to his definition, irrespective of the absence of any 'proof' that they work as intended.

As far as science education is concerned, his views on usefulness mean that science can be made practically relevant by putting it in context without being a lesser subject. This is in contrast with the prevailing view that 'applied science' is a watered-down version of the subject (Douglas, 2014). Since socially relevant science can enable diverse learners and learning communities to feel connected to the creation of scientific knowledge, it is a powerful way to improve the inclusivity of science without compromising learning (Bennett et al., 2005; Siry et al., 2016). It also brings science a little closer to Feyerabend's vision of a society in which 'all traditions have equal rights and equal access to the centres of power (1978, p. 9).

He gave thought as to how science's power might be reined in and be regulated in response to the values of the society in which science is practised. Just as political extremism is held in check by legal frameworks and the checks and balances of the democratic processes. Likewise, Feyerabend thought that the research agenda should be determined by citizens, rather than scientists acting autonomously (Feyerabend, 1975). These mechanisms would ensure that science would only be accorded privilege to the extent that society judged it be of value to them. If the same thinking was applied to science education, pupils might be able to select how much of their timetable they would allocate to science and the nature of the science they studied. The popularity of science might be expected to rise hugely if pupils had agency to shape their science curriculum.

8. Conclusion

Although Feyerabend's view on science were viewed as very controversial at the time he published them, they have acquired a new level of meaning in the climate of contemporary science education. They provide both the concepts and rationale for re-evaluating how science can better respond to contemporary societal and global challenges. His rebuttal of many of the tenets of classical science included its inherent superiority, much of which has its basis in the way that it creates knowledge on the basis of verifiable evidence. His stance opens up a fresh consideration of diverse forms of knowledge and ways of creating knowledge, through which different types of science can be valued and positively promoted. He presents a vision in which groups who are currently under-represented in science could not only enjoy a greater level of affordance but whose contributions would be actively welcomed. He also suggests some of the mechanisms through which science, and by inference science education, could be shaped by society's needs and concerns rather than by self-interested elites. Ultimately, he leaves us a vision for a very different sort of science, and one that could be much more accessible but still powerful, albeit in different ways, to the version we currently operate.

References

Adey, P., & Shayer, M. (1993). An exploration of long-term far-transfer effects following an extended intervention program in the high school science curriculum. *Cognition and Instruction*, *11*(1), 1–29. https://doi.org/10.1207/s1532690xci1101_1

Aikenhead, G. (2001). Integrating Western and Aboriginal sciences: Cross-cultural science teaching. *Research in Science Education*, *31*, 337–355.

Apple, M. W. (2004). *Ideology and curriculum* (3rd ed.). Routledge Falmer.

Ball, S. J. (2003). The teacher's soul and the terrors of performativity. *Journal of Education Policy*, *18*(2), 215–228. https://doi.org/10.1080/0268093022000043065

Barnes, D. (1976). *From communication to curriculum*. Penguin Books.

Bennett, J., Grasel, C., Parchmann, I., & Waddington, D. (2005). Context-based and conventional approaches to teaching chemistry: Comparing teachers' views. *International Journal of Science Education*, *27*(13), 1521–1547.

Biesta, G. (2020). Risking ourselves in education: Qualification, socialization, and subjectification revisited. *Educational Theory*, *70*(1), 89–104. https://doi.org/10.1111/edth.12411

Bybee, R. W. (1997, October). The Sputnik era: Why is this educational reform different from all other reforms? In *Reflecting on Sputnik: Linking the past, present, and future of education reform*.

Campaign for Science and Engineering. (2014). *CaSE report – improving diversity in STEM*. https://www.sciencecentres.org.uk/documents/360/casediversityinstemreport2014.pdf (sciencecampaign.org.uk)

Cassidy, R., Cattan, S., & Crawford, C. (2018). *Why don't more girls study maths and physics?* Institute For Fiscal Studies (IFS).

Chapman, B. (1991). The overselling of science education in the eighties. *School Science Review, 72*(260), 47–63.

Douglas, H. (2014). Pure science and the problem of progress. *Studies in History and Philosophy of Science Part A, 46*, 55–63. https://doi.org/10.1016/j.shpsa. 2014.02.001

Driver, R. (1989). Changing conceptions. In P. Adey (Ed.), Adolescent development and school science. Falmer Press.

Erduran, S., & Dagher, Z. (2014). *Reconceptualizing the nature of science for science education: Scientific knowledge, practices and other family categories.* Springer.

Essex, J. (2018). Why 'science for all' is only an aspiration: Staff views of science for learners with special educational needs and disabilities. *Support for Learning, 33*(1), 52–72.

Essex, J. (2020). Towards truly inclusive science education: A case study of successful curriculum innovation in a special school. *Support for Learning, 35*(4), 542–558.

Feyerabend, P. (1969). Science without experience. *Journal of Philosophy, 66*(November), 791–795.

Feyerabend, P. (1975). *Against method.* NLB.

Feyerabend, P. (1978). *Science in a free society.* New Left Books.

Feyerabend, P. (1987). *Farewell to reason.* Verso.

Feyerabend, P. (2001). *Conquest of abundance: A tale of abstraction versus the richness of being* (B. Tepstra, Ed.). University of Chicago Press.

Feyerabend, P. (2011). *The tyranny of science* (E. Oberheim, Ed.). Polity Press.

Fricker, M. (2007). *Epistemic injustice: Power and the ethics of knowing.* Oxford University Press.

Huxley, T. (1905). *Science and education* (Essays by Thomas Huxley). Macmillan.

Jenkins, E. W. (2013). The 'nature of science' in the school curriculum: The great survivor. *Journal of Curriculum Studies, 45*(2), 132–151. https://doi.org/10.1080/ 00220272.2012.741264

Kidd, I. J. (2013). Feyerabend on science and education. *Journal of Philosophy of Education, 47*, 407–422. https://doi.org/10.1111/1467-9752.12009

Klafki, W. (1995). On the problem of teaching and learning contents from the standpoint of critical-constructive Didaktik. In S. Hopmann & K. Riquarts (Eds.), *Didaktik and/or curriculum* (pp. 187–200). IPN.

Osborne, J., & Dillon, J. (2008). *Science education in Europe: Critical reflections.* The Nuffield Foundation.

Park, H., Kim, Y., & Jeong, S. (2019). The effect of a science festival for special education students on communicating science. *Asia-Pacific Science Education, 5*(2). https:// doi.org/10.1186/s41029-018-0029-0

Polonyi, M. (1958). *Personal knowledge: Towards a post-critical philosophy.* University of |Chicago Press.

Popper, K. R. (1972). *Objective knowledge.* Oxford University Press.

Pritchard, D. G. (1963). *Education and the handicapped 1760–1960.* Routledge.

Reid, D. J., & Hodson, D. (1987). *Science for all: Teaching science in the secondary school.* Cassell.

Runswick-Cole, K., & Hodge, N. (2009). *Needs or rights? A challenge to the discourse of special education.* Sheffield Hallam University Research Archive (SHURA). http://shura.shu.ac.uk/6098/

Siry, C., Wilmes, S. E. D., & Haus, J. M. (2016). Examining children's agency within participatory structures in primary science investigations. *Learning, Culture and Social Interaction, 10,* 4–16. https://doi.org/10.1016/j.lcsi.2016.01.001

Villanueva, M. G., Taylor, J. C., Therrien, W. J., & Hand, B. (2012). Science education for students with special needs. *Studies in Science Education, 48*(2), 187–215. https://doi.org/10.1080/14703297.2012.737117

Walpert, L. (1994). *The unnatural nature of science.* Harvard University Press.

Werler, T. C., & Tahirsylaj, A. (2022). Differences in teacher education programmes and their outcomes across Didaktik and curriculum traditions. *European Journal of Teacher Education, 45*(2), 154–172. https://doi.org/10.1080/02619768.2020.182738

Young, M. (1972). On the politics of educational knowledge. *Economy and Society, 1*(2), 194–215. https://doi.org/10.1080/03085147200000010

Rethinking Science Education: Fostering Feyerabend's View of Pluralism and Proficiency

Deivide Garcia da Silva Oliveira

1. Introduction

Humans have tried to understand the world throughout almost their entire existence. Among the attempts, a variety of approaches to understand the world was developed. These attempts were denominated in a variety of ways, like religion, philosophy, indigenous knowledge, modern science, and others. For many reasons, the so-called science became one of the most spread traditions. Thus, it is also a widespread idea that scientific knowledge is one of the most well-successful human enterprises (Chalmers, 2013).

We also know that science succeeds concerning some of its own epistemic goals and its own established patterns of interest and evaluation. Nonetheless, Feyerabend quotes Konrad Lorenz to remind us of the disastrous consequences of the 'erroneous belief that only what can be rationally grasped or even what can be proved in a scientific way constitutes the solid knowledge of mankind' (1993, p. 131). In other words, depending on how we understand science, we could flirt with the risk of establishing it in advance as a tradition above all traditions (Gürol Irzik & Nola, 2007).

For instance, in science classrooms in schools, students are taught that scientific knowledge is up for scientific criticism but at the same time also that science itself is not up for choice as the more successful way to understand the world. Science is presented as the most successful tradition in revealing facts and rational arguments. Not merely scientific facts, but revealing stable and lasting facts, which will stand up independently of the theory that once revealed them. Feyerabend named this way of seeing scientific fact as the principle of autonomy of facts (1993). This picture of autonomy of facts, which is advocated by schools of thought like logical positivism, is not true in real scientific practice, but it is yet often seen in science classrooms of schools and universities. As a result, this picture brought over science education an unnecessary crisis (Fourez, 2003). In this case, students are supposed to see that, rationally speaking, accepting that kind of science is the only way to talk about the world, at least if they want to be part of a rational and scientific world. Some philosophers highlighted that under such a view, which establishes one tradition above all traditions, it means that a mere disagreement with some scientific foundations will be seen as absurdity (Feyerabend, 1993) and even a product of craziness (Chang, 2012).

But why is that and how so? It has to do with many elements, one of them being the necessary association between positivistic legacy in science and the epistemological values it claims to own. For instance, when science is associated with rationality, objectivity, and truth, this association appears to make science itself, and all it does, synonymous of rationality itself. If this were the case, it would be natural to make science a tradition above all traditions. This kind of association is a basis for uniformity and presupposed superiority. A similar situation is observed with other uniform traditions, like religion. Feyerabend says that hardly 'any religion has ever presented itself just as something worth trying. The claim is much stronger: the religion is the truth, everything else is error' (1993, p. 218). What makes any tradition a would-be religion, or a wannabe tradition above all traditions, is 'the belief that some demands are "objective" and tradition-independent – [which] plays an important role in *rationalism*' (1993, p. 218, brackets added).

If we assumed such a necessary association between science and epistemic values (like rationality, truth, and objectivity as conforming to what a positivistic and rationalistic legacy left for science), the consequence would be that alternative epistemological traditions could not have those epistemic values once they did not belong to that form of scientific tradition. Therefore, even if there is any future association between non-scientific traditions and those epistemic values, such an association would be considered sporadical and only valid if submitted to scientific standards and approval.

This kind of argumentation seems to point to science as universally valid and uniformly constituted, a kind of science that awakens extremist and opposed attitudes, such as scientism and denialism. The uniform view of science assumes a scientific monist worldview which, as a consequence, reduces humans to a single True World, that is, where 'all the manifold abilities of the observers are now directed towards this True World, they are adapted to a *uniform* aim, shaped for *one particular* purpose, they become more similar to each other which means that humans become impoverished together with their language' (1993, p. 199). This account of science, as it sets its own standards by which it judges everything outside of it, is a self-perpetuating oppressing system. A system that demands that any outside view is to be judged accordingly.

We will argue that in order to defend science there is no need to embrace such a monist view of science. We will argue that rationality or objectivity or truth do not belong to one tradition, but rather they are found in our individual and collective efforts, it can be found in all epistemic traditions. Furthermore, such an association of epistemic values and science will not be necessarily found in all scientific endeavours and products. There are other forms of science where more than one theory, worldview and rationality is accepted, used and pursued simultaneously.. In a few words, a science that is taken from a pluralist stance (Kellert et al., 2006).

That being said, our general aim here is to address this pluralism of science in science education as a way of introducing another view of approaching science. With the help of some of Feyerabend's proposals, we will argue that another way of understanding science is possible and needed due to the problems it created, like the problem of education, i.e., how uniform science education indoctrinate people and cause disinterest in it. In the more specific side of our objective, we have two additional goals. First, we will investigate the meaning and practical role played by critical thinking and proficiency in science education according to our interpretation of Feyerabend's philosophy. Second, also we want to explain how pluralism is needed but it is not enough to address the problems of a kind of education that is built to mould people's minds to, and by, only one tradition (Oliveira, 2017, 2021).

As a pluralist, just like some of our contemporary philosophers, Feyerabend believes that a pluralist account of scientific knowledge is not only rich in content, as it helps us to advance critical consciousness, and 'without such awareness, we can reach neither *a true appreciation* of the achievements of science *nor a properly critical attitude regarding the claims of science*' (Chang, 2012, p. xv, italicisation added).

Critical thinking and proficiency are deeply related to Feyerabend's plurality because it opens us to many worldviews throughout a peaceful competition, without eliminating defeated traditions, where each tradition improves the other. It is a pluralism born from an 'ever increasing *ocean of mutually incompatible alternatives*, each single theory, each fairy-tale, each myth that is part of the collection forcing the others into greater articulation and all of them contributing, via this process of competition, to the development of our consciousness' (1993, p. 21). To Feyerabend, this passage makes clear that, traditions serves us, not the other way around. In classrooms, when students learn about science, it should not matter if, after learning science, they will be stuck with their own traditions and worldviews or if they will replace these traditions for science. What matters from a pluralist view of science education is that the students must always remain able to change their views as they please, while also developing a truly respectable dialogue with other traditions, systems of knowledge, and ontologies. What matters is freedom of thought (Feyerabend, 1993).

Until now, there are not a lot of attempts by Feyerabendian scholars to argue how concrete answers would solve this issue of teaching scientific theories without aiming to change students' beliefs or tipping the balance toward scientific knowledge (Oliveira, 2017). Also, we are not familiar with any attempts to address this problem of changing students' beliefs focused on the notion of proficiency. Here we argue that proficiency works as a strategy, together with the development of pluralism and critical thinking in students, while still supporting the practice of teaching and learning science in schools.

Our debate on science education addresses the heart of what Feyerabend called the problem of education, where it lies the issues of indoctrination, disinterest in science, and the lack of critical thinking, resulting in what Fourez and Matthews dubbed the crisis in science teaching (Fourez, 2003; Matthews, 1992a).

To achieve our aim, this work is divided into five sections (including the introduction). In the second section, we will clarify what Feyerabend means with by criticism of science from an educational perspective. In section 2.1 we explore the target of his criticism, the uniform view of science, and in 2.2 we explore how weak arguments, like past successes of science, can be revisit from a pluralist approach. In sections 2.3 and 2.3.1, we presented the origins and detailed definition of the problem of education. We will show not only its constitution, and how Feyerabend established it, but also how it is currently going on and why it is still alive. In third section, we argue how the so-called Berkeley's experience transformed Feyerabend and how it opens up the path for pluralism in education, even about science. In the fourth section, we start to work on our answers to the problem of education. This is why counterinduction is introduced, but also how debates around values and cosmologies of cultures are helpful to allow the student to find their way. Finally, in the fifth section, we can put all these pieces together and explore how the notion of proficiency fits into this problem of education, that is, indoctrination and disinterest in science. Still, in the fifth section, inspired by Feyerabend, we introduced a name for the a practical educational approach that offers the basis for the notion of proficiency in science education, we named it the 'game approach of science education'. This also explains how the notion of an abundant world can only be sustained in science education if we respect and include critical thinking and the notion of proficiency in our strategies to address the problem of education. We conclude our text not only highlighting important achievements of our text, but also offering our reflections from what was presented along this work.

2. Understanding Feyerabend's Critique of Science as an Approach to Unveil the Problem of Education as Part of a Uniform View of Science

Feyerabend considered science a respectable, valuable, and successful enterprise, but he also thought that we needed to keep the doors open for a critical approach of scientific knowledge (Preston et al., 2000). For instance, he says that many 'people trust a physician or an educator as they would have trusted a priest in earlier times. [… and so] the advice in all cases is to use experts, but never to trust them and certainly never to rely on them entirely' (1978, p. 97).

For those who are familiar with Feyerabend's work, there is no surprise here. Feyerabend does not attack science. As he said, the reader should always 'remember that my examples do not criticize science; they criticize those who want to subject it to their simpleminded rules by showing the disasters such rules would create' (Feyerabend, 1993, p. 46). Instead what Feyerabend does is criticise how some philosophical views, about a specific approach of science, advance uniformity which fits well in tyrants' appetites. This view does not need to be accepted in any way in order to take science as a valuable and successful enterprise (Feyerabend, 1978). Feyerabend even says that science succeeds in its efforts and goals, although '*scientific successes cannot be explained in a simple way*' (Feyerabend, 1993, p. 1).

2.1. Uniformity Approach of Scientific Success and Development of Conflicts in Science Education

Scientific successes cannot be explained simply because there is no formula to success, and there is no guarantee that science will succeed in the future. Which means that a rational method, with strict rational rules and justification do not exist. Moreover, the very idea of success and that such scientific tradition should be picked up over other traditions (non-scientific) creates unnecessary pressure and conflict for learning science, which are seen in classrooms. For instance, Feyerabend says that what he is 'talking about is the extent to which scientists and scientific organizations using all available pressure tactics short of murder have succeeded in determining what has to be done with the young (education programmes which try to weed out non-scientific traditions replacing them by silly inventions such as the "new mathematics")' (Feyerabend, 1978, p. 212).

Thus, every time in the classroom, when it is assumed that to learn about science we must weed out non-scientific traditions may leads science students to a uniformist approach of science, one which installs and nurtures conflicts between students' beliefs and scientific beliefs. As a result, such pressure and conflict unveil a fundamental problem in science education: a tacit effort to change students' beliefs (Oliveira, 2017).

The effort to understand science cannot be accomplished by avoiding criticisms, by attempts to replace non-scientific traditions with scientific traditions, and by teaching that critical thinking is only valid within the limits of science. Disagreements about the most fundamental truths of this world cannot be addressed by ignoring that it is science that exists within a complex world, and not that it is the world that exists within science.

Feyerabend's views on science teach us about what it takes to develop our critical thinking, and it claims that science is not the only way to understand the world and guide our lives, that is, science 'is neither a single tradition, nor the best tradition there is, except for people who have become accustomed to its presence, its benefits and its disadvantages' (1993, p. 238). Once this is accepted, it is possible to teach scientific knowledge without having to compromise ourselves with radical relativism, science denialism, or scientism.

2.2. Understanding Scientific Success from a Pluralist Stance Against Indoctrination in Science Education

Science itself is not a single entity and, as pointed out by John Ziman in his book *Teaching and Learning About Science and Society* (1980), scientific knowledge is better represented by a plurality of maps, without each of them having 'to be learnt in every detail' (Ziman, 1980, p. 18). The reason for this view is the purpose of maps, which in most cases is to show 'how to get from A to B, drawing particular attention to general landmarks and junctions, but excluding confusing details such as twists and turns on the way' (Ziman, 1980, p. 19).

Furthermore, we can have multiple maps, with different purposes (like going from A to B walking, or only by bus, train, or even to show historic sites and buildings). Whatever the case, Feyerabend (1993) quotes what Ziman says, there is 'no single "scientific" map of reality [...]. But there are many different maps, of many different aspects of reality, from a variety of scientific viewpoints' (Feyerabend, 1993, p. 245; Ziman, 1980, p. 19). Therefore, thinking in what would be the primary goal of science education, is not to indoctrinate students through a simplistic and uniform view of it.

A complex and rich view of science will be fair when does not ignore science's accomplishments, and Feyerabend reinstated this over and over like when he says: 'I am not suggesting, let me emphasize, that there is a reality which science fails to get at' (Feyerabend, 1993, p. 272). However, on the other hand, there is no reason to kill non-scientific traditions on the way or to think that science only welcomes one view of the world. There is no reason to adopt only a uniform view of science and a monist stance on the world.

The situation is quite the contrary. Feyerabend presents a singular view of pluralism (Oliveira, 2021) when he argues that science is not only plural but also constituted with a divergent and mutually competitive and simultaneously cooperative ocean of alternatives, where each one forces 'the others into greater articulation and all of them contributing, via this process of competition, to the development of our consciousness' (1993, p. 21).

In other words, the development of our consciousness and the use of pluralism, as Feyerabend understands them, are intrinsically related because 'Ideologies are marvellous when used in the company of other ideologies. They become boring and doctrinaire as soon as their merits lead to the removal of their opponents' (Feyerabend, 1999 [1975], p. 188).

This view of science is much more relevant for science education considering that we need to help students to develop critical thinking about science as just another ideology among others.

In this sense, we will argue that it is desirable to promote science education from a critical approach, but if we want to do this without losing our students to any extremist views (relativism and science denialism or scientism), then we need to take science as a complex, rich, and plural entity when we are teaching about scientific theories and successes.

In a few words, indoctrination, taken as a form of scientific education from and to a single ideology, should be rejected if we want the students to make their own decisions and to be 'adaptable and inventive, not rigid imitators of "established" behavioural patterns' (1993, p. 159), it should be rejected if we want to reconcile scientific education with a 'humanitarian attitude' (Feyerabend, 1975, p. 20).

In science classrooms, the teacher should remember that scientific theories are means for the development of the student's consciousness, not a mean to develop science or an end in themselves. They should remember that in order to teach science it is important to be clear that theories which seem to be Truth today may well be entirely false and have unexplained parts and problems. Teachers should 'emphasize that even a theory that now seems to be without blemish is bound to have shortcomings. He will impress upon the pupil that the task is to find out these shortcomings by a process of critical examination' (Feyerabend, 1999 [1962], p. 69; 1999 [1975]). The refusal to do so is part of what led Feyerabend to notice the so-called problem of education which will be addressed in the following section 2.3, and further detailed in four parts in section 2.3.1.

2.3. Uniform Science as a Source for the Problem of Education (PoE)

By and large, a first thing to approach science education is to acknowledge and analyze the existence of what Feyerabend called the problem of education (Feyerabend, 1999 [1980], p. 223), which is observed in science education but in reality, is a byproduct of issues from a uniform view of science.

But before we further explore *the problem of education*, let us spend a few lines explaining how and when it was systematically tackled by Feyerabend.

Feyerabend tells us how since the 1950s–1960s (1978, pp. 107, 118; 1999 [1963], p. 96) he was aware of questionable practices of education that appeared to be rich but in reality ended up indoctrinating and impoverishing science students, science itself and non-scientific traditions of knowledge. For instance, he recalls that the 'problem of knowledge and education in a free society first struck me during my tenure of a state fellowship at the *Weimar Institut zur Methodologischen Erneuerung des Deutschen Theaters* (1946)' (Feyerabend, 1978, p. 107).

The way that this problem was revealed to him had to do with how rationalists argued in favour of their own perspective as if nothing else were the case, and as if to teach science through their way was an act of mercy, of humanity, to those coming from other traditions (Feyerabend, 1993, 1978). However, Feyerabend says that he saw the situation differently.

> What remains in the end behind all the humanitarian verbiage is the white man's assumption of his own intellectual superiority. It is this high handed procedure, this *inhumane suppression of views one does not like*, this use of 'education' as a cub for beating people into submission *which has prompted my contempt for science, rationalism, and all the pretty phrases that go with it* ('search for truth'; 'intellectual honesty' etc. etc.: intellectual honesty, my foot!). (Feyerabend, 1978, p. 136, italics added).

This behaviour of suppression of alternative views, which for a uniformist is identified as *scientific mercy's*, is exactly the kind of behaviour seen in many religions, whereas rationality (or whatever supreme divine entity the religion poses), is considered exclusively under the lines of this form of scientific tradition, as if that rationality were evacuated objectively and independently of science, by a divine force. These types of pretty phrases, epistemic values, and views ('search for truth'; 'intellectual honesty, 'objectivity', etc.) are one of the reasons of Feyerabend's discontentment with science, they lead to totalitarian science. Nonetheless, this discontentment can also be extended to our science education if this education is based on such a totalitarian view of science. We call it totalitarian because they 'are totalitarian, for they make the ideology of a small gang of intellectuals the measure of everything' (Feyerabend, 1978, p. 138).

Thus, in classrooms guided by this totalitarian education, if one part of the class, let us say any student, has 'not yet become a participant of the chosen tradition he will be badgered, persuaded, "educated" until he does' become part of it (1978, p. 29). It would be this way because presenting a true world to the students would be seen as an act of mercy and love.

This supposedly true world 'described in a uniform way' (Feyerabend, 1993, p. 198) is only achievable through unification, 'as educators want it to be' (Feyerabend, 1993, p. 246), after all, this is how they learned science and how they became part of it. This image of a true world is created through training procedures seen in our schools and universities when the students 'are adapted to a uniform aim, shaped for one particular purpose, they become more similar to each other which means that humans become impoverished together with their language' (1993, p. 199).

However, we could ask, is there a such thing as a true world and can science give it to us? The very idea of one scientific worldview can only make sense if there is just one science. However, there is not such a thing as a single entity called science 'there is no uniform enterprise "science"' (1993, p. 249), but rather a plurality of divergent and incompatible entities called science. As Feyerabend said, 'science contains a great variety of [...] approaches and that even a particular science such as physics is but a scattered collection of subjects [...] each one containing contrary tendencies' (1993, p. x). Therefore, even from an exclusive scientific perspective, there is a pluralist openness of sciences and worlds.

To put it simply, 'the assumption of a single coherent world-view that underlies all of science is either a metaphysical hypothesis trying to anticipate a future unity, or a pedagogical fake' (1993, p. 245). For the sake of our purpose, this assumption will be seen as both a metaphysical hypothesis and a pedagogical fake because it is widely spread in educational institutions as a way of teaching people about science. This pedagogical fake becomes the *status quo* that sustains our view about science and education, monolithically founded.

2.3.1. *The Problem of Education and the Universalist Standard Account of Science*

A consequence that follows from this monolithic education is how 'a little brainwashing will go a long way in making the history of science duller, simpler, more uniform, more "objective" [...]. Scientific education as we know it today has precisely this aim' (1993, p. 11).

This is how the uniform view of science nurtured something that in the 80s Feyerabend called 'the problem of education' (1999 [1980], p. 223), although he notices it in the 50s and 60s (see section three below: Berkeley's experience). Now, let us finally state how Feyerabend describes what is the problem of education:

> The problem of education, however ([part-1] people may remain in execrable traditions because they do not know better, [part-2] hence we need a uniform and universal education) [part-3] provides an argument *against* the *status quo*, not *for* it: hardly any adherent of science, of scientific medicine, of rational procedures has chosen this form of life from among a variety of alternatives, the scientific point of view was imposed by 'education', not chosen and [part-4] the groups who want to leave the fold and return to more traditional forms of life do so in full knowledge of the splendours they are leaving behind: they have savoured the bouquet of scientific rationalism and have found it wanting. (Feyerabend, 1999 [1980], p. 223, numbers within brackets added)

The problem of education, which for the sake of brevity we also refer to just as indoctrination (because is the basis of the problem), is not constituted of just one part but rather four, that relates indoctrination with its immediate consequences, like the impoverishment of our knowledge and ourselves as individuals and human beings by the imposed set of current belief system. This is the reason we need to explain the PoE in detail because it means that its effects are not only epistemological but also ontological, educational and humanitarian. For didactic reasons, let us analyse the above quotation and break it down into *four parts* corresponding to the ideas constituting the PoE.[1]

---

1 The general term 'problem of education' (PoE), if isolated from context, may give the wrong impression that we will talk about education/pedagogy in general. However, the reader must keep in mind that our focus is on science education because of Feyerabend's own focus on science. Naturally, science education is part of general education, so only in this sense the PoE also refers to general education. Furthermore, Feyerabend talks about general education, but as we also do, he is concerned with the causes and effects of scientific tradition on our schools in general and on our

First of all, the PoE is a result of applying the uniform view of science-to-science education. Thus, the first idea carried out in the first part of the quotation (*part-1*) argues:

> Part-1: 'people may remain in execrable traditions because they do not know better'. (Feyerabend, 1999 [1980], p. 223)

In other words, it means that people who live in non-scientific traditions, which are execrable ones, needs help to get out of them although they do not know how to do it because they only know one tradition. They do not know better (meaning a non-execrable tradition). *Part-1* only makes sense from a starting point of superiority where science is taken as the better tradition in the case and one which should be extended to everything else in all societies and in all times (past, present, and future). In this scenario, no education could be made if not from and towards uniform science, and teachers must employ all resources to free people from execrable traditions.

In *part-2*, we see that a better tradition, which would save those who live in execrable traditions, is a uniform science that must then be the basis for:

> Part-2: 'a uniform and universal education'. (Feyerabend, 1999 [1980], p. 223)

Feyerabend notices the implicit claim for a uniform science and how it extends to education. For instance, in *Against Method* Feyerabend relates the support for uniform science inside and outside schools, asking 'who can say that the world which so strenuously resists unification really is as educators and meta-physicians want it to be – tidy, uniform, the same everywhere?' (1993, p. 246).

Another aspect is the definition of universalism in science. A classical description of a *universalist Standard Account* of science, according to Cobern and Loving (2001, pp. 53–60), is given by Matthews' case of the volcanic eruptions. Matthews (1994) says that when volcanoes throw out larvae over people who live nearby, it does not matter their beliefs, forms of rationality, and epistemologies because, in the end, it is the behaviour of the volcano that 'finally judges the adequacy of our vulcanology, not the reverse'

lives outside schools. Furthermore, Feyerabend, as we all know, focussed his work about science, and even the text where we find this quotation of PoE debates science and society focusing on science dominance. Thus, because of the contextualisation of the PoE in the text, because of the contextualisation of the PoE as focusing on the topics and tradition that concern Feyerabend, which is science, and because we already explained that we are also concerned with science education, we will keep the general term 'problem of education' but only for keeping Feyerabend's choice of words unchanged, although we have in mind science education.

(1994, p. 182). Cobern and Loving (2001) call such an example a model for the *universalist Standard Account of science*. According to them, a *Standard Account* would have the following seven criteria:

1. it is basically a result of Western culture, so that 'Western culture and science have matured in consort' (2001, p. 53);
2. Western culture was led to believe in the materialistic superiority of the scientific mentality (2001, pp. 53–54);
3. that science 'ideally' intends to be the universally valid material explanatory system about the natural phenomena (2001, pp. 57–58);
4. This explanatory system is also objective and empirically testable (2001, p. 58).
    4.1. That objectivity, by the way, is something related to 'a universal, value-free process' (Cobern & Loving, 2001, p. 58; Stanley & Brickhouse, 1994).
    4.2. The Standard Account objectivity refers 'to the goal that experimental outcomes not be prejudged nor unreasonably constrained by prior belief, that data is collected fairly and accurately, and that research methods are executed with fidelity' (2001, pp. 58–59);
5. This objectivity runs under empirical and theoretical consistency requirements (2001, p. 58). Thus, since an explanatory system tries to explain how the world works, then,
    5.1. the 'Standard Account of science is grounded in metaphysical commitments about the way the world "really is"' (2001, p. 60);
6. and metaphysical commitments means assumptions of natural order of the world, direct causality, and the possibility of knowledge (2001, p. 60).
7. Lastly, but not least, authors say that the Standard Account sees what is also consensually defined by the community of the practitioners (2001, p. 60).

All these seven items of the Standard account support or matches the uniform account of science in the PoE, to which Feyerabend objects. The belief that people who live in a non-scientific worldview need help and want to get out of these views assumes a superior perspective and a monist ontology of just one science and one scientific worldview, based on this universalist account of science. However, this Standard account cannot be sustained under the slightest scrutiny, because it mistakenly assumes that science is uniform and not a plural entity (not even possibly; Kellert et al., 2006), and also because the very notion of better has already been decided as whatever the uniform science and the *status quo* says it is.

Thus, in *part-3* of the quotation, Feyerabend says:

> Part-3: 'the problem of education, however [...] provides an argument *against* the *status quo* not *for* it: hardly any adherent of science, of scientific medicine, of rational procedures has chosen this form of life from among a variety of alternatives, the scientific point of view was imposed by "education", not chosen.' (Feyerabend, 1999 [1980], p. 223)

This *part-3* reveals in reality what is the duty of every education, which is not only to go against the *status quo* (and as a rule in itself does not work), but fundamentally to provide alternatives and means for choosing between them, without being permanently committed to it. Education must provide freedom of thought. By doing it, education would be humanitarian and contribute to the development of our consciousness. Because of this duty, whenever educational institutions do not fulfil it, then these institutions would end up imposing one viewpoint over others and will still call this process 'education'.[2]

Understood in this sense, the problem of education should be taken as a dispute of cultures under a supposed epistemic superiority, which throughout the distinction 'between "mere beliefs" and "objective information", the defenders of scientific rationalism tolerate the former but use laws, money, education, PR [public relations] to put the latter in a privileged position' (Feyerabend, 1987, p. 84, brackets added).

The problem of education from a uniform scientific worldview is a humanitarian problem in the sense that it is a training procedure that aims to turn the choice of what tradition to follow into an automatic result, favouring science. Science, as a dominant tradition in Western societies, starts from our very childhood the 'process of socialization and enculturation (to use ugly words for an ugly procedure) compared with which the training of household pets, circus animals, police dogs is mere child's play' (1978, p. 174).

Feyerabend's description of the difficulty to break out from a tradition, whatever *status quo* tradition we are living in, exposes how training operates

---

2 Naturally, there is a difference between general education and science education. Nonetheless, not only the direct quote presented is focusing on science education and scientific rationalism (more specifically how uniformist view thinks of it), as the discourse of the *status quo* about what to teach in schools and what is 'an educated' person still follows the rules posed by scientists and scientific disciplines. Thus, it is in a sense a general problem of education, but the reason comes from a universal and uniform view of science as the tradition whose dominance is established beforehand.

in our brain and why the educational process should confront the *status quo* in many ways given our fallibility. In this sense, when we take the method of education which 'often consists in the teaching of some *basic myth*' (Feyerabend, 1999 [1975], p. 188), what is underneath it is how we teach people to adhere to only one single worldview (scientific one), one single form of knowledge (scientific one), and more importantly, to make people think that there is only one science, uniform, instead of a rich, plural and complex tradition, ontologically plural, with many realities and worldviews.

The uniform account of science oppresses any individual that wants to break out from it even before the intent manifests itself. The so-called problem of education claims how the *status quo*, a uniform scientific worldview, would restrain any alternative view from trying to diverge. Consequently, our very reality could simply be a result of imposition by education offered by the uniform scientific worldview. In this account, against the *status quo*, '*the best education consists in immunizing people against systematic attempts at education*' (1987, p. 316). The best education is going against monolithic education.

This is why pluralism, especially as we take to be Feyerabend's view (cosmological divergent pluralism[3]), is introduced to shake the grounds of whatever is in place as *status quo*. It is a delicate balance between what we can do, what we want to do, and what we have to do. A more realistic account of science would point out that 'there are many different maps of reality, from a variety of scientific viewpoints' (1993, p. 245), and consequently, the proliferation of 'theories is beneficial for science, while uniformity impairs its critical power' (Feyerabend, 1993, p. 24).

In this account, good criticisms in science classrooms can only be taught upon a platform of cosmological and divergent pluralism where the alternatives at play are all available to mutual criticism, whereas the students can learn about traditions without being indoctrinated. This is why an argument

---

3 The notion of cosmological pluralist view in Feyerabend as proposed here is based not only on the idea of ontological pluralism, something that Feyerabend clearly associates with himself (1999, p. 215) in order to highlight how his pluralism refers to 'various forms of manifest reality' (1999, p. 214), but beyond this we assume his pluralism as cosmologically divergent. The notion is also founded on how his idea of pluralism, even when debating science, depends and entails every aspect of our world, a cosmological view that 'underlies everything' (1999, p. 87), which influences and is influenced by everything, even culture. Passages like these are abundant in Feyerabend's texts and we will not enter in many details here. But if there is interest about the notion and the topic, check the paper: Oliveira, D. G. d. S. (2021). The cosmological divergent proliferation in Feyerabend's pluralism. *Principia: an international journal of epistemology*, 25(3), 421–454.

for science education recommends that what 'we need here is an education that makes people *contrary, counter-suggestive without* making them incapable of devoting themselves to the elaboration of any single view' (1999 [1975], p. 188).[4]

As Feyerabend sums up that his view on such divergent plurality and the epistemic outcome, knowledge (by which he means scientific one) that would come out of this process

> is not a series of self-consistent theories that converges towards an ideal view; it is not a gradual approach to the truth. It is rather an ever increasing *ocean of mutually incompatible alternatives*, each single theory, each fairy tale, each myth that is part of the collection forcing the others into greater articulation and all of them contributing, via this process of competition, to the development of our consciousness. (1993, p. 21)

In other words, there is no reason to think that this form of divergent plurality is only deconstructive because it pushes the *status quo* tradition, or theory, out of the centre of the stage. The plurality here proposed is both deconstructive and constructive. It is deconstructive because it works through competition of mutually incompatible alternatives. Nonetheless, it is constructive because the competition should be used in a way where the theories are mutually incompatible, but they still contribute to each other's articulation, and our consciousness. By working in this contributive way, pluralism nurtures knowledge in an articulated approach, aiming the development of the consciousness of people involved in the process and traditions. Thus, it goes beyond the mere inclusion of alternatives. It is about the need for an interplay between the games (traditions and theories) under an understanding and respectable format so that the individuals, the students, are not excluded because of what they think of science from a pluralistic view.

The exclusion of students who do not accept uniform science happens when we only take one tradition, and one approach of it, as the measure of a well-educated person. In *part-4* of the PoE quotation Feyerabend says that science suffered many pushbacks from people who did not feel science was enough for them, and at least within science classrooms, this pushbacks

---

4 One important question emerges here. Are students' worldviews limited by formal education? Are they not also educated by their parents and groups? These are relevant questions because it requires a step back about the role played by other elements of the students' environment, like family, religion, culture, and so on. We agree that these elements play a significant role. However, we also agree with Brighouse (2006) when he mentions that formal education, especially schools, must take the responsibility to make pluralism of alternatives (knowledge, ways of life, realities, etc) part of their duties in order to make possible the flourishing development of the students.

were later on named the crisis in science teaching (Fourez, 2003; Matthews, 1988). The *part-4* says:

> Part-4: 'the groups who want to leave the fold and return to more tradi-
> tional forms of life do so in full knowledge of the splendours they are leaving
> behind: they have savoured the bouquet of scientific rationalism and have found
> it wanting.' (Feyerabend, 1999 [1980], p. 223)

The general idea behind this part-4 has to do with the idea that people who have learned science, from a uniform and universal approach, people who have savoured the bouquet of scientific rationalism are now pushing back and returning to their traditions (Cobern, 2000; Feyerabend, 1993). Here, Feyerabend is not attacking a pluralist science but only a uniform science. By doing this, he notices what also many authors noticed, that an education based on a kind of science that does not include students' view, other scientific alternatives, and worlds, is a science destined to fail. Educationally speaking, this uniform science fails even in the minimum sense of teaching science, that is, to make students interested in the subject. As Fourez said, 'young people today seem to no longer accept to engage in a process that is imposed on them without having been convinced beforehand that this path is interesting for them or for society. This is true for all courses, but perhaps even more so for scientific abstraction' (Fourez, 2003, p. 110, transl. ours).

2.3.2. Uniform Science Education: Open and Guided Exchanges

In this sense, a uniform science excludes students because it only allows dialogues from a prior agreement, which is, the monolithic scientific view. To this preconditions of dialogue, which assumes a universalist rationalism, Feyerabend repeatedly labelled *guided exchange* to which 'some or all participants adopt a well specified tradition and accept only those responses that correspond to its standards' (Feyerabend, 1978, p. 29; 1987, p. 29; 1993, p. 227). A guided exchange argues for one tradition as being more superior and more powerful than others, and because of this, people should follow its rules before further engaging in dialogue. Because of this view, any attempt of criticism, or of proposal of change, or opportunity of exchange between traditions can only happen under the standards of the tradition in power, like science, therefore, if 'one party has not yet become a participant of the chosen tradition he will be badgered, persuaded, "educated" until he does' (Feyerabend, 1978, p. 29). Because of these standards, there is also a predetermination of what is rational and what is irrational, what is acceptable and what is not, and finally, what is good education and what is bad education.

Feyerabend's conception and critique of *guided exchange* are suitable for the description education under universalist and monolithic science. To put in other thinkers' words, Irzik (2001) says that multiculturalist supporters generally are 'critical of these views [universalists] because they believe that such views are wrong not only philosophically, but also politically and morally, as they serve a politics of exclusion and suppress the fact that there are alternative forms of science, which suit the purposes of a "good life" better than WMS [Western Modern Science]' (Gurol Irzik, 2001, p. 71, brackets added).[5]

In contrast to *guided exchange*, Feyerabend presents an *open exchange*, according to 'the tradition adopted by the parties is unspecified in the beginning and develops as the exchange proceeds', so an open exchange is changeable with time, and in the interactions of the participants they 'get immersed into each other's ways of thinking, feeling, perceiving to such an extent that their ideas, perceptions, world-views may be entirely changed – they become different people participating in a new and different tradition' (Feyerabend, 1978, p. 29; 1993, pp. 227–228). The *open exchange* suits well to our answer for the PoE, that is, our pluralist view of science and education. To put it in Song's words 'proponents of multiculturalism find common ground in rejecting the ideal of the "melting pot" in which members of minority groups are expected to assimilate into the dominant culture' (Song, 2010). From Feyerabend's notion of *open exchange*, which we apply to scientific educational context, an 'open exchange respects the partner whether he is an individual or an entire culture' (1978, p. 29), and the reason for this is not only humanitarian but epistemological, because of the fact that 'exchanging a powerful tradition for a mere dream need not reduce contact with reality. The world in which we live has many sides, many aspects, many potentialities' (1978, p. 169) and we may be wrong about our truths. In this sense, knowledge is neither restricted to science nor emerges only from science. This is our detailed analysis of what Feyerabend called a problem of education. Let us explore more the question of how updated this problem still is, and how pluralism is needed although it is not sufficient for developing critical thinking in students inside science classrooms.

---

5 We are grateful to Karsten Kenklies for pointing out that even WMS falls into the trap of universalism, as if even Occidentalism were somehow a monolithic and homogeneous entity. It is correct that there are many things that could be referred as Occidentalism, however, for the sake of brevity, we will not go further this topic.

3. The Influence of Berkley's Experience in Feyerabend's View on Science Education

We saw before that the PoE revealed the perils of a uniform and universalist science education for individuals, and we also saw that it became damaging for science education practice since it created a crisis in science teaching once people felt a form of indoctrination inside the process of learning about science. In the 1990s, many thinkers pointed out that science, and science education, are not automatically humanitarian or epistemically progressive, and that there is a necessity to pay attention to these features. As consequence, multiple approaches were applied to help people to understand and teach science while avoiding indoctrination (Cobern & Loving, 2001; Matthews, 1992b, 1994; Siegel, 2002; M. U. Smith & Siegel, 2004).

It is remarkable though how Feyerabend noticed this need to avoid indoctrination in science education decades before it became an international concern, thus the PoE was based on such a necessity and concern. Although remarkably, Feyerabend developed a PoE with such a concern, this is not a product of luck, because as we briefly mentioned before, Feyerabend went through changing experiences in the 50s and 60s.

For instance, in 1964, Feyerabend talked about his experiences as a professor at UC Berkeley, under the scenario of new educational policies in which Indians, Mexicans, and blacks entered the university to be 'educated' (1978, p. 118; 1993, p. 263). However, this inclusive policy had a catch which was: how to accomplish to educate a person and what it means by 'education'. For this policy, education was only what rationalists imposed, which were mistakenly taken to be the foundations of Western Modern Science, and the way to accomplish it was through a uniform view of science.

The trade-off proposed for this policy in Berkeley was clear, the freedom of the students in exchange for more knowledge from this monolithic view of science. Feyerabend recalls the mindset of the academic environment at the time. He says that the policy seems to his colleagues like a huge 'opportunity for a prophet in search of a following! What an opportunity, my rationalist friends told me, to contribute to the spreading of reason and the improvement of mankind! What a marvellous opportunity for a new wave of enlightenment! I felt very differently' (1993, p. 263).

At this point, one might ask, why does Feyerabend feel differently? What is wrong to be educated according to Western Modern Science, especially when we are talking about teaching and learning well-established scientific knowledge? The problem, Feyerabend calls our attention, is not about scientific knowledge itself. Bear in mind that his 'examples do not attack science'

(1993, p. 46). Rather the problem is the effort to turn out Western scientific rationalism into the synonymous of scientific and general education.

This effort restricts any alternative in advance by making us worship terms like 'honour, patriotism, truth, rationality, honesty that fills our schools, pulpits, political meetings [which] imperceptibly merges into inarticulation' (1993, p. 266). By considering Western Rationalist intellectuals as 'teachers, the world as a school and "people" as obedient pupils' (1993, p. 161), the policy actually not only tried to impair individuals and cultures, but it also harms science itself since it made science students disinterested in science, as we saw with the crisis of science teaching, and it harms science because it does not present an accurate view of it.

The effort to make the standards of one particular group, like the *universalist Standard Account of science*, the very definition of science should also be considered something non-humanitarian since it forces outsiders to 'become participant of the chosen tradition [and] he will be badgered, persuaded, "educated" until he does' agree with the chosen tradition (Feyerabend, 1978, p. 29). If we embrace uniform science in science classrooms as a guide for scientific knowledge and the world, we must be aware of its cost because uniformity impairs the 'critical power' of the tradition (science), and 'also endangers the free development of the individual' (Feyerabend, 1993, p. 24). This approach, in consequence, has not only an impact on educational institutions and students. It impacts society in general because it impairs the critical capacity of its members when they leave the universities and schools.

These triple undesirable and related things, impairment of science critical power, and impairment of societal and individual development help us to understand why an education that restricts us in advance and as 'as practised in our schools', is something irreconcilable 'with a humanitarian attitude' (Feyerabend, 1993, p. 12). It is irreconcilable not only for epistemological reasons but for restricting in advance individuals and groups' possibilities to play other games, to dedicate to learn other traditions, before even knowing them.

In other words, uniform science and its indoctrination are not only a threat to the existence of non-scientific knowledge, but they are also a threat to the development of plural science itself, individuals, and ultimately, to a free society. In Feyerabend's words, such a scientific education

> is in conflict 'with the cultivation of individuality which alone produces, or can produce, well-developed human beings' it 'maims by compression, like a Chinese lady's foot, every part of human nature which stands out prominently, and tends to make a person markedly different in outline' from the ideals of

rationality that happen to be fashionable in science, or in the philosophy of science. (Stuart Mill apud Feyerabend, 1993, p. 12)

Unfortunately, this is how our educational system, especially in science education, has been working for many decades, where 'elementary education joins hands with higher education to produce individuals who are extremely limited, unfree in their perspective' (Feyerabend, 1978, p. 175).

The way our educational system works is by compressing students and educators into what rationalists and bad empiricists define as the only valid standards to accept answers and questions. So, things like truth, reason, morality, and education would only be properly comprehended when based on their uniform standards. This is why Feyerabend says that while our scientific education 'destroys the most precious gift of the young, their tremendous power of imagination, [it still] speaks of education' (1999 [1963], p. 96, brackets added).

Education, as Feyerabend understands it, must be reconciled with a humanitarian attitude, which means that, on the one hand, it avoids the indoctrination (disguised as education), as seen in our schools, which turns the individual into 'mournful ape, a "bearer" of the *status quo*'; while on the other hand, it makes the individual 'a person who is able to make a choice and to base his whole life on it' (Feyerabend, 1978, p. 176).

One of the consequences of the PoE on the development of individuals is how it affects our capacity to make decisions. According to Brighouse (2006), the capacity of decision-making is fully developed only when individuals had the opportunity to being in contact with multiple choices available. This means that pluralism is one aspect involved in decision-making, but it is not the only one. Decision-making also involves the possibility to evaluate and decide, which means the possibility of accountability for the choices made. However, without proper contact with other games, meaning traditions and epistemologies, it is not even possible to say that one is accountable for the choices since the richness of the world was reduced to please the *status quo*.

4. The Counterinduction as a Tool for Pluralism in Science Education

The crisis in science teaching, the questions about indoctrination, and the search for a humanitarian science education introduced questions about the aims of science education in the classroom, which started with consideration of the plurality of worldviews we commonly found in class (Archila & Molina,

2020; El-Hani & Mortimer, 2007; Matthews, 1998; Oliveira, 2017; M. U. Smith & Siegel, 2004).

According to Feyerabend, considering the kind of education approached by the PoE and how we should change our course, the following question is imposed: what science education do we need? On many occasions (1993, 1978, 1987), Feyerabend seems to give the same answer which is that '*the best education consists in immunizing people against systematic attempts at education*' (1987, p. 316, italics in original). In other words, the best education means that people should be prepared to notice and protect themselves from the attempts of indoctrination by the *status quo* education in place.

The meaning of education as stated by Feyerabend cares more about the people involved in the process than the tradition itself applied in the process. Nonetheless, education as stated by Feyerabend also helps to develop science because it develops the people who will teach and learn science by widening the worldviews beyond what is inductively and systematically taught as education; that is, his understanding of education '*may advance science by proceeding counterinductively*' (1993, p. 20, italics in original), that is, against what has been systematically taught as inductively aimed (admitted), leading to what is naturally the rational path.[6] This is why Feyerabend wants to give people the needed individual development to make their own choices[7] and to do this it seems that we should go against the stream of power.

In his words, we should strengthen students' 'natural contrariness' (1987, p. 316), that is, the education he is arguing claims that what 'we need here is an education that makes people *contrary, counter-suggestive without* making them incapable of devoting themselves to the elaboration of any single view' (Feyerabend, 1999 [1975], p. 188, italics in original). As an example, Galileo states how impressed he is by Copernicus for being counterinductive with respect to his senses. He says:

> Nor can I ever sufficiently admire the outstanding acumen of those who have taken hold of this opinion and accepted it as true: they have, through sheer force of intellect, done such violence to their own senses as to prefer what reason told them over that which sensible experience plainly showed them to be the contrary. (Galilei, 1967 [1632], p. 131)

---

6 The term 'inductively' here is taken from the term 'inductive', from the late Latin *inductivus* meaning hypothetical, leading to; and also 'induct' from the Latin *induct* meaning led to, admit to. In other words, and for our purposes, what is already admitted and led by the education in place. Moreover, counterinduction is used as opposition to the general.

7 Despite his intentions, Feyerabend was aware of the limitations of his proposal and how his view could become also a mean for indoctrination (1993, 1987, 1975).

As Feyerabend notices through the case of Galileo, which we applied for science education, the counterinduction seems to serve well the development of the individual and science, a counter-suggestive education contributes to strengthening 'the minds of the young and "strengthening the minds of the young" means strengthening them *against* any easy acceptance of comprehensive views' (Feyerabend, 1999 [1975], p. 188, italics in original). Thus, the result of such an education would benefit both the development of the individual and science, after all, not only the individual but also science 'needs people who are adaptable and inventive, not rigid imitators of 'established' behavioural patterns' (1993, p. 159, italics in original).

Thus, what rests on the shoulders of science teachers is the responsibility to learn other forms of teaching science. These forms should not simplify science with rationalistic simplifications. Teaching science through a clear-cut of boundaries and where the 'standards which separate what is correct, or rational, or reasonable, or "objective" from what is incorrect, or irrational, or unreasonable, or "subjective"' are now under scrutiny and against our training' (Feyerabend, 1975, p. 21). If we establish a necessary link between scientific knowledge and values like Truth or Reason (with capital letters), then science education would become, from Feyerabend's perspective, a clear contribution to indoctrination and harm to science and society (Oliveira, 2017). Let us now see what has been considered by some science educators and how Feyerabend seems to look for other answers.

4.1. Acceptance and Belief in Science Classrooms Do Not Solve the Problem of Education

Some thinkers have tried different approaches to teach science without maiming students' imagination and without simplifying science. One of the offered answers was the separation of two terms, 'acceptance' and 'belief' when teaching scientific theories. For instance, the acceptance approach takes the basic assumption that students must be able to freely believe in whatever they want since they accept the scientific theory as established knowledge (Gallup, 2017; M. U. Smith et al., 2016). On the other hand, there are authors, like Alters (1997), whose view is that teaching 'students to just understand the material is not a sufficient goal; the teachers must also attempt to have students believe that what is being taught is correct' (Alters, 1997, pp. 15–16).

The proposal to separate acceptance from belief makes no difference if, in the end, the basic myth *guides exchanges* between traditions and determines what is rational, true, and educated and what is the opposite. After all, the exchange would remain based on the idea that when 'teaching a myth, we want to increase the chance that it will be understood (i.e. no puzzlement about any feature of the myth), believed, *and accepted*' (Feyerabend, 1999 [1975], p. 188, italics in original).

To Feyerabend, if traditions such as Western Modern Science, Chinese traditions, indigenous knowledge, and other systems of knowledge were taken seriously, this would offer an opportunity for *open exchange*, by establishing 'connections between different traditions' (1993, p. 228). The establishment of an open exchange realigns science as no longer being our gravitational centre of worldviews. Science becomes one tradition among others, and *prima facie* it is not better, uncontroversial, unlimited, or guided by a single rationale.

The problem of education, like the disinterest in science and indoctrination, cannot be handled with a simple change of concepts. According to Barnes and Brownell (2017), we cannot escape from the problem of students that do not want to understand a theory only by changing our conceptual language. Neither changing of terms nor the simple introduction of epistemological alternatives cuts much ice of our problem. We are missing one important component, the influence of culture on people's life. Feyerabend showed us these limitations when and how he realised the limitations of pure pluralism. He said:

> In 1964–1965 when these ideas first occurred to me I tried to find an *intellectual* solution to my misgivings, that is, I took it for granted that it was up to *me* and the likes of me to devise educational policies for other people. I envisaged a new kind of education that would live from a rich reservoir of different points of view permitting the choice of traditions most advantageous to the individual. The teacher's task would consist of facilitating the choice, not in replacing it by some 'truth' of his own. Such a reservoir, I thought, would have much in common with a *theatre* of ideas as imagined by Piscator and Brecht and it would lead to the development of a great variety of means of presentation. [...]. I now realize that these considerations are just another example of intellectualistic conceit and folly. It is conceited to assume that one has solutions for people whose lives one does not share and whose problems one does not know. It is foolish to assume that such an exercise in distant humanitarianism will have effects pleasing to the people concerned. (Feyerabend, 1978, pp. 119–121, brackets added)

In the same sense of taking cultures seriously, Barnes and Brownell (2017) say that some studies did indicate that there is a weak relationship between acceptance and the supposedly accomplished effect of understanding a scientific theory, such as the theory of evolution. In this account, they say (Barnes & Brownell, 2017), teachers must consider the role played by cultures in the science classroom because 'the research is clear that students' religious beliefs and the beliefs of their family and friends more strongly predict whether they will accept evolution' (Barnes & Brownell, 2017, p. 2).

Thus, before teaching evolutionism in the classroom, the teacher needs to be aware of 'how many students accept views about evolution or creationism because this information is essential for the process of education in this field' (Archila & Molina, 2020, p. 2). On one side, this information is important for the kind of strategy adopted to teach evolution (Archila & Molina, 2020), but on the other side, it does not seem to be enough. We should go deeper.

Teachers should be sensible to the values carried by all systems of knowledge, even science. For instance, Cobern says that recognising 'in the science classroom that all knowledge systems are grounded in presuppositions would re-introduce a valuable discussion on the nature and meaning of scientific knowledge itself' (Cobern, 2000, p. 241). These presuppositions are of many types, and values (epistemic and non-epistemic) are one of them.

These presuppositions will be a starting point against the kind of science education which considers itself an all-powerful 'autonomous science' as if science in the classroom could ignore all these elements and sustain itself above people. This kind of autonomous science poses a threat to students' autonomy, it 'poses a threat to any meaningful sense of life and Nature for most students' (Cobern, 2000, p. 241). We should remind our science teachers that non-scientific cultures also have their own epistemologies, and what the science teacher may think to be a belief is 'actually a form of knowledge' for these cultures (Cobern, 2000, p. 236).

In the science classroom, the differences in seeing all these traditions (scientific and non-scientific) as pervaded by other elements, such as values and group beliefs, take a necessary step back in the discussion of acknowledging the plurality of traditions in the classroom and abandoning the ideal of value-free science, which is something we will briefly approach now.

4.2. The Problem of Education and Value-Free Science

Year in and year out, we keep addressing this need to be pluralist, especially in science education. One of the reasons to do this is the fact that, despite many efforts promoted by philosophers in the 1980s and 1990s (Douglas, 2009; Longino, 1990, 2002), there is still a strong view in scientists, science teachers, and philosophers, that science is value-free ideal. Science as cold way of thinking, a pure fact knowledge machine freed of the mundane disputes around human values and affairs. All matters of science would then then be purely factual, experimental, and evidential, interpreted by our best theoretical efforts. No value would be involved in the justification and evaluation of these theories, establishment of disciplines. The rule is supposed to be simple, theories that for whatever reason fail in the face of evidence should go away, and any other values were thought to not play any role here in the justification (K. R. Popper, 2002 [1959]).

This concept of value-free science plays an important role in the construction of an indoctrinated way of teaching science. The reason is its relationship with an image of a rational science closer than any other tradition to the ultimate truth, reason, and neutrality that helps all humans regardless of their cultural identity. At this point, that famous passage of Matthews (1994) that gave the foundations of a *universalist Standard Account of science* explored above about volcanoes, must be reinstated in its entirety. He says that just

> as volcanic eruptions are indifferent to the race or sex of those in the vicinity, and lava kills whites, blacks, men, women, believers, non-believers, equally, so also the science of lava flows will be the same for all. [...] ... it is the behavior of volcanoes that finally judges the adequacy of our vulcanology, not the reverse. (1994, p. 182)

Naturally, many things changed since Matthews stated this example and definition. Nonetheless, the effects of such a view still resonate with many teachers and contributed to the idea of value-free science. According to Douglas, a value-free ideal is something that emerged in its fully articulated form only in the 1950s (Douglas, 2016). She synthesises this idea of value-free science by explaining that, on the one hand, values in science were a largely uncontroversial topic in the sense that 'values shape what scientists chose to explore' (Douglas, 2016, p. 2). On the other hand, values were only thought to be part of the logic of discovery, not the logic of justification. In this account, this separation was rooted in the fear that if it was admitted that values played a role in the logic of justification then 'the worry was (and remains) that science could be corrupted' (Douglas, 2016, p. 2).

Behind this fear of corruption of science by values in the context of justification, we noticed that something else might nurture this fear. The frightening picture is that many features and elements that usually played important roles in our positivist approaches to scientific knowledge, such as impartial and universal methods, autonomous facts (facts that once discovered are independent of the theory), could only be dreams of a powerful group, as to say it in Feyerabend's words (1993).

This means that for a pluralist approach in science education, the view of a value-laden science (Douglas, 2016) needs to play with more than one player, to be pluralist. We argue that a value-laden science, when taught in science classrooms, is desirable once it puts the cards on the table (which values embrace), it allows us to dialogue about them, criticise them, and make them compete with other scientific and non-scientific views. Such a value-laden science must be able to allow the students to have contact with these values and to be proficient in the game of science, without losing their minds to them.

In other words, the expectation that scientific justification is also pluralist and value-laden, instead of only theory-laden and uniform, makes our science education richer because it allows the students to realise that 'even the apparently hardest scientific "fact" can be dissolved by decisions undermining the values that make it a fact and/or by research that replaces it by facts of a different kind' (Feyerabend, 1993, p. 236). This being said, let us now explore a bit more concrete ways to be versed in science from a pluralist perspective.

5. *The Game Approach of Traditions: Proficiency and Critical Thinking*

Insofar as we explored the problem of education we also broke it down into four parts. In addition, we explored its origin (uniform view), arguing how pluralism is needed in science education, and also how and why pluralism is limited by the need for other aspects that come along with other divergent cosmologies and elements such as epistemologies, cultures, and values. We also proposed a change in our view of science education from uniformism to pluralism, that besides theory, included values.

But all these debates had the intent to open room for debating the constitution of Feyerabend's approach to science education in the day-to-day practices in educational institutions. This approach addresses a more practical answer for dealing with the PoE as we stated, and this is important because it gives a more applicable approach for science teachers without losing sight of teaching science.

In its roots, the description and analysis of the PoE expose an attempt to simplify and unite a world that refuses to be understood in such uniform terms. The abundant and complex world we live in, and how our science education should picture it, can only be contemplated by limited beings with the pragmatic turn of our views about science. Feyerabend (1993) addresses this complex world through pluralism and the need to strengthen students' minds. To do this, within learning and teaching context of schools, he refers to traditions (scientific and non-scientific alike) as if they were games. It is noteworthy to remember that whatever the content you think should be taught in science classrooms, he wants to guarantee freedom of thought, an education should impair individuals to 'devoting themselves to the elaboration of any single view' (1999 [1975], p. 188). Even if it is science itself (a pluralist one).

Science would then be just another game, not necessarily the best game that we humans developed to deal with in our abundant world but it is still a game. This treatment of traditions as games has the purpose of creating a distance between the traditions and their participants and observers. The distance does not mean a lack of interest, but their openness to learn science, and other games. Generally, the development of a plurality of games is a common practice of our species, and learning how to play one does not harm our mind to play others. Maybe the reason for it is that what is so unique about games is that being able to play one does not turn you incapable of appreciating and playing others. Maybe what is so useful about the game approach in education is that, on the one hand, it has a natural attribute of learning to play a game (like theories and methods) does not turn it into your life. It is still as the saying goes, 'just a game'. On the other hand, learning traditions as a game puts it into perspective with other games, so it will hardly hook you up if the teacher shows that there are many fun games to be played. This type of distance is needed in science education.

From Feyerabend's view, the interaction between traditions (games), which for the sake of our argument often happens in the science classroom, should adopt a pragmatic philosophy in which the 'pragmatist must be both a participant and an observer' (1993, p. 217). In the science classrooms, aligned but beyond what Barnes and Brownell (2017) said, the task to be set for teaching science is not only a matter of being aware of the influence of cultures and systems of beliefs. The task in place, especially when teaching topics like evolutionism, requires that the teacher could understand her own culture and beliefs, and the students' limitations for engaging, or breaking out (depending of the level of commitment already in place), from science tradition. Therefore, when 'considering any interaction of traditions we may ask two kinds of questions which I shall call *observer questions* and *participant questions* respectively' (1993, p. 216). These questions are as follows:

> *Observer questions* are concerned with the details of an interaction. They want to give a historical account of the interaction and, perhaps, formulate laws, or rules of thumb, that apply to all interactions. Hegel's triad: position, negation, synthesis (negation of the negation) is such a rule. [...]. The observer asks: what happens and what is going to happen?
> *Participant questions* deal with the attitude the members of a practice or a tradition are supposed to take towards the (possible) intrusion of another. [...] The participant asks: what shall I do? Shall I support the interaction? Shall I oppose

it? Or shall I simply forget about it? (Feyerabend, 1993, p. 216, brackets added; italics in original)

In other words, a pragmatic philosophy, in Feyerabendian terms, means that the practice of interaction between traditions presupposes acknowledging our limitations in making and understanding questions. Because of this, a pragmatic philosophy also acknowledges the fallibility of our own traditions. This is the distance from our own views that a gamification of education brings. The Feyerabendian game approach of traditions in science education means that students must be prepared for a pragmatic philosophy that 'can flourish only if the traditions to be judged and the developments to be influenced are seen as temporary makeshifts and not as lasting constituents of thoughts and action' (1993, p. 217). To put it bluntly, it recommends to all of us take some distance from all traditions, which for each one of us it is not an easy thing to do. It is not easy because 'it is very difficult to see one's own most cherished ideas in perspective, as parts of a changing and, perhaps, absurd tradition' (1993, p. 218).

But how would this pragmatic philosophy be carried out? Our analysis of the constitution of Feyerabend's view of science education, although composed of many aspects, will be here restricted to only two items, proficiency, and critical thinking, which will be useful in day-to-day life of schools.

5.1. Teaching Critical Thinking in Science Education Through Game Approach and Pluralism

That being said, first of all, the idea of critical thinking and also the promotion of proficiency to play a plurality of games are important in a pragmatic philosophy because it works through an open exchange.

Second, is the very practical aspect of it. Manifested into two moments, while critical thinking awakes and grows from plurality and contrariness by revealing the games available, proficiency engages students in learning the games.

In order to build this balance, students must be introduced to science 'without serious commitment and without robbing the mind of its ability to play other games as well' (Feyerabend, 1993, p. 161). This is a challenge for teachers, not the students.

If students, especially at their early ages, are taught to take things so seriously and commit themselves to one game, the desirable emancipation would be turned into an indoctrination process, because there would be a preference for one game, which would not be criticised, whereas others will necessarily be, as we detailed in previous sections (Feyerabend, 1993).

According to Feyerabend, it is by the early introduction of pluralism to our students that they would have a chance to know about the existence of many alternatives. This is the first step, that is, to get rid of a uniform view of science without getting rid of science itself, which could be approached from pluralism.

The second step of pluralism is acknowledging our limitations as participants of one tradition, or as Feyerabend asked us: 'how can we possibly examine something we are using all the time? How can we analyze the terms in which we habitually express our most simple and straightforward observations, and reveal their presuppositions?' (1993, p. 22).

To put these questions into our topic of interest, how can we examine critically something by which we are completely restricted? How can we critically analyse the terms we are using while being completely dependent on them? Whatever the case, it is clear that we 'cannot discover it from the *inside*' (1993, p. 22), that is, the only way to do it is from outside of the game we are playing.

In other words, using the pluralistic account, and the limits of our knowledge and tradition in making questions, we must look to think outside the box as part of the construction of critical thinking in students. This is how the idea of analysis and the need of doing it from outside lies behind the general constitution the notion of critical thinking. The idea is to break free from one game (even our own). This idea where critical thinking is built from outside one's most cherished tradition, which is something suggested by Feyerabend, finds support elsewhere, in the origins of the term criticism. The term criticism is related to the term 'critic', from the Greek *kritēs* (a judge), from *krinein* (judge, decide), which additionally begs for things to be decided based on an equal opportunity of the parts involved to be heard. In this sense, the kind of critical thinking Feyerabend is arguing, and for us also needed in science education, means that we should search for 'an *external* standard of criticism' (1993, p. 22). In one important paragraph, he explains this in detail.

> ... observational reports, experimental results, 'factual' statements, either *contain* theoretical assumptions or *assert* them by the manner in which they are used. [...]. All these are abstract, and highly doubtful, assumptions which shape our view of the world without being accessible to a direct criticism. Usually, we are not even aware of them and we recognize their effects only when we encounter an entirely different cosmology: prejudices are found by contrast, not by analysis. The material which the *scientist* has at his disposal, his most sublime theories and his most sophisticated techniques included, is structured in exactly the same way. (1993, p. 22, brackets added, italics in original)

So, there is no pluralism if the standards we are using do not give us an external perspective or even allow us to explore and have meaningful contact with other cosmologies. In other words, critical thinking in science education needs scientific pluralism, which cannot exist without general pluralism because criticism 'involves a comparison with other existing alternatives' (Feyerabend, [1968] 1999, p. 111), and this comparison should come from ontologically divergent alternatives, such as the one we find in Protagoras' proposal, which 'is *reasonable* because it pays attention to the pluralism of traditions and values. And it is *civilized* for it does not assume that one's own village and the strange customs it contains are the navel of the world' (1993, p. 226).

Critical thinking, in Feyerabendian terms, not only allows us to retain refuted theories, it asks us to examine the strengths and the weaknesses of the accepted game and the process that lead to it, and the exclusion of others. This type of science education can only be accomplished by an integrated account of the history of science and the philosophy of science. For instance, Feyerabend notices that 'scientific textbooks explain the theories which are commonly accepted and only rarely mention existing alternatives or weaknesses of the current theories' ([1961]1999, p. 61). A pluralist account of science such as 'a rich reservoir of different points of view' (1993 p. 265), is better achieved by strengthening students' contrariness and an external reference. The remaining question though, is how we get out from our own most cherished beliefs if, as self-explained, they are so beloved? Our answer is through the proficiency.

5.2. *Game Approach and Proficiency as Qualitative Contact*

As we said, pluralism is not enough. When left alone, Feyerabend remembers that pluralism is just a product of a 'conceit and folly intellectualism' (1993, p. 266).[8] To develop critical thinking, and to take advantage of pluralism, *we must have contact with other games* but first, we need to counter-reason

---

8 One might point to the risk of making pluralism a new *status quo*, the new fairy tale. This question was made by Ernan McMullin to Feyerabend, and there are two answers for this objection. First one is Feyerabend's answer which says that 'not to replace one set of general rules by another such set: my intention is, rather, to convince the reader that *all methodologies, even the most obvious ones, have their limits*' (1993, p. 23, italics in original). The second answer, which we present, is that pluralism itself is a meta-epistemology, or as Kellert, Longino and Waters (2006) said a *Stance*, which open spaces for all traditions and for constant dynamics without placing one of them definitely in the centre of power. Third, to accuse pluralism of universalism is to fall in the same argumentative trap that Popper (K. Popper, 2002 [1945]) avoid between democracy and totalitarianism, where the totalitarian accused the democrat of being totalitarian for not allowing him to play the game.

against *status quo*. For instance, nowadays, who would dare to doubt the very existence of the world such as Descartes once did? Who would dare to ask if Darwin were an evolutionist? From a uniform view, it seems that no one should dare to make these questions and this choice is usually considered to be rational. Well, we argue that it is not rational and neither a critical way of thinking.

This is why Feyerabend's idea of contrariness helps us to play other games and even to teach scientific theories critically and interestingly. For instance, Delisle (2019) proposes something that would appear to be irrational under such a uniform view of science, but in a counterinductive way, Deslile says, 'a liberating question can be raised in order to shake off the weight of the historiographical tradition: Was Darwin really an evolutionist?' (2019, p. 22).

This question seems to be absurd depending on which view of science one has taken and how it should be taught. Of course, those who know the history of evolution in detail would not, at least for epistemological and historical reasons, think that this is an absurd question. But on the other side, if the history of evolutionary theory is crystallized in science classes, Delisle's liberating question could look foolish and embarrassing if a student states it. This position restricts students' imagination and keeps the possibility of learning and thinking critically against the *status quo*, a task impossible to accomplish from outside of what has already been accepted. This is why to be able to play other games, we must be proficient in them. Even if one must criticise science, and exposes its weaknesses, proficiency in it is even so more needed. Feyerabend even remembers that Lenin said something similar and in a practical fashion. He said:

> 'Two very important practical conclusions follow from this [character of the historical process],' writes Lenin, continuing the passage from which I have just quoted. 'First, that in order to fulfil its task, the revolutionary class [i.e. the class of those who want to change either a part of society such as science, or society as a whole] must be able to master all forms or aspects of social activity without exception [it must be able to understand, and to apply, not only one particular methodology, but any methodology, and any variation thereof it can imagine] ...; second [it] must be ready to pass from one to another in the quickest and most unexpected manner.' (Feyerabend, 1993, p. 10)

To be proficient in one game, such as science, students must be able to play it, which means they must be able to understand a fair number of things for playing it. To be proficient one must know well the rules and how to analyse the game, to contrast it with others. But to do this, we must have a good amount of knowledge about them, which means theoretical and practical.

Philosophers of science that even criticize science, like Feyerabend, had a fair amount of knowledge about it.

Of course, practical and theoretical not in the sense of being professionally a scientist. An individual who wants to play chess does not need to be professional in any sense in order to do this. To be proficient we must be interested in the game, but also without losing the ability to play others. When we are playing the games, the

> The standards will be considered, they will be discussed, children will be encouraged to get proficiency in the more important subjects, but only as one gets proficiency in a game, that is, without serious commitment and without robbing the mind of its ability to play other games as well. Having been prepared in this way a young person may decide to devote the rest of his life to a particular profession and he may start taking it seriously forthwith. (Feyerabend, 1993, p. 161)

Nonetheless, the proficiency for playing many games, which is in part responsible for developing critical thinking, cannot happen without 'a fairly complete knowledge of alternatives' (Feyerabend, 1993, p. 161). Or to repeat Lenin's words quoted by Feyerabend: 'the revolutionary class [i.e. the class of those who want to change either a part of society such as science, or society as a whole] must be able to master all forms or aspects of social activity without exception' (Feyerabend, 1993, p. 10). This fairly complete knowledge of the plurality of games cannot happen by bending minds to conform people 'to the standards of one particular group' (Feyerabend, 1993, p. 161). It cannot happen by appealing to values that exist above all games, like truth, objectivity, and morality, and neither as only revealing that pluralism of traditions exists.

On the one hand, a pluralist account of scientific knowledge is not only rich in content as it is helpful to build a critical awareness of our surroundings, and without it, 'we can reach neither a true appreciation of the achievements of science nor a properly critical attitude regarding the claims of science' (Chang, 2012, p. xv). On the other hand, pluralism seems to fall short of the development of our critical thinking, which is why the game proficiency approach is needed.

The notion of proficiency supplements pluralism in science education and the reason for it is that proficiency suggests a *qualitative contact* with other traditions, values, theories, and cosmologies revealed by pluralism.

It is not enough to comprehend a game, that is, to be well-informed of the rules, laws, methods, and principles (let us call this the technical content of a theory). Rather, we should aim for being proficient in the sense of escaping from any 'serious commitment' (Feyerabend, 1993, p. 162) that robs students' minds and obstruct a conscious choice, and which can only happen after a 'fairly complete knowledge of alternatives' (Feyerabend, 1993, p. 162).

In detailed terms, the so-required 'fairly complete knowledge of alternatives' in practical terms means something like being aware of the existence of an 'account of the alternatives replaced, of the process of replacement, of the arguments used in its course, of the strength of the old views and the weaknesses of the new, not a "systematic account" but a *historical account of each stage of knowledge*, [this] can alleviate these drawbacks and increase the rationality of one's theoretical commitments' (Feyerabend, 1993, p. 31, brackets added, italics in original).[9]

In other words, proficiency involves the mastery of the technical content of a game/theory. But only that is not enough. One needs to have contact with the game, one needs to play it.[10] Why is that? Because a dogmatic person with good memory and a basic scientific training formation can explain a game (Darwin's natural selection or Lamarck's evolutionism or a Greek explanation of the origins of the universe).

Since proficiency requires a pluralist attitude, especially divergent ones with respect to our own views, it is reasonable to infer that Feyerabend's proficiency appeals to an exploration of other forms of life, a contact with the plurality of realities.

According to Feyerabend's idea of proficiency, a primary aim of science education is to help the students to avoid any commitment in advance with any game, even taking distance from their own game, in order to prepare them '*to choose between the standards*' (1993 161).[11] This is also why there is no good science education possible if in the classroom we suppress scientific

---

9 We must recall here that Feyerabend does not want to separate these three disciplines science, philosophy of science and history of science (1993, p 34) in the sense that, despite their different identities, we should acknowledge their mutual influence, and then the impossibility to fully understand one without the help of the other.

10 In some way this is also close to Matthew's criticism in favour of the notion of understanding, accordingly to, in science education, understanding goes beyond the immediately available information respect a scientific theory, like, its laws, methods, evidences, and principles (Matthews, 1998).

11 Naturally, science teaching in schools is still about science, but this does not mean that, when necessary, teachers could not discuss scientific or non-scientific alternatives with the students. For instance, in the case of evolutionism, where we may find religious beliefs playing a role in the process of learning evolution, it is important to debate the points of intersection between them, whether in classrooms or through broader projects in a very opening and honest way, where the strengthens and weaknesses of both traditions are explored.

knowledge from debating with other areas, like history and philosophy, and neither if we insulate a single theory from its critics and alternatives.

Proficiency, then, is a form of contact with these alternatives. The self-imposed question is: what do we mean by 'contact'? Feyerabend's proficiency and pluralism go beyond the acknowledgement of the existence of alternatives, like the existence of a plurality of products in an aisle of a supermarket (Oliveira, 2021; Preston, 2000).[12] Contact is more than a supermarket with shelves full of products (like ontologies and theories available). A contact is a kind of touch to the game, where one understands the theoretical aspects, knows how to play it, and play it. In other words, qualitative contact comes in gradation.

According to Feyerabend, 'the explanation is rather simple. Understanding cannot exist without contact' (1999, p. 268); that is, in a classroom where a clash of traditions may occur, the people involved in the clash need to have proficiency in both games to deeper the dialogue. If this isn't the case, if neither the student nor the teacher has proficiency, the better thing to do is to acknowledge these limitations respecting the games while looking forward to such proficiency in case the debate seems to be interesting enough for the individuals involved.

5.2.1. Qualitative Contact: The Supermarket Example

Let us build our case from the example of the supermarket that Feyerabend (1999) used elsewhere. For instance, if a person enters a big supermarket aisle looking for coffee and finds a shelf full of brands of coffee beans, then say that this is a form of a plurality of options available (assuming that what other supermarkets sell does not matter now). By starting to look at the brands on the shelf, and seeing his favorite brand, this person sees the plurality, and contemplates the possibility it carries (like trying another brand). Only this contemplating attitude, like reading and observing the variety, is an important step for proficiency and plurality. The plurality might give to this person the thought that her choice for a single coffee brand could be at least poorly informed and the world of coffee is more abundant than imagined. Next step, given that this person has time to spend, and coffee is a sufficiently important subject for her, then she may feel the need to read and compare the labels of each brand. This person may discover flavours she did not even imagine could exist in coffee.

Although these two steps, seeing and reading the packages of the brands, are already a beginning for proficiency, this would not be called a fairly

12 To more details about this concept of science as supermarket, see John Preston's (2000) excellent paper about it.

complete knowledge of the coffee brands available in the supermarket aisle. This is a better description of the pluralist proficiency and contact, although it started only by contemplating the implications of the existence of pluralism and by reading the packages. So now the person needs to get in touch with the coffee, something like tasting the coffee found on the shelf. By doing this, she would note that some flavours written on the package label were stronger than previously thought. She may find also other flavours that she could not even perceive despite the description in the label, and other flavours were as good as expected. This person may discover flavors she did not even imagine could exist in coffee, experiences of combining it with other foods and drinks. The possibilities and knowledge on coffee definitely changed, as the references for comparison of what coffee is more acid or sweet, what aspect she likes more, and what she will look in her next visit to the supermarket. She may even improve the consciousness over her own preferences.

Now, this person has some theoretical and practical knowledge about the coffee tasted. She can now compare her previously favoured coffee with the ones she tasted. At least concerning the coffee brands tasted, she has proficiency in this minimal sense (which could be increased with time and other contacts and experiences).

Thus, proficiency could be gradually increased (like tasting more and more of the same brand or new brands), although it does not need to. In the future, the ability to make a choice, and to commit to more than one coffee is the point. Students should learn the need to taste the games before making any commitment to any of them; they should have contacted them. This is one way for students to learn science without having their minds robbed by one tradition in the process, something similar to how Nietzsche saw baths, that is, 'I approach deep problems like cold baths: quick into them and quickly out again' (Nietzsche, 1985 [1946], p. 231).

As it is concluded from Brighouse's defence of pluralism in schools, it is the wide range of alternatives and our contact with them that allows us to live a flourishing life (Brighouse, 2006). It is the possibility to see our own worldviews in perspective, as temporary makeshifts of an absurd tradition, that in practice gives us the opportunity to better respect and understand the different values and systems of knowledge without murdering them for being different from ours (which applies to every culture and not only scientific ones).

6. *Final Considerations*

This text presents a problem, which is the problem of education, and also an answer to this problem from a Feyerabendian perspective. To do this, we show how Feyerabend's criticism of science is not one of all forms of science but only one of a uniform science. Based on Feyerabend's argument, we exposed how uniform science often uses its successes as an argumentative strategy to convince people about its superiority, and by extension also produce something very non-scientific, which is the indoctrination of people into science. But as we argued, scientific successes can also be interpreted in a pluralistic fashion, which avoids indoctrination while sustaining the value of science as a very successful activity. This leads us to reveal the conflict between at least two approaches to science, the uniform and the pluralist one. The uniform view of science leads science education to the so-called problem of education. The problem of education (PoE), as Feyerabend states it, is constituted by the idea that scientific knowledge should be used to help people to make their own choice. Rather science education has been used to indoctrinate students that a scientific worldview is the more successful form of knowledge that humans developed about the world and that to choose something else than science is only the result of a lack of contact with science. This uniform approach shows that the PoE slavered our perceptions of science while murdering other cultures, and pushing people away from science (Feyerabend, 1993). Naturally, the PoE has not only implications for science education, but it has for science itself, individuals, and society, producing a crisis in science teaching (Fourez, 2003). In a certain way, the view of science defended by rationalists in science education has its origins in the universalist view of science. Thus, we addressed in detail the problem of education, breaking it down into four parts, and how one of these parts has to do with such a universalist view, which was dubbed by the literature in education as *a universalist Standard Account of science*, composed of seven elements. However, although this crisis emerged only recently, Feyerabend notices the PoE much earlier than most philosophers and science educators. The reason for it is related to his experience in Berkeley in 64 as a professor during a period of changes in educational policies.

Based on this PoE, our interpretation of what would be Feyerabend's answer to it follows these elements covered in sections four and five. The first one is that to avoid the PoE, we should pick up a different view of science, the pluralist one. Second, pluralist views of science allow scientific pluralism, allow alternative worldviews, and recommend the students that going against the *status quo* does not mean they are being irrational, and neither against science. Pluralism in science education gives space for debating something beyond a theory-laden science, which is something Heather Douglas called value-laden science, whose understanding is that justification, and not only discovery, are also part of the values in the process of inventing, testing, and sustaining theories. It is a view that science is not value-free activity. In this sense, the uniform view that science education should change students' beliefs is attached to universalist and occidental values, and as such it is irreconcilable with a pluralist view of science as supported by Feyerabend. A more moderate view of science, given by Barnes and Brownell (2017) seems to embrace that acceptance of theories avoids the problems of believing in scientific theories, but only if the teacher considers the importance of the values in the cultures of the students. From our interpretation of Feyerabend's education, this position seems to be more inclusive, but we should dig deeper into the PoE and into what acknowledging these values and worldviews from non-scientific culture means in practice. Our third element for the PoE based on Feyerabend's work is a more practical one. It is something we decide to name it 'game approach' of science in science education. The game approach focuses on the teaching of science in the proficiency to teach and learn about science, as if science were a game, just as much as any other tradition and epistemology that may be revealed in a class by the students. So, everyone should take a distance from their own traditions and be able to see all of them as successful in their own right but also limited, with flaws, temporary and, ultimately, not as an end in themselves but as means for developing our individual consciousness. Our Fourth element suggests considering traditions as games and under a pluralistic view, meaning that in order to think more clearly about them, to be able to better develop our critical thinking which will address our most cherished beliefs and traditions, we must be able to think outside them. But to be able to think outside them means that we must be able to be proficient in other traditions. This is also the reason why we need epistemic and cultural diversity in our schools and to be able to debate them, if necessary, in science education. But to talk about them is easier than actually working with them.

From our interpretation, what Feyerabend is saying is that in order to teach science we need to think of science education as composed by also a pluralist stance of history and philosophy of science. One which allows an *open exchange* between the traditions in the classroom and allows the students to put their own tradition in perspective. In conclusion, and to give a broad view of our text about Feyerabend's perspective of science education, and education in general, we argued that students should learn how to make decisions, and their autonomy and happiness is the most important aspects of any education, not the traditions themselves that are being taught, or that was imposed on us in our early age.

References

Alters, B. (1997). Should student belief of evolution be a goal. *Reports of the National Center for Science Education*, *17*(1), 15–16.

Archila, P. A., & Molina, J. (2020). Evolution and creationism: Views of students in a Colombian University – findings from 7 years of data using a three-question survey. *Research in Science Education*, *50*(4), 1619–1638. https://doi.org/10.1007/s11165-018-9746-3

Barnes, M. E., & Brownell, S. E. (2017). A call to use cultural competence when teaching evolution to religious college students: Introducing religious cultural competence in evolution education (ReCCEE). *CBE – Life Sciences Education*, *16*(4), es4.

Brighouse, H. (2006). *On education*. Routledge.

Chalmers, A. (2013). *What is this thing called science?* Queensland Press.

Chang, H. (2012). *Is water H_2O? Evidence, realism and pluralism*. Springer.

Cobern, W. W. (2000). The nature of science and the role of knowledge and belief. *Science and Education*, *9*, 219–246.

Cobern, W. W., & Loving, C. C. (2001). Defining 'science' in a multicultural world: Implications for science education. *Science Education*, *85*(1), 50–67.

Douglas, H. (2009). *Science, policy, and the value-free ideal*. University of Pittsburgh Press.

Douglas, H. (2016). Values in science. In P. Humphreys (Ed.), *The Oxford handbook of philosophy of science*. Oxford University Press.

El-Hani, C. N., & Mortimer, E. (2007). Multicultural education, pragmatism, and the goals of science teaching. *Cultural Studies of Science Education*, *2*, 657–702. https://doi.org/10.1007/s11422-007-9064-y

Feyerabend, P. ([1961] 1999). Knowledge without foundation. In J. Preston (Ed.), *Philosophical papers – knowledge, science, and relativism* (Vol. 3, pp. 50–77). Cambridge University Press.

Feyerabend, P. ([1968] 1999). Outline of a pluralistic theory of knowledge and action. In J. Preston (Ed.), *Philosophical papers – knowledge, science, and relativism* (Vol. 3, pp. 104–111). Cambridge University Press.

Feyerabend, P. (1975). *Against method: Outline of an anarchistic theory of knowledge*. Humanities Press.

Feyerabend, P. (1978). *Science in a free society*. NLB.

Feyerabend, P. (1987). *Farewell to reason*. Verso.

Feyerabend, P. (1993). *Against method* (3rd ed.). Verso.

Feyerabend, P. (1999 [1962]). Knowledge without foundation. In J. Preston (Ed.), *Philosophical papers – Knowledge, science, and relativism* (Vol. 3, pp. 50–77). Cambridge University Press.

Feyerabend, P. (1999 [1963]). How to be a good empiricist: A plea for tolerance in matters epistemological. In J. Preston (Ed.), *Philosophical papers – knowledge, science, and relativism* (Vol. 3, pp. 78–103). Cambridge University Press.

Feyerabend, P. (1999 [1975]). How to defend society against science. In J. Preston (Ed.), *Philosophical papers. Volume 3: Knowledge, science, and relativism* (Vol. 3, pp. viii, 257 p.). Cambridge University Press.

Feyerabend, P. (1999 [1980]). Democracy, elitism and scientific method. In *Philosophical papers – knowledge, science and relativism* (Vol. 3, pp. 212–226). Cambridge University Press.

Feyerabend, P., & Terpstra, B. (1999). *Conquest of abundance: A tale of abstraction versus the richness of being.* University of Chicago Press.

Fourez, G. (2003). Crise no ensino de ciências. *Investigações em ensino de ciências, 8*(2), 109–123.

Galilei, G. (1967 [1632]). *Dialogue concerning the two chief world systems: Ptolemaic & Copernican* (S. Drake, Trans., 2nd ed.). University of California Press.

Gallup. (2017). In US, belief in creationist view of humans at new low. *Gallup News.* Retrieved from https://news.gallup.com/poll/210956/belief-creationist-view-humans-new-low.aspx

Irzik, G. (2001). Universalism, multiculturalism, and science education. *Science Education, 85*(1), 71–73.

Irzik, G., & Nola, R. (2007). Worldviews and their relation to science. In *Science, worldviews and education* (pp. 81–97). Springer.

Kellert, S. H., Longino, H. E., & Waters, C. K. (2006). *Scientific pluralism* (pp. xxix, 248 p). University of Pittsburgh Press.

Longino, H. (1990). *Science as social knowledge: Values and objectivity in scientific inquiry.* Princeton University Press.

Longino, H. (2002). *The fate of knowledge.* Princeton University Press.

Matthews, M. R. (1988). A role for history and philosophy in science teaching. *Educational Philosophy and Theory, 20*(2), 67–81.

Matthews, M. R. (1992). History, philosophy, and science teaching: The present rapprochement. *Science & Education, 1*(1), 11–47.

Matthews, M. R. (1994). *Science teaching: The role of history and philosophy of science* (p. 256). Routledge.

Matthews, M. R. (1998). In defense of modest goals when teaching about the nature of science. *Journal of Research in Science Teaching: The Official Journal of the National Association for Research in Science Teaching, 35*(2), 161–174.

Nietzsche, F. W. (1985 [1946]). Beyond good and evil. In A. Nehamas (Ed.), *Nietzsche, life as literature.* Harvard University Press.

Oliveira, D. G. d. S. (2017). *Anarquismo, Autonomia e Esclarecimento no Objetivo do Ensino de Ciências* (Doutorado). Universidade Federal do Recôncavo da Bahia.

Oliveira, D. G. d. S. (2021). The cosmological divergent proliferation in Feyerabend's pluralism. *Principia: An International Journal of Epistemology, 25*(3), 421–454. https://doi.org/10.5007/1808-1711.2021.e72764

Popper, K. (2002 [1945]). *The open society and its enemies.* Routledge.

Popper, K. R. (2002 [1959]). *The logic of scientific discovery.* Routledge.

Preston, J. (2000). Science as supermarket. In *The Worst enemy of science* (pp. 80–101). Oxford University Press.

Preston, J., Munévar, G., & Lamb, D. (2000). *The worst enemy of science? Essays in memory of Paul Feyerabend.* Oxford University Press.

Siegel, H. (2002). Multiculturalism, universalism, and science education: In search of common ground. *Science Education, 86*(6), 803–820.

Smith, M. U., & Siegel, H. (2004). Knowing, believing, and understanding: What goals for science education? *Science and Education, 13*, 553–583.

Smith, M. U., Snyder, S. W., & Devereaux, R. S. (2016). The GAENE – generalized acceptance of evolution evaluation: development of a new measure of evolution acceptance. *Journal of Research in Science Teaching, 53*(9), 1289–1315.

Song, S. (2010). Multiculturalism. In E. N. Zalta (Ed.), *The Stanford encyclopedia of philosophy* (Fall 2020 ed.). Metaphysics Research Lab, Stanford University. https://plato.stanford.edu/archives/fall2020/entries/multiculturalism/

Ziman, J. M. (1980). *Teaching and learning about science and society.* Cambridge University Press.

The Place of Scientific Errors in Feyerabend's Pluralism for Educational Purposes

LÍLIA FERREIRA SOUZA QUEIROZ AND DEIVIDE GARCIA DA SILVA OLIVEIRA

1. Introduction

In schools, universities, and the news, we are told that scientific theories have been superseded by other scientific theories or just by some experiment. We all know that science makes errors and that scientists can make errors when carrying out their experiments, that is, errors are part of science's ordinary life. However, what does this teach us about science being fundamentally experimental and fallible? Often, the issue of errors often goes unnoticed in scientific education, or it is just approached superficially, disregarding the relevant role of errors in the development of scientific knowledge.

This type of contact with errors can raise many doubts among students and the general population regarding the reliability of scientific knowledge. Questions like: Is scientific knowledge true? Are the mistakes made by science all corrected? Does science always succeed in its research? How far can we trust the science that makes errors? Faced with these questions, philosophical investigations about errors have become an important part of the research. It is not enough to say that science is wrong or fallible, which on the one hand, can generate a certain level of distrust in science and, on the other hand, perhaps is not enough to break with the conceptions that science seeks an absolute truth, placing errors as naturally surmountable obstacles.

Many authors advocate for the inclusion of the topic of scientific errors in science teaching (Allchin, 2012, 2017, 2020; Kipnis, 2010; Zachos et al., 2003), especially because errors are significant to understanding the nature of science and a fundamental part of competence for scientific literacy. However, the issue of errors in science teaching is still a major challenge for educators, managers, and trainers of educational curricula.

Faced with this challenge, this work sought to understand the relationship between scientific errors and Paul Feyerabend's pluralism, including the role and analysis of errors in scientific knowledge as part of science education. Based on the definition of scientific error used by Feyerabend in his article *Classical Empiricism* ([1970] 1981, pp. 38–39): 'deviations from the accepted point of view'.

In the next section, we first delve into the problem of scientific errors (2), in particular the issues of reliability of scientific claims, emphasising the relationships of errors to the nature of science (2.2). We defend the need for a[1] progressive view of scientific errors in science teaching. This is reflected in Feyerabend's pluralistic perspective, as discussed in section 3. In his perspective, errors are part of the human character of science (3.1); they are productive for the progress of science (3.2) and are not transitory in the development of scientific knowledge (3.3). This understanding forms a basis within the Feyerabendian proposal of a pluralistic scientific education, expanded by Oliveira (2017), which includes scientific errors (3.4).

2. *Why Teach Scientific Errors in Science Teaching?*

The challenge of finding reliable knowledge is a basic concern of humanity (Zachos et al., 2003). Nevertheless, modern society, in general, sees in scientific knowledge this possibility of being one of the only, if not the only, safe and reliable knowledge, basing political, social and economic decisions on what science says, even for problems beyond the scientific scope (Haack, 2012).

---

1 Term used by Oliveira and Queiroz (2021) differentiating a traditionalist view of errors, present in the philosophies of Bacon, Descartes, Bachelard, and a progressive view of errors in the philosophies of Allchin and Feyerabend. In the authors' definition, the traditional view: 'More specifically, taking error as something removable (traditional) or not (progressivist) from the process and result of scientific knowledge. Thus, we propose that the more one defends the possibility of total removal of errors from the process of construction of scientific knowledge, the more traditional it is likely to be' (Oliveira and Queiroz, 2021, p. 77).

But, social phenomena[2] such as denialism, Fake News, opponents of climate change, and flat-Earthers, among others, show some instability in sciences or the consensus of the scientific community. These phenomena have revealed a movement of total distrust in sciences, in opposition to scientific dogmatism, in which people blindly trust sciences and what is said to be scientifically proven.

A current example is what has been happening in the face of the new coronavirus pandemic, which started in 2019, in which governments and health organisations have been concerned about the reliability of the population with sciences, especially concerning the denial of the vaccine against COVID-19. According to Bardon (2021), the rejection of scientific experience in respect with COVID-19 vaccines includes factors such as distrust in public institutions and perceived threats to one's cultural identity and a dramatic politicisation of trust in science itself.

Consequently, it is understood that society's trust in scientific knowledge implies cultural, social, political, but also epistemic issues (Allchin, 2017). Thus, discussing reliability involves many factors.

Though the analysis of reliability in the sciences requires a look at many factors, the search for trust in sciences needs to be in the balance between unconditionally believing and disbelieving in sciences; that is, a critical view of the sciences is necessary. In this sense, science education plays a fundamental role in the view of sciences by students and the population in general, since science education carries the main task of preparing students and citizens for socio-scientific and technological decision-making. In Allchin's words:

> One may characterize the primary (although perhaps not the only) goal of public science education as developing analytical skills based on understanding the nature of science (NOS): Students should develop a broad understanding of how science works to interpret the reliability of scientific claims in personal and public decision making (Allchin, 2017, p. 1).

In Allchin's argument, for students, as future citizens, to interpret reliability in science, science education must develop an understanding of the so-called Nature of Science (NOS), that is, in a simplified way, how science works. In section 2.1, we will explore this relationship.

---

2 The examples that we use in the text demonstrate social phenomena of the western culture itself in which the sciences influence and are influenced. However, other phenomena such as indigenous ways of knowing, meditation, horoscopes and tarot can also be included as phenomena that can affect this relationship of reliability, especially when it is based on the idea of the need to establish sciences as the only valid knowledge.

2.1. Scientific Errors, Nature of Science and Science Education

Although errors are known to scientists as a possibility to occur in all aspects of scientific research, errors have not been properly addressed in science education. On the one hand, the possibility of errors can be hidden, by treating them as non-existent in the sciences, free from errors, or when, at most, errors are admitted as part of the process that will be eliminated in the path of truth. Something common in the sciences classes, when teachers tell a simplified, cropped story from the history of sciences (Feyerabend, 1993). This can generate an interpretation problem leading to distrust or denial of the validity of scientific knowledge, since, ultimately, these errors are shown as something negative that compromises science, its development and results (Allchin, 2017). On the other hand, faced with this problem, the need for scientific education to convey a non-negative image of scientific errors in science is highlighted, showing both success and errors.

Zachos et al. (2003) advocate the inclusion of an approach to scientific errors in science teaching curricula as a way to help science students develop sensitivity, understanding and competence to constructively deal with the role of error in development. of science.

Kipnis (2011) in his analysis of the role of errors in science teaching concluded that scientific errors 'if made available to students, through their science teachers, such as knowledge, would give students a deeper insight into the scientific process and remove their fear of making errors in their own laboratory work' (Kipnis, 2011, p. 655). Kipnis also points out at least three contributions of the teaching of scientific errors to scientific education: (1) Understanding the Nature of Sciences; (2) Critical interpretation of the reliability and morality of the sciences; (3) Improve students' attitudes in their lab work when errors occur.[3]

Allchin (2012) pointed to the teaching of scientific errors as a primary opportunity for students to understand science and for citizens to interpret, review scientific recommendations and studies. And at other times (2017, 2020), he pointed out that understanding mistakes can help transform trust in science.

As seen above, it is observed that several authors defend the teaching of scientific errors in science teaching. Despite this, the issue of errors is still far

---

3 The objective of this part of the text is to demonstrate that Kipnis defends and demonstrates the reasons for including the theme of errors in science education. However, these reasons given by the author are detailed in his article Kipnis, N. (2011). Errors in sciences and their treatment in science teaching. *Science and Education*, 20, 655–685.

from science teaching, teachers often ignore the presence of errors in sciences or treat it as a surmountable event, as if sciences were self-correcting or excusing sciences for its errors in the name of an inevitable truth. And, even if they refer to some errors of scientists, it is not enough to reach the fallibility nature of sciences and the tendency, therefore, is to excuse the failures of sciences in the name of the progress of humanity, as Allchin states:

> Mere classroom allusions to possible failure, however, cannot dislodge the potent cultural image of science as an amalgam of fact, certainty, and incontrovertible evidence. Just mentioning that 'science is tentative' seems to function culturally like an escape clause, excusing science any time it does not meet the ideal. The ideal will persist. Indeed, that naive view has prompted will informed lawsuits against scientists for their published mistakes or, in a recent case, their failure to predict an earthquake (Hall, 2011; Steinbach, 1998)! If students are ever to learn that science is 'tentative', they must encounter real, concrete examples of scientific error or failure. One may surely couple them with examples of scientific change or the remedy of error, to show how knowledge grows. But the fundamental challenge is to teach fully about cases of error in science (Allchin, 2012, p. 905).

Thus, the simple citation of scientific error does not characterize it in scientific activity and, therefore, for Allchin, it is necessary to understand the dimension of error in sciences and make it explicit in teaching and, thus, its role in changing the inadequate image of sciences. Sciences will be more efficient. The defence of teaching errors is justified, as we have seen, precisely by the understanding of NOS, as Allchin explains:

> in science is a prime occasion to teach the nature of science, especially the central feature of tentativeness. (…). Errors are thus valuable for counteracting the distortions of scientific 'myth-conceptions,' the idealized and monumentalized images of science typically found in the media and textbooks (Allchin, 2003a). Cases of reasonable error or fallibility, especially among scientific heroes, function as NOS discrepant events or NOS anomalies that trigger reflection and deepen understanding of NOS. (Allchin, 2012, pp. 904–907)

In this sense, Allchin indicates that the teaching of scientific errors can contribute to the understanding of the nature of the sciences. In several of his works (2001, 2004, 2009, 2012, 2017, 2020) the author emphasises that error is common in scientific activity, but little present in scientific education.

Previously, Matthews (1992) has also argued that the aim of sciences teaching is to promote content learning while learning about the nature of sciences. In this sense, when teaching about how sciences work, teaching error is also essential to understand how wrong ideas were once considered correct, in the development of scientific knowledge (Allchin, 2016).

Therefore, we find a lesson in error for science teaching in understanding the NOS concerning its characteristic of being fallible and imperfect, in addition to another aspect of sciences: its human character. In this sense, Allchin highlights some aspects of the profile of sciences:

> Science is a human enterprise. Some scientists are motivated by curiosity or a passion to solve problems, others by profit or ambition. Some collaborate; others compete. Knowledge develops historically. Sometimes concepts change dramatically. Science resolves only problems of fact, not values. Nonetheless, the practice of science and its results have moral dimensions. (Allchin, 2004, p. 2)

Understanding sciences as another human activity helps not only in understanding the nature of sciences, but also in the critical and reflective relationship of students with sciences.

In this way, understanding NOS also involves understanding scientific errors, as something not only part of science but also essential for its development. Making mistakes and looking for mistakes is knowledge (Allchin, 2012). In this sense, an understanding of scientific errors can help us to reframe the way we communicate and use scientific information in personal and public environments, in the words of Allchin (2012). That is, scientific literacy as part of education epistemically grounded by the understanding of NOS must also be based on the teaching of scientific errors, as errors are the 'foundation for skills in analyzing claims in public and personal decision making, in a context of scientific literacy' (Allchin, 2012, p. 916).

However, as Allchin (2012) warns, teaching about errors in science is still a challenge, even after more than half a century of investigations into errors in science teaching. Among these challenges, education stands out as the epistemic foundation on errors that conceive them as something negative and contradictory; natural sciences commonly show only scientific success as a sequence of steps closer to the truth. Part of the problem of errors in science teaching comes precisely from a view of scientific errors inherited by scientific education from traditionalist philosophical conceptions, such as the views of Bacon, Descartes and Bachelard, who conceive errors as eliminable in the process of developing scientific knowledge, that is, something transitory (Oliveira & Queiroz, 2021).

Faced with this problem of errors in sciences teaching, it is important to teach about errors not to challenge the authority of sciences, but to draw a clearer profile of the NOS. Thus, the treatment of errors in science education must be guided by a progressive conception, which conceives errors as part of its development (Oliveira & Queiroz, 2021). In the next section, we will present the contributions of the progressive perspective of Feyerabend's errors to science education, through pluralist education proposal, expanded by Oliveira (2017).

3. *Scientific Errors in Feyerabend's Progressive Perspective*

As can be seen in the previous topic, the problem of approaching scientific errors in science education presents essential epistemic aspects for the inclusion of the theme. Although Feyerabend has not dedicated specific work to this topic, at least not as we see in other thinkers (Allchin, 2004, 2012, 2015b; Allchin & Werth, 2017; Mayo, 1996; Rescher, 2007), his perspective provides insight into scientific errors that re-signifies errors, contributing to the understanding of NOS. In addition, the scientific training indicated by Feyerabend values the students' intellectual autonomy and critical view, which can help in the relationship of reliability in scientific statements.

Oliveira and Queiroz (2021) saw that in Feyerabend's article *Classical Empiricism* ([1970] 1981), when Feyerabend describes the meaning of errors as 'deviations from the accepted point of view' ([1970] 1981, pp. 38–39). This definition helps to understand the current aspect of the relationships established with the basic ideology, especially when in the competition between theories; thus, the paradigmatic theory gives the others the status of wrong theories. In other words: The 'error needs a point of view, generally accepted, as the basis for its existence' (Oliveira and Queiroz, 2021, p. 100).

The word error does not refer to a future situation where the theory now accepted will eventually be refuted, but to the current state of research, in which competition between theories is taking place (Oliveira & Queiroz, 2021).

This understanding of errors is important for sciences education, especially for science teachers, who, when pointing out what an error is in their classes, must consider their moment of debate between theories. For example, in the dispute between the phlogiston theory and the oxygen theory, it is important to emphasise that conceptualising the phlogiston theory as an error should only be considered when considering the moment of clash with the oxygen theory.

In this view, the interpretation of facts is determined by accepted theories, capable of defining the existence of error, because, it

> stems from certain values (right, wrong, true, false) that may well be evaluated intersubjectively, but are by no means universal or theory-independent. In a sense, the error status within theoretical disputes resembles the notion Schrödinger's cat, where the cat could be both alive and dead, simultaneously. In the same way, because something can be interpreted as an error, and as not

being, at least in principle by two incommensurable theories, then the error problem in science is not simply resolved by pointing to 'The Error'. (Oliveira & Queiroz, 2021, p. 100)

Based on this concept of errors, and other passages from *Against Method* (1993), we highlight three aspects of errors in the Feyerabendian pluralist perspective, namely: 3.1 Errors are part of the human character of science; 3.2 Errors are productive for the progress of science; 3.3 Errors are not transitory in the development of scientific knowledge. Such aspects will be used below as a framework to help reframe errors, bringing a positive understanding of errors in science and understanding in science education.

3.1. *Errors are Part of the Human Character of Science*

In principle, one can be wrong about anything, mainly because we are limited, with finite and fallible minds in the face of a world of infinite complexity. That is, we cannot have access to complete information, this is mainly due to our limited condition that only one theory cannot respond to all facets of the phenomenon.

This notion of errors within the human character of the sciences may seem that we are talking about an inherent error, in the strong sense of the word error, contrary to what we said earlier about the relationship of theories in the definition of errors, but we understand that error is at the same time inherently and theoretically pointed out. Well, there are errors that occur because a theory cannot account for the phenomenon, and often these errors will only be revealed in the light of another alternative theory, and errors are also defined within the theoretical clash.

On this human aspect of science, Feyerabend (1993) draws attention to scientific activity as a human enterprise, therefore, changeable and fallible. In this sense, it is acceptable to say that science errs, after all, to err is human. As a human activity, science has poor access to information and incompetence in processing information. This is why Feyerabend says that scientific knowledge constructed by scientists is like buildings of different sizes and shapes, therefore, knowledge constructed 'can only be judged after the event, that is, only after they have finished their structure. It may get up, it may fall – nobody knows' (1993 p. 2).

Thus, in scientific activity, errors made by another theory or even revealed in the light of an alternative theory show us the need for the proliferation of alternatives. The reason for the proliferation of theories empirically resides in that 'no theory ever agrees with all known facts in its domain. And the problem is not created by rumours or the result of sloppy procedure. It is created by experiments and measurements of the highest precision and reliability' (1993, p. 39). That is, the sciences follow precise procedures and a high degree of reliability, but the world to be explored is so complex that only one theory would not be able to account for all parts of a phenomenon. Thus, Feyerabend opposes the restrictions arising from monist understandings and proposes a plurality that remains open to alternatives.

In scientific knowledge, the alternatives come from the past or from what is considered 'error' or 'absurdity' in his time, as Feyerabend states: 'There is no idea, however old and absurd it may be, that is not capable of improving our knowledge. The entire history of thought is absorbed by science and used to improve each theory' (1993, p. 33).

A close look at the history of the sciences reveals how many of the ideas considered wrong persisted and later turned out to be correct and according to a now-accepted 'reason', that is, in the light of accepted theory. Therefore, 'it is advisable to let your own inclinations go against reason under any circumstances, which makes life less constrained and can benefit science' (1993, p. 33). Here, we see in Feyerabend a proliferation that places the errors and wrong ideas of the past as necessary for scientific investigation and for understanding the nature of science, and the condition of being considered brings a historical and philosophical dependence depending on the context in which such ideas were incorporated.

This human dimension of science is an issue that permeates NOS, as science education often treats science as something special, perfect and made by geniuses. This makes the acceptance of scientific errors difficult, generating several problems in relation to the criticality of students and citizens about the validity of scientific knowledge. Therefore, Feyerabend (1993) warns of the need to talk about errors instead of pretending that these errors do not exist, as questioned by Feyerabend: 'Should we assume that everything that happened after Newton (or after Hilbert) is perfection? Or should we admit that modern science may have basic flaws and may need global change?' (1993, p. 214).

One way to address errors in science teaching is through the history of science. The history of science can humanise science. Well, the story, along with the philosophy of sciences, provide tools necessary to increase students' criticality, through the understanding of a more humane sciences (Matthews, 1992). And when this story is not limited to the demonstration of success but also of error as an inherent part of scientific investigation, then the process of identifying aspects of human activity in science is better contemplated (Feyerabend, 1993).

3.2. Mistakes Are Productive for the Progress of Science

Feyerabend (1993) highlights the relevance and presence of errors and human limitations, but without necessarily compromising scientific knowledge. By using the terms 'errors' and 'deviations' in the sentence 'These "deviations", these "errors" are preconditions of progress' (1993, p. 158), Feyerabend exposes three characteristics of error, as described by Oliveira and Queiroz (2021):

> First error is the relationship between the cognitive limitation and fallibilism (...); Second error is a result of an analysis coming from a certain reference; (...) Third error does not refer to a future situation but to the present state of research where competition between many theories, interpretations of facts, and cosmologies is always operating. (Oliveira & Queiroz, 2021, p. 99)

Feyerabend considers that both errors from the past and current alternatives considered wrong should be seen as essential for the progress of science. As the author states: 'For what appears as "sloppiness", "chaos" or "opportunism" when compared with such laws has a most important function in the development of those very theories which we today regard the essential parts of our knowledge of nature' (1993, p. 158).

> Therefore, errors are not just preconditions of progress in the epistemic sense, they are part of what leads us to explore new alternatives and, consequently, tests of strength, criticism and changes in knowledge (Oliveira & Queiroz, 2021).

It is important to highlight that progress in Feyerabend goes through the epistemological sense of the proliferation of theories and the principle of tenacity, both of which will help in the evaluation of aspects of the theory, such as attractiveness, fruitfulness and retention (tenacity) (Oliveira, 2021). This does not mean that there are guarantees that knowledge will improve with each theory, because errors will always exist, and science works with this possibility and even with a margin of error. In other words, it is a progress and an increase in the proliferation of alternatives that remain alive in the debate between theories.

3.3. Errors Are Not Transitory in the Development of Scientific Knowledge

Understanding the importance of errors for scientific research enriches science and understands that errors are not transitory in the development of scientific knowledge. Scientific development occurs with errors that cannot simply be overcome as steps closer to the truth. That is, Feyerabend has a progressive view on errors by treating them as present at any stage of scientific knowledge and development and that will not necessarily be overcome or rectified (Oliveira & Queiroz, 2021). This helps us understand the place of scientific errors in Feyerabend's pluralist perspective.

Scientists, when identifying errors in their theory, do not necessarily or immediately correct them, but not rarely maintain them, because, despite these errors, the theory still manages to answer certain important aspects to solve the problem. And despite the general consensus, this does not mean that an accepted theory is free from problems, unexplained facts and shaky evidence. As Feyerabend said: 'The contradiction may stay with us for decades or even centuries' (1993, p. 61). In addition, the sciences, for statistical reasons, work with a margin of error, but this does not affect the reliability and accuracy of the research.

Knowing that errors are not transient helps to understand how science coexists with errors, but maintains reliability. This is especially important for understanding the Nature of Science and therefore for science education. In this sense, scientific education conceived on a Feyerabendian pluralist basis of inclusion of errors can help in this understanding.

3.4. Contributions of Feyerabend's Progressive View on Errors in Science Education

The aspects raised so far show how the Feyerabendian view contributes to important epistemic bases on errors, mainly related to NOS, something expensive for the search for a critical scientific education and for scientific literacy. For this very reason, Feyerabend defends an exposition of errors, because, by omitting scientific errors, it ends up simplifying all the complexity that involves the sciences, leading to an also incomplete understanding of the nature of science and every aspect of science that remains are its good ones. results, there being no place for their difficulties, weaknesses and errors that are subject to a human activity and limited in the face of the complexity of nature. This type of education cannot be reconciled with a humanitarian attitude. It is in conflict 'with the cultivation of individuality which alone produces, or can produce, well-developed human beings'; it

> maims by compression, like a Chinese lady's foot, every part of human nature which stands out prominently, and tends to make a person markedly different in outline' 8 from the ideals of rationality that happen to be fashionable in science, or in the philosophy of science (Feyerabend, 1993, p. 12).

In this comparison of a Chinese lady's shoe, the author exposes the oppressive character of an education that epistemically limits the scientific successes of only one main scientific theory, without demonstrating the gaps in this theory, pointed out by the alternatives, and the scientific mistakes made by science throughout of your story. If, on the contrary, an education that values the plurality of theories, positions, that demonstrates both successes and errors, would not have the objective of distancing students from science, on the contrary, it would bring them closer to their human lives and attitudes, moreover, it would favour the criticality of students and their choices would not be imposed, but for clarification.

In this pluralist perspective of a humanitarian education Feyerabend proposes the admission of errors in science, recommending an exposition of scientific errors:

> The objection that citizens do not have the expertise to judge scientific matters overlooks that important problems often lie across the boundaries of various sciences so that scientists within these sciences don't have the needed expertise either. Moreover, doubtful cases always produce experts for the one side, experts for the other side, and experts in between. But the competence of the general public could be vastly improved by an education that exposes expert fallibility instead of acting as if it did not exist (Feyerabend, 1993, p. 251).

In this passage Feyerabend opposes the argument that citizens would not be prepared to know the plurality of opinions in science and its flaws. In his opposition, this type of argument is not enough to exclude information from citizens, on the contrary, an education that exposes errors is the way to prepare the population for critical decision-making:

> Maturity is not found lying about in the streets, it must be learned. It is not learned in schools, at least not in the schools of today where the student is confronted with desiccated and falsified copies of past decisions, it is learned by active participation in decisions that are still to be made. (Feyerabend, 1978, p. 87)

Feyerabend's intention for a pluralist education that provides an active decision-making and an exposure of errors is part of a need to minimise aspects of the problem of scientific education.

Oliveira (2017) highlights that this humanist perspective suggested by Feyerabend has precisely the purpose of preparing the citizen to make choices in the face of pluralities in order to examine and debate with the established standards, that is: 'only in the sense of someone who achieves proficiency in a game, that is, without serious commitment and without robbing the spirit of the ability to also indulge in other games' (Feyerabend, 1993, p. 161).

Thus, we have in Feyerabend a pluralist education with humanitarian and citizen perspectives, against a pedagogical dogmatism that restricts the standards of group theories in particular that restricts freedom, subjugating the minds of students. In his words, general education

> should prepare citizens to choose between the standards, or to find their way in a society that contains groups committed to various standards, but it must under no condition bend their minds so that they conform to the standards of one particular group (Feyerabend, 1993, p. 161).

Feyerabend is direct in saying that education should not serve a specific group of prevailing monist ideology, but that it should be committed to the formation of man to provide the necessary conditions for an intellectual maturation to choose on their own (Oliveira, 2017). In short, Feyerabend's proposal is for a pluralist scientific education that emphasises the plurality of alternatives and exposes scientific errors, with the intention of providing basic tools for the action and critical decision of citizens in society, in turn helping in the relationship of science reliability.

4. Conclusions

Faced with recent problems regarding the reliability of science and the need for a critical scientific education, we warn that the teaching of scientific errors is urgent to minimise these problems, in addition to not being able to tolerate more a scientific education that addresses only scientific successes distorting what is scientific work. In this sense, the pluralist educational approach can contribute significantly.

The educational proposal to approach the errors that we tried to describe in this work sought to bring epistemic aspects of Feyerabendian pluralism and its perspective on basic scientific errors for the inclusion of the theme in scientific education. Aware of the need for further studies, even of an empirical nature, for the incorporation of the proposal in curricula and in science classes. Finally, we take a further step in the analysis of errors according to Feyerabend's view.

References

Allchin, D. (2000a). *The epistemology of error*. Paper presented at the Philosophy of Science Association Meetings, Vancouver, BC.

Allchin, D. (2000b). *To err is science*. Paper presented at the American Association for the Advancement of Science, Washington, DC.

Allchin, D. (2001). Error types. *Perspectives on Science, 9*, 38–59.

Allchin, D. (2004). *Error and the nature of science.* American Institute of Biological Sciences.

Allchin, D. (2012). Teaching the nature of science through scientific error. *Science Education, 96,* 904–926.

Allchin, D. (2017). *From test tubes to YouTube: Nature of science in socioscientific issues and history* [episteme]. Homi Bhabha Center for Science Education.

Allchin, D. (2020). The credibility game. *The American Biology Teacher, 82*(8), 535–541.

Allchin, D., & Werth, A. (2017). The naturalizing error. *Journal of the General Philosophy of Science.*

Bardon, A. (2021, September 16). *Political orientation predicts science denial – here's what that means for getting Americans vaccinated against COVID-19.* BST. https://theconversation.com/political-orientation-predicts-science-denial-heres-what-that-means-for-getting-americans-vaccinated-against-covid-19-165386

Feyerabend, P. ([1970] 1981). Classical empiricism. In *Philosophical papers – problems of empiricism* (Vol. 2, pp. 34–51). Cambridge University Press.

Feyerabend, P. (1978). *Science in a free society.* NLB.

Feyerabend, P. (1993). *Against method* (3rd ed.). Verso.

Haack, S. (2012). *Seis Sinais de Cientificismo.* Publicações da Liga Humanista Secular do Brasil.

Kipnis, N. (2011). Errors in science and their treatment in teaching science. *Science & Education, 20,* 655–685.

Matthews, M. R. (1992). History, philosophy, and science teaching: The present rapprochement. *Science & Education, 1*(1), 11–47.

Mayo, D. G. (1996). *Error and the growth of experimental knowledge.* University of Chicago Press.

Oliveira, D. G. S. (2017). Anarquismo, Autonomia e Esclarecimento no Objetivo do Ensino das Ciências. Tese (Doutorado em Ensino, História e Filosofia das Ciências). Instituto de Física, Universidade Federal da Bahia e Universidade Federal de Feira de Santana, Salvador, 217 f.

Oliveira, D. G. d. S. (2021). The cosmological divergent proliferation in Feyerabend's pluralism. *Principia: An International Journal of Epistemology, 25*(3), 421–454. https://doi.org/10.5007/1808-1711.2021.e72764

Oliveira, D. G. d. S., & Queiroz, L. F. S. (2021). Epistemologically progressivist and traditionalist analyses of scientific error in Rescher's Allchin's and Feyerabend's philosophies. *Disputatio – Philosophical Research Bulletin, 10*(17), 77–106. https://doi.org/10.5281/zenodo.5135886

Zachos, P., Pruzek, R., & Thomas, H. (2003). *Approaching error in scientific knowledge and science education.* Seventh International History, Philosophy of Science and Science Teaching Conference Proceedings, Winnipeg, pp. 947–957.

Part IV: Performances: Feyerabend and Pedagogical Practice

The Tyranny of Truth and the Preservation of Human Happiness (à la Bertolt Brecht and Paul Feyerabend)

KATJA FRIMBERGER

1. Introduction

My aim for this chapter is to show how Paul Feyerabend, the philosopher of science, borrowed features from German theatre maker Bertolt Brecht's theatre theory and theatrical methods for his own conception of scientific theorising and practice. A curious question poses itself immediately of course. Is such endeavour plausible, even possible? Are the theatre/the arts and science not two different beasts? As I will show, both Feyerabend and Brecht were indeed convinced that the arts and the sciences had a lot in common; that they could even learn from each other. In their view, art and science share many similarities – even if they are not exactly the same thing of course.

Feyerabend, the man of science, looked towards the arts – and Brecht, the man of the theatre, looked towards science for the formulation of their theories and their resulting practice. Feyerabend's openness to the arts and his affinity with Brechtian theory and practice in particular is hereby no mere cultural coincidence, although Brecht (1898–1956) was German/Bavarian, Feyerabend (1924–1994) was Austrian. Both lived through the turmoils of WWII, even if in very different circumstances (young Feyerabend fought on the French and Polish frontline on the German side; the 'communist' Brecht resided abroad in exile from the Nazis). Both were also immersed in the post-WWII (East German) theatre scene. They were influenced by, and partook in, movements for theatrical reform. Calling out the ideological nature of dramatic storytelling under the Nazis (and in post-WWII theatre more generally), both were concerned with the (practical and theoretical) questions regarding theatre's post-war mimetic purpose and practice.

In short, both Feyerabend and Brecht pondered how this *new* theatre could raise to the social and aesthetic challenge of a post-war world. Would the *new* theatre be able to fulfil its mimetic purpose (of imitating human actions truthfully and plausibly), whilst still drawing on the *old* dramatic and narrative structures? And most importantly, perhaps, both men just loved the world of the stage – as producers/practitioners, philosopher-speculators and critics. To this effect, Feyerabend even tells his readers in *Against Method* (1993, p. 252ff) and in his autobiography *Killing Time* (1995, p. 54ff), that it was in this post-WWII East German theatre scene of 1946, where the key ethical and epistemological questions; those that would shape his scientific ethos, were first sparked.

> The problem of knowledge and education in a free society struck me during my tenure of a state fellowship at the Weimar Institute zur Methodologischen Erneuerung des Theaters [Weimar institute for the methodological renewal/ reform of the theatre], which was a continuation of the Deutsches Theater Moskau under the directorship of Maxin Vallentin. (1993, p. 252)

Through the Marxist philosopher Walter Hollitscher, Feyerabend first encounters Brecht (1978, p. 113ff) when the German theatre maker rehearses his play *Die Mutter* [The Mother] at the Burgtheater in Vienna (Austria). And it so happened, that Feyerabend was invited by Brecht to become his artistic assistant at the *Berliner Ensemble* in East Berlin. Interestingly, in *Science in a Free Society* (1978), Feyerabend implies that his decision to *not* follow Brecht's call to become a man of the theatre and apprentice at the Berliner Ensemble was perhaps one of the biggest mistakes in his life.

> Enriching and changing knowledge, emotions, attitudes through the arts now seems to me a much more fruitful enterprise and also much more humane than the attempt to influence minds (and nothing else) by words (and nothing else). If today only about 10% of my talents are developed then this is due to a wrong decision at the age of 25. (p. 114)

It must however also be mentioned that a later Feyerabend, in his biography *Killing Time* (1995), qualifies this regret of not working under Brecht in East Berlin. Here, he concedes that he would have been indeed rather keen to 'learn about the theatre, and from such an extraordinary man' (p. 73). That is, he would have liked to receive training in how to communicate and enrich an audience's knowledge, emotions and attitudes through the full artistic repertoire of the theatre. At the same time, however, Feyerabend reflects that his 'almost instinctive aversion to group thinking' (p. 73) would have likely led him to detest the cult-like nature of the 'partly fearful, partly dedicated, and certainly pushy and closely knit' Brecht circle and its 'collective [moral] pressure' (p. 73) to realise the playwright's idea(l)s.

Considering his own righteous (moral) indignation as a young man regarding the needs for post-WWII-theatrical reform (hinted at the beginning of this chapter), Feyerabend (1978) is however also aware of his own early tendency towards 'ideological purity'. Concomitantly, his own rejection of the idea that the playwright *should* in fact act as a moral force, took him some time to come to – given his youthful affinities for scientific formalism and 'ruthless' agit prop approaches, when applied for the 'right cause' of course (p. 108). Having sketched out Feyerabend's and Brecht's biographical overlaps, their shared interest in post-WWII-theatrical reform and curiosity about the relationship between theatre's (production) aesthetics, its ethics and epistemology – I will now turn to outline the chapter's structure.

2. Chapter Structure

This chapter starts off with some more biographical scene setting that builds on my short introductory section. My aim here is to further contextualise the Feyerabend-Brecht biographical connection, before moving to detail their theoretical affinities.

The main part of the chapter is then laid out in two sections. Section 1 establishes Bertolt Brecht's 'scientific theatre' theory. Section 2 maps Feyerabend's Brechtian theatre-influenced scientific theorising and practice.

The Brecht section 1 is organised into two sub-points. Here, I firstly explore Brecht's view on the relationship between the arts and science, which hinges on the role that pleasure is to play in the creation of knowledge. Secondly, I look at Brecht's self-styled *Anti-Aristotelianism*.

In the second section, I explore how Feyerabend's *epistemological anarchism* maps onto Brecht's (so-called) 'Anti-Aristotelian' view – in theory and practice. In three further sub-points, I firstly show how Feyerabend, like Brecht, questions the ideal of the role of myth (including drama and science) to reproduce specific metaphysical theories (to ensure the coherence of a closed society). In my second point, I demonstrate how Feyerabend, like Brecht, entertained a more practical ideal as to the role of artistic and scientific storytelling in a modern, pluralistic society. Rather than re-producing *specific* norms and values, it is to sustain the more practical aim of nourishing individual *human productivity* in its manifoldness. Theatre and science are to preserve human happiness (and life, more generally) – by embracing, and bringing forth, the pleasure and joy that resides in people's acts of knowledge production (in the arts and sciences). Feyerabend's resulting Brechtian scientific practice, as I explain in point 3, can be observed in his rejection of scientific formalism in favour of an experimental, participatory (and popular) science and his embrace of a historicised science that does not disregard archaic metaphysical theories – as is, for example, shown in his call for *estrangement* through counterinduction.

3. Biographical Scene Setting

Let us start then with grounding our inquiry into Brecht's intellectual influence on Feyerabend in some further biographical scene setting. This will allow the reader to get a better idea of Feyerabend's personal connection to, and intellectual interest in, the arts and also prepare us for section 1, which establishes Brechtian theory and practice in more detail. Drawing on Feyerabend's autobiography *Killing Time* (1995), it is however important to be aware that we are dealing with a highly polished piece of (partly tongue-in-cheek) self-mythologising; one in which *Herr Direktor* Feyerabend indeed stylises himself as a man of the theatre – and leftist intellectual at that. *Killing Time* then not only gives us an insight into Feyerabend's personal and intellectual curiousness about the theatre, but also a sense of his own aesthetic of self-presentation and staging of (autobiographical) knowledge.

3.1. Herr Direktor Feyerabend

Drafted into the German army at 16, Paul Feyerabend was seriously wounded when serving as an officer on the Eastern Front during Nazi Germany's retreat from the Russian Army in 1945. Admitted to the hospital of Apolda, a town about 15 km from the city of Weimar in the federal state of Thuringia, Feyerabend slowly recovered from his war injuries. Searching for employment at the same time, he is unexpectedly helped into a job by the town's mayor. Despite his former involvement as an officer in the very government, which had expelled the mayor – a worker and anti-fascist – from his office, he is entrusted with leading the local council's education section (1995, p. 57). Although still healing from his war wounds, he throws himself into his new responsibility to entertain. Feyerabend writes speeches, dialogues and sketches for various events. He creates children's plays and even composes larger parts for actors at the Weimar national theatre. He practices performances with actors and supervises the staging of plays. But his physical constitution is not suited to the strenuous rehearsal process. He reminisces in *Killing Time* (1995) about his time as a budding director: 'I might have become a good director, perhaps a great one; I enjoyed what I was doing and was much too ignorant to have scruples or be nervous' (p. 57).

After his full recovery, Feyerabend pursues his interest in the arts, even if he does not, in the end, become a man of the stage. He receives a scholarship to attend the Weimar music academy and theatre institute. There, he studies his beloved opera singing, takes acting classes and regularly visits theatre performances in various East German cities. Whilst discussing both classical and new plays with actors, audiences and fellow students from the Weimar music and theatre academy, Feyerabend publicly ponders the connection between theatre's production aesthetic and its (moral) function as (public) *knowledge*. He notes that the new post-war, anti-fascist plays, those that depict the fight of the German resistance against Nazism, seem to draw on the same aesthetic devices as some of the old plays staged under the Nazi regime.

It is here then (Feyerabend implies), in the smoky theatres of post-1945 Weimar, where his curiosity about the connection between the arts, ethics and (scientific) human inquiry was first sparked. Let us then look a bit closer at the details of Feyerabend's observations within the broader context of cultural criticism of the WWII German stage, and the more general question that, naturally, emerges. What exactly is to constitute 'good drama' in a post-Nazi world?

3.2. Aesthetics, Ethics, Knowledge

Although the new plays wish to champion a *new* politics and a *new* anti-fascist morality, Feyerabend observes an eerie structural similarity to the Nazi's 'new German plays' (Gadberry, 2000), which had celebrated the heroism of Nazi underground operations abroad. Both old (fascist) and the new (anti-fascist) plays, Feyerabend recounts (1993, p. 253; 1995, p. 60), indulged in the so-called *hero trope*. They both told the monomyth of the classic hero's journey (Campbell, 2004) as an archetypal story of good versus evil. There were clear-cut heroes and villains and undecided individuals (usually male – Feyerabend informs us) embarking on a journey of adventure and soul-searching. Nudged by a virtuous good person (usually a *good woman* – he recounts), the hero's journey – on both sides of the political spectrum – always concluded with the protagonist being moved towards the *right kind* of moral decision (within the framework of the respective ideology). Glen Gadberry (2000) in his analysis of the Third Reich's 'historical plays', points to a similar issue with dramatic structure *during* the Nazi period. Despite the Nazi's ideologically cemented view of a conflict-ridden world of racial hierarchies, clashes of cultures and ideological weaponry (from Christianity to Capitalism, Communism and Democracy), the newly written Nazi history plays themselves dramatised these supposedly *epic* historical struggles in ideologically adjusted, but flat historical stories.

In other words, heroes, and the overcoming Volk, were depicted as victorious indeed. Their enemies were however regularly defeated without much dramatic toil. There were recurring rhetorical devices, heavy symbolism and of course rituals conjuring up Volk, Vaterland, blood and soil and so on. With the play's dramatic structure guided by a predictable *ideological/political correctness*, it was however left bereft of any essential dramatic conflict at its centre (p. 123). Gadberry points out that 'the ironic and recurring complaint about the history plays of Nazi Germany, even from their most sympathetic critics, was that they were constructed without essential conflict (...) and without conflict, there was no drama, according to the prevailing dramaturgic wisdom of the time; only rhetoric, bathos; zealotry or petulance' (...) (p. 123). In other words, the Nazi's deterministic worldview (predicated on certain predetermined historical and moral constellations) did not lend itself to the writing of plays with believable antagonists, which made their actions seem plausible (we will explore the question of dramatic structure in section 1). In summary, both old and new plays prioritised the portrayal of *good and bad character* for the purpose of instruction into a specific worldview. Feyerabend critiques in *Killing Time*: 'But isn't it absurd to base the fight of good versus evil on mere names, and isn't it rather obscene to use the same form, even the same type of story, to describe it' (1995, p. 60)?

In other words – Can a play's *new* moral content be framed in the same, old aesthetic structures? Can fascists *just* become communists? Can good be simply *exchanged* for evil; can villains and heroes be *switched around* just like that? Can allusions to Hitler in a speech simply be *substituted* by references to Marx and Lenin – with the aesthetic, narrative structure staying the same, without losing its claim to morality? Both kind of (new and old) plays' formulaic nature – driving the plot and its characters towards a predetermined moral conclusion – seemed to Feyerabend bereft of artistic quality, with their 'ideological speeches, outburst of sincerity and dangerous situations in the cops and robbers tradition' (1993, p. 253; 1995, p. 60). He ponders in *Against Methods* (1993) as to the difficulty of theatre's mimetic work in this new (post-Nazi) world and asks: 'How should a play be structured, so that one recognizes it as presenting the "good side"? What has to be added to the action to make the struggle of the resistance fighter seem more morally superior to the struggle of an illegal Nazi in Austria in 1938?' (p. 253).

Having established Feyerabend's personal connection to – and his intellectual interest in – the arts (esp. the theatre), we will now transition to section

1. Here, I explore Bertolt Brecht's own investment (as theatre practitioner and theorist) in exploring the relationship between drama (and its structure), knowledge and ethics. We will then come back to Feyerabend in section 2 to see how Brecht's theatre theory maps on his epistemology and scientific practice. Let us start the section then with Brecht's (1978) most well-known piece of theatre theory in the Anglophone world – *the Short Organum*. My aim is to clarify Brecht's view on the relationship between science and *good drama* – and its function as *knowledge*.

4. Section 1: Brecht's Scientific Theatre of Estrangement

4.1. The Role of Pleasure in the Creation of Knowledge

The *Short Organum for the Theatre* (written in 1947/1948) was produced at the tail end of Brecht's WWII exile years, just before he settled in (post-WWII) East Berlin. The curious title *Organum* (meaning *a body of principles*), written in 78 aphorisms – short pithy statements in prose – refers, in form and title, to renaissance scientist Francis Bacon's 1620 book *Novum Organum* (2019). Brecht was likely attracted to making the link with Bacon and his empiricist natural philosophy, as a way of giving aesthetic expression to his own (implied) anti-Aristotelian *scientific* position in the theatre (Brecht, 1978, p. 205). Bacon's *interpretation naturae* is considered the ground work for what we now think of as the scientific method. With its emphasis on empirical and rational observation, and methodical, inductive reasoning, it was composed as an ideological refutation of Aristotelian deductive logic as *anticipation naturae* in his *Organon* (2017).

Brecht indeed shared Bacon's concern regarding the authoritative finality of concept-making that can (potentially) result from a *purely* anticipatory approach (e.g. Aristotle's syllogism, 2017). This danger of ideological imposition, for Brecht, was however not eradicated by simply substituting an idealist speculation with a (purely) empirical observation of a strictly materially determined world *out there* (e.g. Lenin, 1970). As Brecht's exchanges with *dissident* Marxist philosopher and lifelong teacher Karl Korsch (2012), and his *Me-ti* texts (which were likely inspired by their discussions), reveal, Brecht struggled with Marxist-Leninist's false idealist/materialist distinction. Dialectical determinism turned materialism into a 'doctrine equated with Being, which consciousness simply reflects, but does not shape or question' (Brecht, 2016, p. 25).

And Brecht experienced of course the disastrous results of its politics. Many of his collaborators (e.g. the actress Carola Neher and director Asja Lācis), communists who had moved to the Soviet Union after the revolution were, under Stalin, branded Trozkyist spies and part of a literary opposition. Seen to undermine the higher purpose of (Soviet realist) art for the direct illustration of Marx's class laws (Paškevica, 2006, p. 118f), they were imprisoned and forced into labour camps (Gulags). As Reinhold Grimm (1979) aptly summarises Brecht's (necessarily 'tragic') political position:

> The Marxist Brecht was faced with a terrible decision. In service of the final humanising of human beings, in which he believed, he either had to demand their total de-humanisation and objectification ... or to question – even to negate – this ideology, his life's and work's prime value. (p. 100)

It might be argued then that Brecht reveals, in his pedagogical and aesthetic ideas, what we shall call a certain (social-) anarchist tendency (likely inspired by Korsch, 2012). In other words, he can be said to share anarchism's pedagogical 'faith in the idea that human beings already possess most of the attributes and virtues necessary to create and sustain such a different society, so do not need to either undergo any radical transformation or to do away with an "inauthentic consciousness"' (Suissa, 2010, p. 149). In fact, in *Meti*, Brecht comments on Marx's observation that consciousness is shaped by being or *life*, for example, the way we make a living. For him, this interdependency does not prove people's in-capacity for reasoning or joy in life. Brecht simply points to the undeniable dependency between our ideas about the world and how we engage with it materially.

He admits that Marx's observation sounds rather depressing, but suggests pragmatically that 'the simple realisation that all great works were nevertheless created in this dependency and that conceding this dependency doesn't make them any less great, settles the matter' (Brecht, 2016, p. 76). Brecht also argues that Marx's principle of the dependency of thought won't seem so depressing, when dependency on the economy won't be felt as so oppressive anymore by people. Brecht's unorthodox Marxist, perhaps anarchist, proclivity (although he himself would have likely rejected the label), then takes shape in his pedagogical position. He believes in the *capacity to reason* of his theatre-going audience and emphasises theatre's role to contribute to human happiness.

Brecht refuses to (fully) instrumentalise theatre for an abstract, *higher cause* when it is disconnected from people's conscious experience of their own valued lives. And he believes that too much (moral, political, social) governance stifles people's capacity to be good, and live a flourishing life (e.g. Brecht, 2016, p. 50). A certain anti-teleological notion is equally articulated in his belief that the artist cannot control the pedagogical/political outcome of his artistic work. In other words, the *exact* pedagogical outcome between what is presented to an audience in the materiality of theatre, and the way that the audience interprets and acts (or not) on the insights thus gained, must remain unpredictable.

> Not even instruction can be demanded of it [the theatre]: at any rate, no more utilitarian lesson than how to move pleasurably, whether in the physical [aesthetic] or the spiritual [moral] sphere. The theatre must remain something entirely superfluous, though this indeed means that it is the superfluous for which we live. Nothing needs less justification than pleasure. (Brecht, 1978, pp. 180–181)

The conditions for change can be created, and the effects of this (indirect) education can be of course hoped for. But it is firstly in the careful attending to the productive conditions particular to the theatre – e.g. when (co)-creating the aesthetic imitations of theatre's ultimately *superfluous* and necessarily *playful* metaphors – that the artist can hope to influence his audiences. In other words, Brecht draws attention to what it means for an artist to partake in the (indirect) creation of conditions (e.g. in the theatre) for the purpose of 'social virtues and human propensities to flourish' (Suissa, 2010) – in a way that does not deny the relation between theory and practice.

Me-ti editor Antony Tatlow (Brecht, 2016) reminds us (p. 53) hereby of the very purpose of the *Verfremdungseffekt*. It is to not only invite inquiry into the productive relationship between theory and practice in *other* acts of cultural production. The V-effekt is to render possible the questioning of Brechtian theatre's own artistic and pedagogical ways and means of presenting the world on stage. The audience is to be invited to read and judge: do theatre's metaphors still move *pleasurably* and *superflously*? – or have they hardened into a *Weltanschauung*? Are the images disconnected from the particularity of their emergence in (everyday life) practice, and the question of people's flourishing therein? Do they seek to organise and govern the world in their own image? Do they create the conditions for social virtues to flourish?

If Brecht himself honoured, or failed, his own principles has of course been discussed (see e.g. Arendt, 1948; Bloch et al., 1977; Feyerabend, 1993). What can perhaps be stated for the purpose of this chapter, is Brecht's intention. Tatlow gets to its heart in his editorial footnote to *Me-ti*: 'Brecht disliked any (artistic) practice without space to question its aesthetic intentions. In such a world you either manipulate or are manipulated. To provoke such inquiry was of course the purpose of the so-called estrangement effect' (Brecht & Tatlow, 2016, p. 53). For our chapter, the question poses itself of course how Brecht conceived of his *estranged* theatrical mimesis? *What* are theatre's imitations to show (of the world) and *how*?

4.2. Brecht's Anti-Aristotelianism

As part of Brecht's (self-styled) anti-Aristotelianism (as shown in his reference to Bacon for example), he firstly critiques a way of making modern art that represents a static and unchangeable world. That is to say, Brecht critiques a theatrical presentation of world that is either determined by invisible metaphysical forces or by individual motive forces alone – especially when these are represented as the result of (an already) fully formed moral character in action (Brecht, 1987, p. 70) – or *specific* metaphysical theories. Concomitantly, Brecht rejects certain modern poet's overreliance on individual feeling and individual artistic intuition, when it is devoid of the commitment to investigate the complicated workings of those cultural productions that mark the (modern) world and its idea(l)s (including scientific innovations). These modern phenomena, for Brecht, also include the individual politician's 'lust to power', embedded in the very *workings* of politics; as much as the *coming into being* of a (Nazi) propaganda newspaper (like the *Völkische Beobachter*); the workings of global capitalist business (his example is Standard Oil); as well as the complicated moral discourse around war-profiteering (p. 73).

But Brecht's self-professed anti-Aristotelianism must also be considered as part of Brecht's own *theatricalisation of ideas*. Like Feyerabend, Brecht was at times prone to certain exaggerated rhetorical flourishes and presentation of ideas, in order to draw attention to both the argument that he was trying to make – as well as his own playful (he would have named this dialectical) *testing* of his theories (against rival ones). What I wish to emphasise in relation to Aristotle is that he was by no means simply an *ideological opponent* for Brecht. In apparent contradiction, his famous juxtaposition of the Aristotelian dramatic (theatre of illusion) versus the Brechtian epic theatre (of estrangement) (1978, p. 70) of course takes a clear stance against Aristotle's (empathy- and catharsis inducing) drama (Poetics, 1996). Here, we must however keep in mind that Brecht in fact accords with Aristotle's key emphasis on *theatre's (eudemonistic) mimetic function*. 'Tragedy [drama] is not an imitation of persons, but of actions and of life' (Poetics, 50a16f).

The portrayal of character is seen by Aristotle as necessarily embedded in what people *do* – their actions – that is in the way they make decisions and act within the various (tricky and difficult) events they encounter in life (or the life of the story). People, for the Greek patriarch Aristotle, however indeed possessed certain *definite* qualities in accordance with their character (i.e. a 'good' woman displays certain qualities appropriate to a good woman, 50a24i). But it is the way that characters *act in life* (and thus in *plausible* stories) that ultimately leads to their happiness or downfall – their 'well-being and ill-being' (50a24i). In short: People's *active involvement in life*, according to Aristotle, and not people's character as such, decides their success, happiness or failure in the end: 'the goal of life is an activity, and not a quality' (50a24i).

When presented correctly then (by imitating *actions* not characters), fiction – according to Aristotle – has a more profoundly exemplary function and universal character than historiography, presenting, as it does, actions of *particular* people in particular situations; ones that *could* however, potentially, pertain to everybody. For him, the universal aspect and educative potential of storytelling therefore consists, somewhat paradoxically, in the fact that one would indeed act like a particular character in a particular play if one *was* the character in the very circumstances of the story. According to Aristotle then, the philosophical potential of theatre (and tragedy in particular), and its formative function, is neither dependent on the *real-ness* of the event, the poet's allegiance to the truth of what *really* happened, nor his/her direct concern with portraying virtuous characters (e.g. the Gods). In the Poetics, drama's formative potential is discussed in relation to the quality of its compositions in poetic verse drama first; the quality of tragedy is linked to the poet's mastery of the craft of plot-writing as a *tekhnē* (usually translated as *craft, skill, art*) and his ability to imitate actions plausibly. The word drama in Greek means action, deriving from the word *draō (to do)*. 'This is the reason – some say – for the term 'drama': i.e. that the poet imitates people *doing* things' (Poetics, 48a12).

4.3. The Nature and Purpose of Theatrical Pleasure

Flourishing – and with that the *good life* – for *both* Brecht and Aristotle, can then only be achieved in human action and *living* (as an activity). And the imitation of such life-in-action is the stuff of (both their) theatrical mimesis. In other words, both are concerned with the playwright's *tekhnē* to plausibly imitate people's acting and interacting in the world. And as already laid out at the beginning of section 1, Brecht hereby also affirms Aristotle's emphasis on the *pleasure and entertainment function* of drama as a form of (eudemonistic) knowledge creation. 'Thus what the ancients, following Aristotle, demanded of tragedy is nothing higher or lower than that it should entertain people (...)' (Brecht, 1978, p. 181).

That said, however, Brecht also refuses Aristotle's position on poetry's 'philosophical potential' regarding its role to express *universals* (Poetics, 5.5, 9-51b). And he importantly differs with him too with regards to the nature and purpose of *theatrical pleasure* – and as to the kind of aesthetics that is to constitute a *plausible* theatrical imitation of life's actions. According to

Aristotle, the well-constructed tragedy is to indeed bring forth a *pleasurable experience* in the audience. This pleasure (unique to good drama) however consists in evoking *empathy/identification* with the ultimate fate of the (flawed) hero and the arousal of the *tragic emotions* of fear and pity, as well as their subsequent physical relief as catharsis (Poetics, 53b10f; 49b27f).

In contrast, for Brecht, the pleasure of recognition evoked by drama's plausible imitations of life's actions, does neither derive from the audience's *full dramatic immersion* and identification with (a flawed, but likeable) hero. Nor is the purpose of drama constituted in the arousal of tragic emotions and their shedding in catharsis. Accordingly, Brecht refuses these quintessentially Aristotelian dramatic features:

> This [Brecht's] dramaturgy does not make use of the 'identification' of the spectator with the play, as does the aristotelian, and has a different point of view also towards other psychological effects a play may have on an audience, as, for example, towards the 'catharis'. Catharsis is not the main object of this [Brecht's] dramaturgy. It does not make the hero the victim of an inevitable fate, nor does it wish to make the spectator the victim, so to speak, of a hypnotic experience in the theatre. (Brecht, 1978, p. 78)

The pleasure of recognition (of the plausibility of human actions in the theatre), according to Brecht, does not reside in a theatrical mimesis that stimulates tragic emotions and their cathartic release, because (as Aristotle would have it) it allows us to see (recognise) the world *as it is* (e.g. in relation to an inescapable metaphysical order of the world; and/or people's unchangeable character, which is revealed in people's actions). In contrast, the pleasure of the poetic element, for Brecht, emerges from theatrical imitations of human actions, which do *not* instruct the viewer into a specific metaphysical worldview (as Feyerabend had observed in the Nazi and post-WWII plays). That is, Brecht instead hopes to delight (give pleasure to) the audience's intellect and their senses by presenting them with a form of mimesis – whose point of view is opened out for both social and aesthetic scrutiny.

It is in this context that Brecht wishes to encourage a non-Aristotelian poetic reception. Here, human actions, social circumstances, the characters' desires and decision-making – as presented on stage – are not merely read as 'revealing' an essential character and/or specific metaphysical framing. Instead, the audience is to examine the protagonist's *process of formation* of their character in view of the (materially/ideologically – shaped) world they find themselves in. In Brecht's theatrical imitations then – 'individuals remain individual, but become a social phenomenon; their passions and also their fates become a social concern. The individual's position in society loses its God-given quality and become the centre of attention' (Brecht, 1978,

p. 104). In other words, theatre is tasked by Brecht with not only making a metaphysical reality *recognisable* in the theatre ('as does the Aristotelian', 1978), but with opening out for consideration to an audience the productive, aesthetic and social processes that (a) produce the imitated *reality* we encounter on stage [aesthetic] and (b) bring forth the (only seemingly static) nature of our everyday (esp. material/ideological) reality and associated human behaviour [social].

Through a theatrical mimesis that is to appeal to people's reason and their senses pleasurably (so that they find entertainment in this *movement* of their intellect, intuition, and feelings), Brecht aims to educate his audience into a habit of a certain practical (critical) curiosity. The (aesthetic) gesture of showing/pointing to (and with that revealing) theatre's own mimetic efforts to *produce reality* – whilst also (necessarily) presenting a certain point of view (or several) on human action – is hereby at the heart of Brecht's famous *Verfremdungseffekt* (estrangement effect) aesthetic. Having established Brecht's theory of estrangement, I will now turn to section 2, in which I will show how Feyerabend's scientific theorising and practice maps onto Brecht's. Let us start this section by looking at Feyerabend's own non-Aristotelian viewpoint.

5. Section II. Paul Feyerabend

5.1. Scientific Myth-Making in Modern Society

In an early 1968 essay entitled *Science, Freedom and the Good Life,* Feyerabend maintains the essential similarity between the arts and sciences. Both are, ultimately, a form of knowledge production through *storytelling* (myth-making). Like Brecht, Feyerabend draws on Aristotelian tragedy to elaborate on the purpose of myth-making in modern vis-à-vis ancient Greek society. In antiquity, so his argument goes, storytelling served as a pedagogy of inducting a populace into a specific metaphysical theory – with the purpose to reproduce the forms of life in a *closed society.* The intention to educate people into an (infallible) myth – in order to ensure cultural unity – hereby presumed a notion of the student who was a passive receptacle, and whose (tabula-rasa) soul was either to be *imprinted* with ideas – or led towards the uncovering of certain *innate* (and eternal) truths. Feyerabend argues that the psychological effects of Aristotelian *catharsis* (as described in the Poetics, 1996) – when understood as the *shedding* of the dramatically induced emotions of fear, pity and horror – hereby built on – and reinforced – the psychological mechanisms inherent in the structure of certain ancient initiation rituals.

> There is a psychological mechanism in man which secures that if he is taught
> something after being subjected to a traumatic situation, it will be almost
> impossible for him ever to eradicate or to criticise what has just been taught
> (...). (Feyerabend 1968, p. 128)

The metaphysical theories underpinning Aristotle's conception of mimesis
(e.g. regarding the *essential* qualities of human beings, i.e. *good women*) –
as well as his dramatic movement's psychological effects – aimed to cohere
people around a *specific view of the world*; one that was to ensure the cultural
coherence, direction, unity and reproduction of *specific forms of life* (including
of course specific social institutions) in a closed society.

> The cultural unity of the closed society has disintegrated; yet, in parts, develop-
> ing independently of each other, live on. Only now these parts seem a little more
> unreasonable. Therefore it seems that certain scientific and artistic doctrines
> today, though much more developed, are in one sense much less reasonable than
> they were when they belonged to the closed society. (p. 129)

Despite the (more or less) disintegration of culturally closed societies,
Feyerabend contends that certain ways of scientific theorising in the contemporary, pluralistic society – indeed still rely on certain *cathartic features* to
induce a *psychological* acceptance of their metaphors. At the same time, however, scientific storytelling has not only severed its kinship with the arts, but
also given up any broader cultural ideals, which it might have once occupied.
With the aim to merely promote dogmatic (abstract) arguments, and ensure
the (professional) status of *certain* methods and methodologies, scientific
storytelling in the pluralistic society, Feyerabend insists, fails to give consideration to the question of general human happiness – i.e. as to (various)
forms our (e.g. intercultural) lives and living in the pluralistic society could/
should take.

> What provided coherence and direction in a primitive society was an ideal –
> the conservation of society and the form of life it stood for. Similarly, what
> we should do under present circumstances is to look for a different ideal (...).
> (p. 130)

But what kind of ideal can give direction and justification to our methods,
when modern, pluralistic society – and its cultural expressions – just can-
not act as provider of norms and laws that can gather people around a stable and shared meaning – to give direction for action (Baummann, 2000).
The 'autonomous society' (p. 212), Baumann famously suggested, is marked
by its very *cultural liquidity* and the fact that there are *no* assured mean-
ings anymore. Its freedom, Baumann argued, can only be assured when we

acknowledge society's *radical liquidity* – when we admit that 'it lives on the surface of chaos, that it itself is a chaos seeking a form, but a form that is never fixed once and for all' (pp. 212–213).

5.2. The Pleasures of Knowledge Production?

The higher enlightenment ideals that are put forward by science to ensure its status (e.g. as Truth and Reason) – Feyerabend maintains, obscure science's lack of broader (social, cultural) ideals; ones that could ensure not a mere abstract claim to truth, but the (practical) happiness of human beings in a pluralistic society.

> Once we have found a new ideal which can provide direction, then of course, we will have found proper justification for procedures in every domain. Moreover, we might have to change these procedures relative to the new ideal. This new ideal should be simply to make people more pleasant and more interesting, to make life happier, to make the world better, to make the beer better and so on. (1968, p. 130)

Resulting from his critique, Feyerabend (1968) entertains a rather Brechtian ideal as to the role of artistic and scientific storytelling in a modern, pluralistic society. Rather than re-producing *specific* norms and values as in the closed society (but without an – even if flawed – ideal of cultural unity), it is to rather sustain more *practical ideals* – aimed at nourishing individual human productivity in its manifoldness. Theatre and science are to preserve human happiness in the broadest sense (and the plurality of life, more generally) – by embracing, and bringing forth, the pleasure that resides in the audience's acts of knowledge production (in the arts and sciences) – as producers, speculators and critics. In his essay *Let's Make More Movies* (1975), Feyerabend echoes Brecht's Anti-Aristotelian theatre's aim (as shown in section 1). Here, Feyerabend argues that plays, rather than serving to instruct people into a *Weltanschauung*, can potentially mobilise a more holistic and pleasurable kind of reasoning; one that draws on the audience's intellect and their senses, so that they can consider (for themselves) the productive and material conditions that have given rise to certain (seemingly universal) arguments and ideas.

> Having been trained by our teachers, by the pressure of professions, and by the general climate of a liberal-scientific age to 'listen to reason', we quite automatically abstract from 'external circumstances' and concentrate on the logic of a demonstration. A good play, on the other hand, does not permit us to overlook faces, gestures – or what one might call the physiognomy of an argument. A good play uses the physical manifestations of reason to irritate our senses and

disturb our feelings so that they get in the way of a smooth and 'objective'
appraisal. It tempts us to judge an event by the interplay of all the agencies that
cause its occurrence. (Feyerabend, 1975, p. 201)

Feyerabend inscribes the theatre (of estrangement) with the pedagogical potential to irritate our senses and our intellect. This is not in order to
traumatise us, for example, by means of a *cathartic effect*, so as to instruct
the audience into specific ideas, and resulting values and practices. In other
words, the *irritation* brought forth by theatrical estrangement is not aimed
to excite and harmonise our psychological state – but to appeal to our intellect, senses and ability to self-govern. Aesthetic estrangement (in the arts
and science) is to show that it shows. Doing so, it is to *estrange* the logic of
abstract argumentations – and to draw our attention to the very productive
processes (social interplay, aesthetic presentation), which bring forth an ide-
a(l) in the first place.

   Theatre's potential to free us from a mechanically lived life, saturated in
unquestioned ideological assumptions (and perhaps psychological manipulation), then lies, for Feyerabend, in its capacity to make *striking and strange*
what seems indeed most familiar to us. Or as he puts it in rather forthright
terms: theatre is to 'bludgeon us into detachment from our daily lives, our
habits and mental laziness, which conceal from us the strangeness of the
world (…)' (2008, p. 302).

   As can be seen, despite Feyerabend's reservations (in hindsight) about
the cult-like Brecht circle and its moral-aesthetic pressures, Brecht's theatre
of estrangement, seems a key reference point in Feyerabend's own thinking
as to the nature (and moral function) of the dynamic and integrative relationship between the arts, science and knowledge. In *Let's Make More Movies*
(1975), Feyerabend further emphasises the role of *estrangement*, as a form
of general public reasoning (i.e. as a key component of human inquiry/life
more generally). Here, our everyday and expert acts of *thinking* about, *acting*
in, and (re)*making* the world, are not kept apart in separate disciplines and
spheres of status. In another act of productive estrangement, various (artistic, scientific, practical and theoretical) knowledge(s) are to be brought into
(public) conversation. Rejecting the universal (even if harmonising) value of
a mere abstract knowledge/ truth (usually promoted by experts), Feyerabend
emphasises the pedagogical potential of estrangement – to move us towards
a more integrated ideal: of living a life of human inquiry as a creative and
enjoyable endeavour.

   What is needed to proceed since the further [the 'artificial' separation of subjects, that began with the enlightenment, roughly] is not the return to harmony

and stability as so many critics of the status quo, Marxists included, seem to think, but a form of life in which the constituents of older myths-theories, books, images, emotions, sounds, institutions enter as interacting but antagonistic elements. Brecht's theatre was an attempt to create such a form of life. (1975, p. 209)

Feyerabend cites Brechtian theatre as an example of such pedagogy of (public) reasoning. Here, estrangement is to catalyse a form of life, in which people's proliferating acts of encountering, contemplating, weighing up and testing *the emergence* of their ideas, values and practices (scientific, artistic etc.), is not simply a means to an end to an abstract (a-priori) ideal of truth. A public pedagogy of estrangement is to be instead part of the more practical ideal of *preserving human life and happiness* more generally; one in which people's irritation of their intellect, senses and intuition – and the inquiry into the 'physiognomy of an argument' (Feyerabend, 1975, p. 201) is (hoped) to be enjoyed for its own sake.

In *his Tyranny of Science* lectures, Feyerabend (2011) further draws our attention to this important (aka life-affirming) interaction between our abstract theory/knowledge and our concrete practices of life in the here and now – and the potentially 'inhumane consequences of a society that succumbs to the seduction of the theoretical', as editor Eric Oberheim formulates it in his introduction (p. xii). Here, in a playful, and somewhat sardonic Brechtian (1978, 2014) style, Feyerabend critiques philosophers (and sociologists for that matter) who 'give the impression they understand the deep reasons behind troublesome affairs' (2011, p. 154). Confident they can capture some underlying (permanent) structures in 'big words, simple concepts and trite explanations' (ibid.), these philosophers, Feyerabend teases, do not take into account the *historicised nature* of *all* knowledge (be it theatrical or scientific), bound up in the particularities of human actions and idea(l)s at a specific point in history (which could also be otherwise). Feyerabend then (1991) concludes that there is a danger to a conception of truth (scientific, philosophical, and artistic) that (even if inadvertently) merely reproduces specific metaphysical theories, and does not recognise its own ideals' embeddedness in history, as well as in the life practices of a specific group of experts (e.g. scientists, professional academics/philosophers of the time).

Feyerabend (1978) insists that the *value of knowledge* cannot be answered in a universal way (e.g. by references to enlightenment truth and reason). As such, the question of knowledge's value is to be mapped onto the concrete ways that people can not only *use* such knowledge, but are enabled to critically weigh up the offered theories in the context of their own conscious experience of a valued (everyday and expert) life's theories and practices. In other words, people's *specific ways of life* – their individual human interactions with the material and ideal features of their world, might not always benefit from the kind of knowledge that science (or philosophy or art) declares as *being* universally valuable. Editor Eric Oberheim (2011), in his introduction to the *Tyranny of Science* lectures, summarises Feyerabend's key concern:

> He [Feyerabend] argues that far from solving the pressing problems of our age, such as war and poverty, scientific theorising glorifies ephemeral generalities instead of confronting the real particulars that make life worth living (…). Theoreticians, as opposed to practitioners, tend to oppose tyranny through the concepts they use, which abstract away from the subjective experiences that make life meaningful. (p. xi)

Feyerabend, not unlike Bertolt Brecht, then wishes to connect the question of epistemological value to knowledge's practical benefit to context-specific, subjective human experiences and practices; especially those that people have developed to make themselves *at home* in the world. How do certain types of knowledge (abstract, object-directed) serve (or hinder) people's capacity to flourish within the *particular* lives and practices that they have developed to live a happy life? What happens when philosophers and/or scientists (or artists for that matter) seek to import ways of *justifying, gathering and presenting* knowledge (methodologies; methods) that assume a universal validity that functions devoid of such concrete contexts?

Knowledge can end up freezing ideas and practices into an ideological prison, Feyerabend warns in *Three Dialogues* (1991, p. 151). Quoting the playwright Eugène Ionesco (2008), he also states that theatre (even artistic practice in general) is of course not exempt from such potentially totalising practice: even an 'ideological play can be no more than the vulgarisation of an ideology' (p. 308). In short, even a well-meaning intention (e.g. for social change), when too willingly burdened by a theatre claiming a *higher status*, can too easily obscure that it is in the business of metaphor-creation. And as such, it can slide into normative *impositions* as to how people *should* think and act. Feyerabend indeed even accused Brecht at times for betraying his own principles of estrangement. Feyerabend (1991) lauded Brecht's anti-ideological, dialectical approach to presenting knowledge in poetry (e.g. in his 1939 poem *To those who follow in our wake*). He praised Brecht's poetry for the way it 'enlarges faults and lets different incommensurable jargons run side by side' (Feyerabend, 1991, p. 95), without harmonising different aspects into a more systematic account. But he also accused Brecht (in some of his plays in particular) of humourless, Marxist intellectualism and, indeed, of 'moralising' from the stage (pp. 81, 143).

In the same way that a mimetic theory and practice in the theatre can refuse to take into account the subjective experience and freedom (and with that self-governing power) of the individual moral agent – scientific rationalism can attempt to conceptually subjugate and dominate the individual's conscious experience of their own valued lives (Feyerabend, 1991, p. 82). This act of ideological freezing, Feyerabend implies, can also apply to a (so-called) liberal relativism when it presumes a closed system of varying ideas, cultures and traditions. Here, in the liberal knowledge economy, knowledge systems are imagined to exist rather neatly side by side. Without causing any *epistemological discord*, they however lack the productive estrangement (the productive and antagonistic interplay), which Feyerabend (as well as Brecht) would have ascribed a key moral-aesthetic/formative function in a free society.

The act of knowledge creation in theatre and science is then not to be an act of purveying universal truths, but to create (pedagogical) *models* and *examples* – without obscuring the *aspect of play* that accompanies the creation of concepts and metaphors. These representations are indeed to delight and move people's intellect and their senses of course, but not in order to imprint the empty canvas of their soul and intellect – but to enable their own *pleasurable acts of knowledge creation* (their testing of certain images and ideals) in turn.

The philosopher-educator (according to Feyerabend) is hereby to act as a creator of conditions, in which these pedagogical models can be weighed up by students, who are encouraged to draw on their experience, instinct and self-governing reasoning power. As such, they are both to scrutinise the offered ideas, and the productive/aesthetic processes that brought forth the model in the first place. In summary, big words like reason, freedom and science should not be used to deny people's capacity to reason and govern themselves, as to what constitutes knowledge that is of value (to particular forms of common and individual life). Feyerabend suggests in fact that he can only think of himself as a philosopher if the individual's capability to self-govern is placed at the heart of the philosophising activities.

> (...) Well, if you think a philosopher is a universal dilettante who tries to see things in perspective and tries to stop people from forcing others into their beliefs, be it now by arguments or by other means of coercion, then certainly I am a philosopher – but so are journalists and playwrights (...). (1991, p. 153)

In my final section, I will consider the implications of this Feyerabendian embrace of the aesthetic of estrangement in relation to his notion of scientific progress demonstrated in the history of thought.

5.2.1. An Example of Aesthetic of Estrangement: Counterinduction

In *Science, Freedom and the Good Life* (1968), Feyerabend gives us an example of what an aesthetic of estrangement might consist of, when we do not only consider the established logic and principles for scientific reasoning, but look more closely at how science has been practiced (and progressed) throughout the history of thought. Feyerabend points us towards Sir Isaac Newton's (1846) famous 'Rules of Reasoning in Philosophy' (particularly rule four) in book three of his *Mathematical Principles of Natural Philosophy* (pp. 384–385). Providing a methodology as to how to handle the explanation of unknown natural phenomena, rule four (Feyerabend states) is although never explicitly stated, and even more rarely debated, nevertheless accepted as an obvious (more or less unquestionable) scientific truth (Feyerabend, 1968, p. 130).

> **RULE IV.** In experimental philosophy we are to look upon propositions collected by general induction from, phenomena as accurately or very nearly true, *notwithstanding any contrary hypotheses that may be imagined, till such time as other phenomena occur, by which they may either be made more accurate, or liable to exceptions.* This rule we must follow, that the argument of induction may not be evaded by hypotheses. (Newton, 1846, p. 385)

Despite this (albeit unstated) dogma regarding the procedure of scientific reasoning – 'never introduce an assumption inconsistent with highly confirmed physical laws/observed facts' (Feyerabend, 1968, p. 130) – Feyerabend argues that the history of science is in fact littered with examples of (rather *successful*) violations of this principle. In other words, the scientific practice of a more estranging (and epistemologically proliferating) *counterinduction* – having contradictory realities run side-by-side – did not only *not* impede but made *possible* the enhancement of scientific theorising. Additionally, such experimental approach (i.e. taking into account counterinduction and the acceptance of alternative, even archaic hypotheses and theories – and with that also a plurality of methods), Feyerabend (1968, p. 131) insists, preserves the *pleasure* and playfulness, which reside at the heart of our human acts of knowledge creation (esp. when these draw on our *manifold* productive capabilities – including the use of our imagination and intuition).

As such, it is not enough to critically test a theory by looking at (new) empirical evidence; the scientist must be able to intuit and imagine alternative *theories* – given not all scientists ever agree on the accuracy of observations, their results and accompanying theories anyway. Feyerabend quotes many examples of such *epistemological anarchism* from the history of science: from the Copernican Revolution to Bohr's model of the atom. He proposes that, for example, Einstein in fact only arrived at his *atomic theory* and Special

Theory of Relativity through *counterinduction*, that is, by holding on to a theory, which in the nineteenth century was thought to be *inconsistent* with the then highly confirmed thermodynamic theories.

> (...) had it been entirely given up in accordance with the principle under attach (never introduce a theory inconsistent with highly confirmed theories), we might not have any atomic physics today. And so we can cite one case after another where progress in the sciences coincides with violation of the [rule four] principle. So the principle *has not* been followed in period of decisive progress. (p. 131)

In other words, Feyerabend argues that a strict empiricist attitude (one that denies intuition and imagination for example) does not only deny the actual development, which has taken place in the *history* of science and scientific progress. Instead of holding on to the dogmatism that marked the closed society, Feyerabend concludes, we should focus instead on recapturing its unity of purpose. Embracing the epistemological discord of an *estranged scientific reasoning* – in service of the more integrated ideal of preserving human life, productivity (in a holistic sense) and happiness – we might not only make public life (and people) more pleasant and interesting but also preserve – perhaps restore – science (and human inquiry more generally) as the *creative endeavour* that it is.

References

Arendt, H. (1948). Beyond personal frustration: The poetry of Bertolt Brecht. *The Kenyon Review, 10*(2), 304–312.

Aristotle and Freire Owen, O. (Trans.). (2017). *Organon, or logical treatises* (Rise of Douai).

Aristotle and Heath, M. (Trans.) (1996). *Poetics*. Penguin Books.

Bacon, F. (2019) *Novum Organum*. Dumfries & Galloway.

Baumann, Z. (2000) *Liquid modernity*. Polity Press.

Bloch, E., Lukács, G., Brecht, B., Benjmain, W., & Adorno, T. (1977). *Aesthetics and politics*. Verso.

Brecht, B. (1978). *Brecht on theatre*. Methuen Drama.

Brecht, B., & Tatlow, A. (Ed.). (2016). *Bertolt Brecht's Me-ti: Book of interventions in the flow of things*. Bloomsbury.

Brecht, B., & Kuhn, T., Silberman, M., & Giles, S. (Eds.). (2014). *Brecht on performance: Messingkauf and Modelbooks* (S. Giles & T. Kuhn, Trans.). Bloomsbury.

Campbell, J. (2004) *A hero with a thousand faces*. Princeton University Press.

Feyerabend, P. (1968). Science, freedom and the good life. *Philosophical Forum, 1*(2), 127–135.

Feyerabend, P. (1975). Let's make More Movies. In C. J. Bontempo & S. J. Odell (Eds.), *The Owl of Minerva: Philosophers on philosophy* (pp. 201–210). McGraw-Hill Book Company.

Feyerabend, P. (1978). *Science in a free society*. NLB.

Feyerabend, P. (1991). *Three dialogues on knowledge*. Blackwell.

Feyerabend, P. (1993). *Against method*. New Left Books.

Feyerabend, P. (1995). *Killing time: The autobiography of Paul Feyerabend*. University of Chicago Press.

Feyerabend, P. (2008). The theatre as an instrument of criticism of ideologies. *Inquiry: An Interdisciplinary Journal of Philosophy, 10*(1–4), 298–312.

Feyerabend, P. (2011). *The tyranny of science*. Polity Press.

Gadberry, G. (2000). The history plays of the Third Reich. In J. London (Ed.), *Theatre under the Nazis* (pp. 96–135). Manchester University Press.

Grimm, R. (1979). *Brecht und Nietzsche oder Geständnisse eines Dichters: Fünf Essays und ein Bruchstück*. Suhrkamp Verlag.

Korsch, K., & Halliday, F. (Trans.). (2012). *Marxism and philosophy*. Verso.

Lenin, V. I. (1970). *Materialism and Empirico-Criticism*. Progress Publishers.

Paškevica, B. (2006). *In der Stadt der Parolen: Asja Lacis, Walter Benjamin und Bertolt Brecht*. Klartext Verlag.

Suissa, J. (2010). *Anarchism and education: A philosophical perspective*. Routledge.

Feyerabend on Education, Professionalisation, and Intellectual Pollution

JAMIE SHAW

1. Introduction

Like most thinkers in the liberal tradition, Paul Feyerabend places a great deal of importance on education. However, his pedagogical writings are sparse and far from systematic. The goal of this paper is to draw together themes in Feyerabend's corpus concerning freedom and intellectual maturity to his views on education. Furthermore, I tie these more abstract reflections to his own pedagogical practices on grading, topic selection, and professionalisation. Finally, I point to some tensions in Feyerabend's thought that manifested themselves in practice.

Most of Feyerabend's corpus is dedicated to showing that all intellectual rules, no matter how basic or obvious they may seem, have their limitations. Discovering what these limitations are is not straightforward. Feyerabend explicitly repudiates the idea of conceiving of rationality as a set of hypothetical imperatives (Feyerabend, 1978, p. 164). Rather, the discovery of when we should be 'rational' comes from violating proposed rules of rationality and comparing the results to the track record of those rules. To know when we should avoid contradictions, for example, we must first engage in practices that *contain* contradictions and see what happens. This 'anarchism' entails that we never follow rules because one feels 'compelled by reason' or forced to on 'pains of contradiction' and the like – we are explorers and creators of existing and unknown forms of life.

Without rules of rationality, anarchism opens the door for dangerous possibilities that Feyerabend thought were dangerous. Feyerabend's best academic rival, Imre Lakatos, insisted this would degenerate into a relativism of the worst kind. Without rules of rationality, the floodgates open and no action or argument can be condemned. More poignantly put, 'anything goes' would enable 'intellectual pollution' where sloppiness and uncritical declarations can overpower the most thoughtful reflections. Despite Feyerabend's flirtations with relativism (see Kusch, 2021), he shares Lakatos' concern. Readers can easily relate to Feyerabend's vivid depictions of what he calls the 'cranks' with their own exemplars of pernicious intellectual engagements:

> The distinction between the crank and the respectable thinker lies in the research that is done once a certain point of view is adopted. The crank usually is content with defending the point of view in its original, undeveloped, metaphysical form, and he is not prepared to test its usefulness in all those cases which seem to favor the opponent, or even admit that there exists a problem. It is this further investigation, the details of it, the knowledge of the difficulties, of the general state of knowledge, the recognition of objections, which distinguishes the 'respectable thinker' from the crank. The original content of his theory does not. (Feyerabend, 1964, p. 305).

While Feyerabend often had the 'tendency ... to pick up strange views and push them to the extreme' (Feyerabend, 1995, p. 39), he recognised that intellectual pollution – where 'illiterate and incompetent books flood the market, empty verbiage full of strange and esoteric terms claims to express profound insights, "experts" without brains, without character, and without even a modicum of intellectual, stylistic, emotional temperament tell us about our "condition" and the means of improving it' (Feyerabend, 1975a, p. 219) – is a troubling phenomenon that requires a response. It is one thing to concede that 'ridiculous' views are often defended by intelligent people. If we look at Feyerabend's exemplars of defences of Voodoo, for example, he chooses researchers with arguments that are more sophisticated than is often appreciated (e.g. Walter Cannon) rather than some snake-oil dealer off the street corner. It is another thing altogether to open the doors to the cranks and the intellectual pollution they create.

Lakatos thought that his own conception of rationality would provide a set of objective standards that could dispel intellectual pollution. This is the ultimate ambition of 'rationalism', or the view that we can formulate distinctive forms of reasoning that are to be used to the exclusion of others that are 'irrational'. This is motivated by Lakatos' conviction that one must accept objective standards of rationality, or one must give way to any form of life that presents itself. Feyerabend disagrees, but his epistemological anarchism does not equip him with any standards from which he can call some thought 'pollution' and others that are worthy of admiration or replication. How, then, does Feyerabend deal with the problem of intellectual pollution? While he introduces the notion of the 'cranks' to shift criteria of appraisal from scientific theorising to scientists, we still need an ability to discern who counts as cranks and why to best combat the problem.

In *Against Method*, Feyerabend declares that the solution does not come from some conception of rationality. Rather, it comes from *education*:

> Lakatos is concerned about intellectual pollution. I share his concern ... But I do not see how the methodology of Lakatos can help. As far as I am concerned the first and most pressing problem is to get education out of the hands of the 'professional educators' ... It seems to me that [a change] in education and, as a result, perspective [will cause] ... such phenomena [to] disappear like a bad dream. (Feyerabend, 1975a, pp. 217–219)[1]

For this solution to genuinely differ from Lakatos', education cannot involve the inculcation of any particular set of beliefs or style of reasoning. Indeed, Feyerabend emphatically rejects this approach (Feyerabend, 2011, p. 125ff).[2] How can Feyerabend walk this tightrope, avoiding reimplementing rationalism on the one hand while defusing intellectual pollution on the other? How education solves the problem of intellectual pollution and what practical consequences this contains is the primary topic to be explored in this paper. Moreover, we will see what practical consequences Feyerabend thought this entailed for his own professional practice as an educator.

2. *Education, Freedom, and Intellectual Maturity*

Let's start from the beginning. For Feyerabend, the best way to live life is to be free and happy (Feyerabend, 1970, p. 210). Freedom and happiness are two sides of the same coin; one cannot be free without being happy and one cannot be happy without being free. In other words, one cannot be happy as an intellectual slave – that is, someone whose actions and thoughts are determined by anything outside of themselves. This does not just include people who are literally enslaved or brainwashed, but those whose thought and identity is conditioned by an abstract view – such as a view of rationality. A free human being is one who does not act or think in a particular way because it is consistent with the Will of God, because it is 'rational', or because it is follows from a moral law. They act and think in a particular way because

---

1 While the ellipses cover pages of argumentation, therein contain the arguments for the changes Feyerabend wishes to make which will be covered in this paper.
2 However, at times, Feyerabend forgets this mantra and discusses curriculum as if they should presuppose his personal convictions.

they *want* to.[3] Political institutions are meant to enable and allow for this freedom: '[In] a free society ... everyone should have a chance to make up his own mind and to live in accordance with the social beliefs he finds most acceptable' (Feyerabend, 1978, p. 299). One who lives a free life will also live a happy one.

Freedom is not a given nor does it follow from a lack of external interference. Rather, it is something each individual must work hard to achieve. Freedom is an *accomplishment*. We are always born and raised in traditions with rules for thinking and behaving that are embedded in our psyches. While some philosophers of education conceive of education as the process of introducing students into these traditions (e.g. Bakhurst, 2011), Feyerabend wishes to train pupils to embrace whatever norms insofar as they are *their own norms*. This may be impossible in practice, as we would need to identify which norms are 'theirs' which raises a host of metaphysical puzzles that Feyerabend never considered, but Feyerabend appears to think that individuals are not solely conditioned by the traditions that surround them. This entails critically reflecting, from an open-ended variety of perspectives, upon our beliefs, attitudes, and emotions. Critical thinking, though, is not what is often taught in critical thinking courses. It is not narrowly understood as developing a set of intellectual tools (e.g. various logics, informal fallacies) (e.g. Bailin & Seigel, 2003). Rather, critical thinking requires the ability to *understand* and *choose* between alternative paths.[4] The idea seems to be that through reflection and exposure to alternative ways of thinking and living, we lessen the hold traditions seem to hold over us (namely, that they are 'natural', 'inevitable', or the like) and can better make free choices. These tools may be helpful for this task, but they alone are insufficient. To understand something fully, Feyerabend frequently claims, one must *live* according to its norms and compare this form of life with alternatives. We need more than an intellectual comprehension of the relative merits and deficiencies of a particular form of life – we must also feel and breathe it. To understand and choose a life of monogamy, for example, one would need to live as a polygamist, celibate, etc., compare them, and consider them from many angles through the standard ways one would learn about something (e.g. reading, writing,

3 Feyerabend then seems committed to the view, *contra Hume*, that we can believe, act, etc. in ways that goes against our passions. See Radcliff (2018) for further discussion.

4 This view, perhaps coincidentally, was also outlined by J. S. Mill, Feyerabend's hero, who declares that logic includes any kind of intellectual activity that 'enable[es] a person to know truths which are *needful to him*, and to know them at the precise moment at which they are needful' (Mill, 2006, p. 6; emphasis added).

listening to testimonies). Only once this critical process has been completed can one be said to make a decision *freely*.[5]

It isn't surprising, then, that we see Feyerabend claim that (formal and informal) educators must introduce their pupils to a variety of forms of life, different ways of thinking about them, and trying to remove whatever dogmas hold them back from experimenting openly with what life has to offer. In essence, the goal of the educator is to provide students with the tools necessary to be free. The value of freedom, for Feyerabend, is not simply for the individual but also for producing good *citizens* – i.e. members of society who enrich the lives of those around them (cf. Callan, 1997). In *Against Method* and *Science in a Free Society*, Feyerabend outlines his idea of a 'mature people' who are, in effect, those who are genuinely free (Brown, 2021). By fortuitous coincidence, the intellectually mature (the 'free') are the primary precipitators of intellectual progress. Feyerabend understands progress as an 'ever-increasing ocean of alternatives each of them forcing the others into greater articulations, all of them contributing, via this process of competition, to development of our mental faculties' (Feyerabend, 1963, p. 107; see also Tambolo, 2015). The freedom to explore and develop the space of possible alternatives is necessary for the production of the best possible knowledge. No standard, practice, or interpretation is held as a *dogma* – they are all just ideas that are being floated, considered, temporarily put aside, and so on. To progress one must not take their cue from any principle, whatever it may be, but to *freely* play around with ideas to inform our decisions as thoroughly as possible. In Feyerabend's words,

> A mature citizen is someone who has learned how to make up his mind and who has then decided in favor of what suits him best. He is a person who has a certain mental toughness (he does not fall for the first ideological street singer he happens to meet), and who is therefore able to consciously choose the business that seems to be most attractive to him, rather than be swallowed up by it. To prepare him for his choice, he will study the major ideologies as historical phenomena, he will study science as an historical phenomenon and not as the one and only sensible way of approaching a problem. He will study it together with other fairytales, such as the myths of 'primitive' societies, so that he has the information needed for arriving at a free decision. An essential part of a general education of this kind is acquaintance with the most outstanding propagandists in all fields, so that the 'pupil' can build up his resistance to all propaganda, including the propaganda called 'argument.' It is only after such a hardening procedure that he will be called upon to make up his mind on

5 Clearly, this makes freedom and 'genuine choice' a matter of degree. This entails that we aim not for 'freedom', strictly speaking, but the highest degree of freedom that is possible in a given situation.

the issue rationalism-irrationalism, science-myth, science-religion, and so on. (Feyerabend, 1975b, pp. 175–176)

The free person has a set of skills that are enabled by particular forms of education: they are *able* to proliferation novel approaches, they are *able* to compare newly proliferated from the old vanguard, they are *able* to compare them according to many standards, and they are *able* to put all of this into practice. Thus freedom is not just valuable for the individual to choose their own path in life, but it is valuable for others as well for they will benefit from the fruits of a free spirit.

As mentioned, these skills do not come from nowhere. They come from hard work and require guidance and support from established institutions. It should be obvious, at this point, that education is a crucial (perhaps *the* crucial) fulcrum for developing a mature populace. From this, a pedagogy grounded in Feyerabend's anarchist philosophy has its goals set out for it such as:

1. Instilling a critical attitude within students to not accept anything as a dogma (often through challenging views or habits they hold).
2. Teaching students a wide variety of traditions that provide the intellectual tools for further experimentation.
3. Allowing students to experiment outside of the pedagogical practice that they are embedded in.

I do not want to suggest that these are the *only* goals an anarchist education may have, but they are certainly the most prominent ones that Feyerabend discusses. Through this method of education, Feyerabend believes that intellectual pollution will be eroded. This method does not force anyone to believe this or that or follow this or that rule, but it will create mature people who be thoroughly thoughtful. In a sense, the kinds of citizens this would create, in Feyerabend's vision, would not be so abnormal. We rarely close debates when someone raises a reason against a view or throw up our arms when one challenges the superiority of, say, the passions over reason. Indeed, the history of perfectly reputable thought is filled with these open-ended debates where no stone is left unturned. While Feyerabend's view of education does not principally exclude flat-earthers, fascists, or others with minority views that seem beyond the pale, it is hard to believe that such views would survive in the minds of the free and, if they did, they would emerge in formulations that would be much less easy to deny. Feyerabend's philosophy of education, therefore, contains a bit of optimism within it or else he may be far too comfortable with the consequences of open-ended, freedom.

All of this, though, is quite abstract and leaves much room for interpretation for how it could be practically manifested. Moreover, there are several theoretical questions that are left unresolved in Feyerabend's corpus about the nature of individual freedom and choice. In keeping with Feyerabend's general outlook, one cannot make sense of abstract views such as this independent from a particular context. To bring this all down to earth, it is worth seeing how Feyerabend acted as an educator in the context in which he found himself.

3. *Practical Consequences*

There are several dimensions of Feyerabend's pedagogical practices that are worth exploring and connecting them to his more abstract 'sermons'. There are a few that will be treated here; namely, Feyerabend's views on *professionalisation*, *grading*, and *lecturing*.

3.1. *The Ethics of Professionalisation*

Feyerabend strictly separates two kinds of teaching. One is teaching someone how to succeed in an already established form of life. This is *professionalisation* – the education that allows one to succeed in a trade or profession with established norms. This is distinct from a *general education*. A general education aims at producing free people. In Feyerabend's words,

> General education should prepare a citizen to choose between the standards, or to find his way in a society that contains groups committed to various standards *but it must under no condition bend his mind so that it conformism to the standards of one particular group.* The standards will be *considered*, they will be *discussed*, children will be encouraged to get proficiency in the more important subjects, *but only as one gets proficiency in a game*, that is, without serious commitment and without robbing the mind of its ability to play other games as well. (Feyerabend, 1975a, p. 218)

More bluntly put, 'we must ... separate the process of learning from the preparation for a particular trade' (p. 217). For Feyerabend, there is nothing intrinsically wrong with adopting the norms of a profession. However, this choice must be made freely. That is, to repeat, one should only accept an education in a trade once one understands the professional norms in the aforementioned sense. One should not join a profession because one has the immediate desire that one 'must' or 'should' join the profession, but because they have gone through a certain amount of pluralistic education, recognise the profession under consideration is an experiment in living, and can compare this profession to other life options. This makes professionalisation both a *sub-species* and *parasitic* on a general education. Professionalisation requires introducing students to a form of life and is therefore a part of a general education. Here, the professional norms would be taught side-by-side with other professional norms, especially those that are diametrically opposed to one another. Moreover, one can only choose a profession *after* some degree of general education (which must be forced at some point in a child's cognitive development). A general education is necessary for freedom, and freedom is necessary for making a genuine choice, and so a genuine choice of a profession requires a general education.

To professionalise a student, for Feyerabend, is to remind them that the norms they are being taught is simply *a* way of living life and contributing to society. To be clear, there should be no tension here as the ambitions of professionalisation are not in conflict with the goals of freedom (though see below). In Feyerabend's words, 'One thing that must be avoided at all costs: the special standards which define special subjects and special professions must not be allowed to permeate *general* education' (Feyerabend, 1975a). Teaching students to be sceptical of a profession is both making them a better professional and a better citizen and human being. Because of this, the goals of professionalisation cannot conflict with the goals of freedom. When and where they do, the trouble resides with the process of professionalisation.

Professionalisation is also connected to intellectual pollution. For Feyerabend, intellectual pollution does not just come from the 'uneducated'. It also, frequently in Feyerabend's estimation, protrudes from academics. His responses to many reviews of *Against Method*, compiled in a section of *Science in a Free Society* entitled 'Conversations with Illiterates' tells you all you need to know. Professional philosophers, for example, may be able to recite various technicalities about verisimilitude or paradoxes of induction, but they also will repeat empty rumours about astrology (see 'The Strange Case of Astrology' in *Science in a Free Society*), voodoo, and so on. They didn't recognise the rhetorical techniques used in *Against Method* because, according to Feyerabend, they only know one way of writing and reading philosophy. Indeed, Feyerabend thought lowly of many of his intellectual colleagues from the 1970s onwards and would include them with other purveyors of intellectual pollution. This is because they do not have a good enough *general* education – they were only ever professionalised. While this cynical take on academia during Feyerabend's time may be unnecessarily harsh, it illustrates how professionalisation can contribute to the problem of intellectual pollution.

3.2. Grading[6]

Feyerabend was uncomfortable with the idea of providing grades. He was harshly critical of how grades were often used as means of intimidation: '"Teachers" using grades and the fear of failure mould the brains of the young until they have lost every once of imagination they might once have possessed ... The constraints of grades, competition, regular examination must be removed' (Feyerabend, 1975a, p. 217). Beyond this, Feyerabend engaged in a fairly controversial 'no grading' policy himself. When he was teaching at Berkeley, Feyerabend gave each of his student an 'A' regardless of their performance in class. Later, at the behest of John Heilbron, Feyerabend compromised and made the course a 'pass/fail' course. This sounds like an absurd practice for many reasons, and, to a certain extent, Feyerabend would agree with this. His tendency, in thought and practice, was to overreact to draw out the implicit assumptions of a view he wished to criticise. What was Feyerabend reacting to?

Grading has a few features that troubled Feyerabend. First, grading involves an evaluation of a student's performance or their demonstrated proficiency with regard to the subject material that was taught. As we will see later, Feyerabend was unsure about what content the students needed to know. Because of this, it would be troubling to test the student's knowledge of material that they may not need to know. What does it matter if a student grasps the lessons of a tradition that is worthless to them?[7] A second reason Feyerabend had against grading was that he wanted students to take ownership of their own evaluation. Feyerabend emphasises over and over again that one must be willing to take responsibility for their own beliefs and not be a mere follower of a dogma. This is a part of being free. As such, it is the student's responsibility to decide whether the content of what they've learned was valuable to them and whether they've mastered this material according to their own standards. Giving the students As was simply reacting to an administrative necessity to give a grade while leaving it up the students to decide what their actual grade was.

6 Parts of this section were informed by conversations with Gonzalo Munévar, who recalled conversations he had with Feyerabend at Berkeley during the mid-1970s, and Grazia Borrini-Feyerabend.

7 A part of this is Feyerabend's conviction that students choosing to study at the institutions he taught at did not (or could not) choose to study there (let alone choose to study this or that topic) freely due to the supposedly poor state of other educational institutions.

To be clear, Feyerabend was not against grading *tout court*. He grants that

> business, religions, special professions such as science or prostitution, have a
> right to demand that their participants and/or practitioners conform to stan-
> dards they regard as important, and that they should be able to ascertain their
> competence. I also admit that this implies the need for special types of edu-
> cation that prepare a man or a woman for the corresponding 'examinations'.
> (Feyerabend, 1975a)

So professionalisation can include forms of grading. However, as we saw
above, there is a tension in Feyerabend's view that he seems unaware of.
Professionalisation is supposed to be a sub-species of a general education,
and Feyerabend declares that grading should not be a part of a general education. It seems as if Feyerabend has two choices. The first is to claim that
grading should not be allowed in professionalisation and the second is that
professionalisation is (or, at least, can be) separated from a general education
and be a practice onto itself. There are also questions that would (or should)
have been more pressing to Feyerabend about where a philosophy course at,
say, UC Berkeley would fit into his more abstract schema. I will not try to
resolve this tension here, but merely highlight it as a point that requires further research.

3.3. *Lecturing as a Performance*

As is well known, Feyerabend was trained in the theatre and his thought was
greatly influenced by Bertolt Brecht.[8] This had a more sweeping importance
for Feyerabend's views on scientific method,[9] specifically on the importance
of storytelling, but also on his view of the methods of a lecturer. A teacher,
according to Feyerabend, should be a performer – as if they were enacting a
one-person play for an audience. Such a play would not only pay attention to
the words that are uttered, but the way they are spoken, the *mise-en-scène*,
and so on. Plays also have the advantage of communication *contradictions
at the same time* (see Couvalis, 1987, p. 117ff). Feyerabend during his lectures often used various theatrical methods to convey the argument he was
lecturing about. For example, Donald Gillies recalls Feyerabend leaping to
illustrate the infamous Tower Argument for the immobility of the earth: 'I
remember Feyerabend explaining this argument in characteristically dramatic

8 See Feyerabend (1967, 1975c) for relevant discussion and Couvalis (1986, 1987) for
   extended analysis.
9 Feyerabend quotes Brecht as the epigraph of the 1st edition of *Against Method*: 'Order
   is nowadays mostly where there is nothing. It's a deficiency' (Feyerabend, 1975a, p.
   17, my translation).

fashion by jumping in the air, and saying: "Look if the Earth really rotated, I should have landed on the other side of the room." This mode of exposition made the argument unforgettable for me' (Gillies, 2019, p. 107), Several audience members recall various times Feyerabend used his cane, which may have otherwise been an impediment to his performance, to make some points more emphatic than others.[10] He would use ridicule, hyperbole, taunts, and a variety of rhetorical devices to impress particular messages upon his audience. Feyerabend notoriously used these techniques in print as well. But it is in person where these techniques availed themselves to Feyerabend to suit his lecture style.

Such performances are not the mere enactments of an eclectic personality (although they were also this) but perform a particular function. Consider what happens when one watches a play for the purposes of more than mere entertainment. While there is usually a moral to the play, the primary purpose is to provoke – both intellectually and emotionally. While it goes without saying these days that one must lecture multiple perspectives on a given topic, Feyerabend's twist on this norm is particularly interesting. Provoking is not the same thing as making an argument that one should believe such and such – it is merely the invitation to take the idea seriously. It is because of this that Feyerabend thought that the performance-style of lecturing is not only more effective, but more compassionate: 'Enriching and changing knowledge, emotions, attitudes through the arts now seems to me a much more fruitful enterprise and also much more humane than the attempt to influence minds (and nothing else) by words (and nothing else)' (Feyerabend, 1978, p. 114). The reason for this is that a play, or story, in Feyerabend's mind is not a kind of propaganda for a worldview but something that has provides mere 'food for thought':

> The playwright (and his colleague, the teacher) must not try to anticipate the decision of the audience (of the pupils) or replace it by a decision of his own if they should turn out to be incapable of making up their own minds. Under no circumstances must he try to be a 'moral force.' A moral force, whether for good or for evil, turns people into slaves and slavery, even slavery in the service of The Good, or of God Himself is the most abject condition of all. This is how I see the situation today. (p. 108)

We can see how Feyerabend's view of the lecturer-as-performer follows from his views on freedom. A performer is better able to transmit not just the intellectual but the *emotional* content of a view, thus enabling 'understanding'

---

10 This story was recounted to me by Hanne Andersen, referring to lectures at ETH Zurich sometime during the early 1990s.

in Feyerabend's embodied sense. This allows the lecturer to promote free-dom more effectively. Moreover, we can see how the style of performance Feyerabend envisions does not interfere with a student's ability to make their own choices.

Finally, an important part of drama, for Feyerabend, is the *distancing effect* which he learned from Brecht (see Bai, 1998). The distancing effect involves intentionally trying to alienate an audience such that they recognise that the performance they are witnessing is being done by *performers* – they are not brought into the story, but are consciously aware that they are watching an act.[11] This is a crucial component of lecturing, for Feyerabend. The distancing effect allows the lecturer to captivate an audience without taking over their mind through various subconscious mechanisms that are blunted by a proper implementation of the distancing effect (see Frimberger, this volume).

4. *Internal Tensions*

Beneath all of this is a tension that lurks deep in Feyerabend's thought. This tension was not merely intellectual, but it affected his emotional compass with regard to his teaching duties. The tension, in essence, is an attempt to balance two inconsistent beliefs Feyerabend held:

1. Students should be free to pursue life as they see fit. Pushes to study alternative forms of life should only be done by those with a close familiarity of the student's ambitions, personality, capabilities, and so on.
2. Students should be exposed to a particular sub-set of forms of life that conflict with those that seem attractive to them.

Both (1) and (2) concern the proper practice of pluralism. With an indefinite number of forms of life to choose from, lecturers must make choices about *which ones* to teach. There are different options, all of which are principally open to an anarchist: teach them the views of their ancestors, teach them 'out there' views his students likely know nothing about, teach them 'absurd' views that conflict with their established beliefs, and so on. (1) dictates that this choice can only be made by those with a great deal of familiarity with the student's personal situation. (2) dictates a more particular sub-set of forms

---

11 For a parallel discussion, see Judith Butler's characterisation of drag qua artform and performativity (Butler, 2020).

of life – namely those mentioned in the final category. (1) does not abandon Feyerabend's normative ambitions to enable freedom, but claims that the details of how such norms would be converted into action should only be done by those who are situated to know how this can best be done in any particular case. (2) is a more heavy-handed normativity, that claims that Feyerabend knows *enough* about cultural norms and student proclivities to know how to maximise the freedom of his students. Consider a passage in *Science in a Free Society*, where (1) and (2) are both underlying Feyerabend's description of the situation he found himself in at Berkeley:

> In the years 1964ff Mexicans, Blacks, Indians entered the university as a result of new educational policies. There they sat, partly curious, partly disdainful, partly simply confused, hoping to get an 'education' ... What an opportunity, my rationalist friends told me, to contribute to the spreading of reason and the improvement of mankind! ... I felt very differently. For it dawned on me that the intricate arguments and the wonderful stories I had so far told to my more or less sophisticated audience might be just dreams, reflections of the conceit of a small group who had succeeded in enslaving everyone else with their ideas ... Were the arid sophistications which philosophers had managed to accumulate over the ages and which liberals had surrounded with schmaltzy phrases to make them palatable the right thing to offer to people who had been robbed of their land, their culture, their dignity and who were now supposed to absorb patiently and then to repeat the anaemic ideas of the mouthpieces of the oh so human captors? They wanted to know, they wanted to learn, they wanted to understand the strange world around them – did they not deserve better nourishment? Their ancestors had developed cultures of their own, colourful languages, harmonious views of the relation between man and man and man and nature whose remnants are a living criticism of the tendencies of separation, analysis, self-centredness inherent in Western thought .... These were the ideas that went through my head as I looked at my audience and they made me recoil in revulsion and terror from the task I was supposed to perform. For the task – this now became clear to me – was that of a very refined, very sophisticated slavedriver. And a slavedriver I did not want to be. (Feyerabend, 1978, pp. 118–119)

Here, Feyerabend is uncomfortable with knowing *what topics to teach*. Of course, as this passage makes clear, we know that Feyerabend rejects an approach to pedagogy that focuses on knowledge transfer. But the struggle here is more subtle. Feyerabend is not worried about what 'truth' to impart – he is committed to the view that this is not his task in the first place. Rather, he is concerned with what worldviews are *worth studying*. Perhaps much of what Feyerabend knows is pointless for students to learn and perhaps it is better worth their time to recapture the worldviews of their ancestors which was destroyed by cultural colonialism. His lack of certainty is propelled by (1)

However, the reason he is *uncomfortable* is because he is also propelled by (2) and wishes to challenge students and expose them to different forms of life. Which path should he take?

The path Feyerabend in fact took involved lecturing about worldviews he assumes his students would reject – voodoo, witchcraft, mysticism, and so on. He also invited many guest lecturers who were experts on such topics (this is less explained by any 'principle' Feyerabend held, but more likely was a result of his laziness). He also allowed students to lecture on issues concerning racism and police presence on campus. This can all be read as an attempt to balance (1) and (2). He makes various coarse-grained assumptions about his students and infers what worldviews should be taught and gives students some additional control over the course content. Additionally, Feyerabend made various assumptions about his students' desires as to why they were taking his course(s) and whether those desires were grounded in free decisions (in his sense) or because they had been brainwashed.

While this solution sounds reasonable, it does not definitively solve Feyerabend's dilemma. Perhaps he led students into pointless intellectual meanderings or undermined their own abilities to understand worldviews that were live options (to appropriate James' expression) to them. Or, perhaps he indeed stimulated his students and enabled their critical skills as he wished. What cannot be reasonably doubted is that Feyerabend tried his best to educate himself about his students. Below is a picture exemplifying this, where Feyerabend would meet with students outside of class and speak to them for hours about their lives and thoughts. He often frustrated students by spending most of the conversation asking about *them* rather than imparting some wisdom.

He met with students regularly, asking them detailed questions about their lives and dreams. He did whatever he could (within the bounds of his laziness and his limitations from his illnesses) to learn what his students needed. But, at the end of the day, there remains a tension: how can a teacher facing a bewildering amount of diversity with thousands of students who will not all be able or willing to have in-depth conversations about their lives (even assuming that students introspect effectively) decide on the course content? A top-down approach ignores the realities students are facing and a bottom-up approach, where students controlled the course, might enable dogmatism, and would not allow them to be exposed to new worldviews. This is, technically speaking, a practical problem with a theoretical upshot: How can one know what to teach while being unable to know what students need to know? 'Anything goes' does not give any direction; it only removes constraints on what can be taught.

Feyerabend Speaking to Students in a Park at Berkeley

4. Concluding Remarks

The primary purpose of this paper was to provide an overview of Feyerabend's understanding of education, connect it with his pedagogical practices, and detail some ways this theory of education is meant to address the problem of intellectual pollution. In a Feyerabendian spirit, his own views must be considered with the utmost scrutiny. Indeed, Feyerabend's account raises many questions that he did not answer and could undermine the plausibility of his broader views on education. Is there a reasonable distinction between what is willed by an individual and what is willed by society through an individual? Can the tension between forcing students to engage with forms of life they don't want to and respecting people's choices be resolved? If so, is it resolved in the same way when thinking about childhood education, postsecondary education, and so on? Can one be an educator without imposing beliefs upon their students, even if only implicitly? Empirically speaking, is Feyerabend's optimism that many worldviews he personally detested would wash out with good educational institutions? I do not have the space or the knowledge necessary to make any definitive endorsements or rejections here, but I wish to gesture towards a criticism of Feyerabend's theory that deserves further attention.

As mentioned, Feyerabend equates happiness and freedom. This equation can be understood in two ways. Either Feyerabend is analytically equating these two notions as intrinsically connected or Feyerabend is making an empirical hypothesis that the free will be happy, and the happy will be free. If it is the former, then much rests on the operationalisation of freedom and happiness or whether it is truly one concept ('free-happiness') that we are looking for. If we take freedom and happiness at their face value, it seems as if they are distinct states of being. Someone isn't happy when they are phenomenologically miserable and yet, conceivably at least, one can be unhappy and free (e.g. skilled in living life in many ways while depressed). Perhaps these two goals come apart, forcing Feyerabend to make a choice that he never did. Perhaps living the *simple, unexamined* life is all one really needs and the education system can be made optional for those who'd rather lay in a field and stare at the stars. This question, moreover, becomes all the more complicated when thinking about children.

References

Bai, R. (1998). Dances with Mei Lanfang: Brecht and the alienation effect. *Comparative Drama, 32*(3), 389–433.

Bailin, S., & Siegel, H. (2003). Critical thinking. In N. Blake, P. Smeyers, R. Smith, & P. Standish (Eds.), *The Blackwell guide to the philosophy of education* (pp. 181–193). Blackwell Publishing.

Bakhurst, D. (2011). *The formation of reason.* John Wiley & Sons.

Brown, M. J. (2021). Against expertise: A lesson from *Science in a Free Society?*" In K. Bschir & J. Shaw (Eds.), *Interpreting Feyerabend: Critical essays* (pp. 191–212). Cambridge University Press.

Butler, J. (2020). Performative acts and gender constitution: An essay in phenomenology and feminist theory. In C. McCann, Kim, S.-K., & Ergun, E. (Eds.), *Feminist theory reader: Local and global perspectives* (pp. 353–361). Routledge.

Callan, E. (1997). *Creating citizens: Political education and liberal democracy.* Clarendon Press.

Couvalis, S. G. (1986). Should philosophers become playwrights? *Inquiry, 29,* 451–457.

Couvalis, S. G. (1987). Feyerabend's epistemology and Brecht's theory of the drama. *Philosophy and Literature, 11*(1), 117–123.

Feyerabend, P. (1963). How to be a good empiricist: A plea for tolerance in matters epistemological." In B. Baumrin (Ed.), *Philosophy of science: The Delaware seminar* (Vol. 2, pp. 3–39). Interscience Publishers.

Feyerabend, P. (1964). Realism and instrumentalism: Comments in the logic of factual support. In M. Bunge (Ed.), *Critical approaches to science and philosophy* (pp. 260–308). The Free Press.

Feyerabend, P. (1967). On the improvement of the sciences and the arts, and the possible identity of the two. In *Proceedings of the Boston colloquium for the philosophy of science 1964/1966* (pp. 387–415). Springer.

Feyerabend, P. (1970). Consolations for the specialist. In I. Lakatos & A. Musgrave (Eds.), *Criticism and the growth of knowledge* (pp. 197–231). Cambridge University Press.

Feyerabend, P. (1975a). *Against method*. Verso Books.

Feyerabend, P. (1975b). 'Science.' The myth and its role in society. *Inquiry, 18*(2), 167–181.

Feyerabend, P. (1975c). Let's make more movies. In J. Bontempo & S. Odell (Eds.), *The owl of Minerva: Philosophers on philosophy* (pp. 201–210). McGraw-Hill.

Feyerabend, P. (1978). *Science in a free society*. Verso Books.

Feyerabend, P. (1995). *Killing time: The autobiography of Paul Feyerabend*. University of Chicago Press.

Feyerabend, P. (2011). *The tyranny of science*. Wiley.

Gillies, D. A. (2019). Lakatos, Popper, and Feyerabend: Some personal reminiscences. *Dilemata, 29,* 93–108.

Kusch, M. (2021). Epistemological anarchism meets epistemic voluntarism: Feyerabend's *Against Method* and van Fraassen's *The Empirical Stance*. In K. Bschir & J. Shaw (Eds.), *Interpreting Feyerabend: Critical essays* (pp. 89–113). Cambridge University Press.

Mill, J. S. (1973/2006). *Collected works of John Stuart Mill* (Vol. 7, J. M. Robson, Ed.). Liberty Fund.

Radcliffe, E. (2018). *Hume, passion, and action*. Oxford University Press.

Tambolo, L. (2015). A tale of three theories: Feyerabend and Popper on progress and the aim of science. *Studies in History and Philosophy of Science Part A, 51,* 33–41.

The Staged Cage? Education, Reality, and 'Illusions' of Freedom: A Dialogue

Nicola Robertson, Vijayita Prajapati, and Yueling Chen

1. Introduction

In this dialogue, we posit a hypothetical conversation between three contemporary female philosophers: Pauline Feu-d'un-Coude, whose name, and attitude, is loosely based on Paul Feyerabend himself; Hina Arora, who is influenced by the life and work of Hannah Arendt; and Carmen Manusia – the quasi-Greek chorus of the piece –whose name is a play on the idea of the 'Common Man'. Carmen represents those qualities that Buchler (1942) identified when discussing the relations between philosophers and 'common men': the common (hu) man is, paradoxically, both naturally sceptical of what is presented to them as purely ideal, but will generalise, with little evidence, notions that seem obvious based on their experience. Comparing this to a Platonic ideal of philosophers as the only people capable of attaining knowledge from ideas (Erler, 2004), would seem to suggest that philosophers and so-called common people are pit antonymously as deep and shallow thinkers. As Carmen will come to show, this is not what we are attempting to underscore in this dialogue. The intention is to create a third, neutral voice who philosophises differently to the other two antagonists; in a way that enables her to draw more on her experiences to eloquently pose her valid questions. While discussing the storming of the Capitol building in Washington DC, January 2021, their thoughts turn to questions of reality, education, and freedom inspired not only by this one shocking event, but within a general socio-political context where questions of what is 'real' or 'true' coincide with contrasting ideas of what it is to be 'free'.

Central to this conversation is the model of the stage, which Feyerabend introduces in his unfinished manuscript, Conquest of Abundance (1999). He makes the argument that artworks, and the aspect of 'reality' that the artist seeks to represent, can be interpreted as a stage set. The stage is set by the artist who selects the aspects to be represented and creates the conditions, which determine how the aspects are to be viewed; it is the viewer who makes the projection of [their] reality onto the stage.

While primarily concerned with artworks, Feyerabend also tells us that this model of the stage can be transferred readily to science – the scientist may set up a stage, an experiment, with resulting data interpretation a projection on a stage. In the case of both the sciences and art, external structures (social constraints, particular equipment) have an effect on the 'reality' that is subsequently projected. These external structures are what he calls 'projective devices' (Feyerabend, 1999, pp. 101–102) and include manufactured – as in his given case of Brunelleschi and the painting of the Baptisterium – and traditional/natural devices – such as beliefs, theories, and cultural norms.

The significance of the stage model of reality is the implication it carries for our notion of education. If an educator has the means to manufacture either the stage, or the projections, or both, this suggests a manipulative undertone in the educational act, which often goes overlooked as, it conflicts with any suggestion of education towards an idea of freedom as the ability to think independently, without recourse to external influences.

Taking all of this into consideration and introducing notions from Arendt (1961) such as natality, and education as the older generation's responsibility to the younger, the interlocutors begin by discussing the stage model of reality, before moving on to think about it in relation to education and how this ties in with notions of freedom and what (education in) a free society might look like (with some reference to Feyerabend's own ideas about this from Science in a Free Society, 1978). All of this is loosely captured under the lens of the unfolding chaos of Trumpism and Republican unrest.

Our intention was to create a piece which at least captures some of what we interpret the spirit of Feyerabend might have enjoyed: a humorous, thoughtful, entertaining dialogue which disrupts generally accepted notions of the conventional written form of a piece of academic work.

2. A Brief Justification of the Dialogue Format

The philosophical dialogue, in our view, is in crisis. With few exceptions[1] we rarely read them in academic journals; even less do we see them performed

1 Our observations here are based on the anglophone discourse in which we are centred. In Germany, societies for philosophical dialogue keep the art form alive: see especially the Society for Socratic Philosophy (https://www.socraticdialogue.org/en/) which reflects our own reverence for the dialogue form.

at conferences. Despite philosophy's so-called performative turn over the last decade, in which some circles have accepted that thought is staged in many forms beyond the written article, book or spoken presentation (Feitosa, 2020), there still appears to be a reluctance to embrace the performance aspect fully. Given how he lovingly described his enthusiasm for the theatre in his autobiographical work (Feyerabend, 1995), it is not illogical to suggest that Feyerabend himself may have been buoyed by the nascent field of performance philosophy.

We view the dialogue as a form of abundant potentiality. It is a representation of the immediacy of a natural discourse, and indeed has more in common with the notion than the asynchronous methods of communication we often relate to modern academic 'discourse'. A dialogue can be read, staged as an event, or occur in the most spontaneous of interactions. It can maintain numerous threads of multiple arguments as each interlocutor strives to make their point. Most importantly of all 'Philosophical dialogue is … that form of writing that best brings about the act of thinking itself' (Ewegen, 2019, pp. 56) and so is justifiably employed in any arena, such as that of this publication, in which the objective is to spark thought in the reader.

In Three Dialogues on Knowledge (1991), Paul Feyerabend exhibited his unique wit and artistry in this forgotten craft, and it is from this we are inspired not only in the creation of our dialogue, but in what it represents as a general rallying call for the revival of the dialogue in wider academic discourse.

3. Context of the Dialogue

Cue Background Sounds from a video of the Capitol riots. The voices of the protestors ring clear:

> *Stop the steal …… Where is Mike Pence? Nancyyyyyyyy Nanccyyyyyy …… Guys come on let's move ahead.* (Lewin, 2021)

As the American Drama played out on 6 January 2021 in the United States of America, three thinkers looked in disbelief at the montage. Their thoughts are initially drawn to how the perpetrators came to construct their version of reality.

4. Speakers

PF: Pauline Feu-d'un-Coude
HA: Hina Arora
CM: Carmen Manusia

HA: History seems to be repeating itself. Another leader is able to create conditions for such an event. And this is in the USA – the self-proclaimed defender of democracy! Here seems to be a group of people for whom 'the distinction between fact and fiction and the distinction between true and false no longer exist' (Arendt, 1958, p. 474). They seem to be subject to a totalitarian view of a leader feeding them an alternate picture of reality.

PF: Well, in this so-called post-truth era there is an increasingly blurry distinction between true and false. Post-truth might be defined as 'an ideological supremacy, whereby its practitioners are trying to compel someone to believe in something whether there is good evidence for it or not' (McIntryre, 2018, p. 12). The compulsion to believe does not necessarily rest in whether something is 'true' or not. Most people nowadays, I suspect, define true as what makes them comfortable, and false as what makes them uncomfortable and this is manipulated by such arbiters of post-truth. I suspect this is not what you mean, though. Tell me – what is the distinction between fact and fiction that you are talking about?

CM: *(despairingly)* Here you go again – asking questions that do not need to be asked. It is obvious – to distinguish fact from fiction, or true from false, we need to first understand the idea of truth and reality. My idea of reality and truth is sense and fact-based. Something concrete and sensual, that we can see, feel, and touch, such as an object; food perhaps in front of our eyes that we can feel and taste. It must be something proven to be right. Like science.

HA: And what happens when one discovers Telescopes and Microscopes or Mars Rover missions? Suddenly what you can see completely changes and the world beyond our planet, or microorganisms beyond human vision, come to light. Are they a new reality? No ... just a challenge to what our sensory understanding of reality is. I believe for anything to be considered reality, what we have sensorily perceived must also be similarly perceived and acknowledged by the others for us to consider it real. Take this group of people storming the Capitol, for example. They seem to perceive themselves as patriots and saving the law instead of breaking the law.

PF: Ah – so Hina, if I and everyone else were to lose all our sense faculties then reality would disappear? Reality cannot be purely external. All arguments about reality have an existential component: we view things as real when they play an important part in the life, we prefer (Feyerabend, 1999) and some of the things we find to be important have nothing to do with our senses. These people in the US – for them, the myth of nation, that is to say the bewitching tableau they hold of the idea of nation (Ellul, 1973) is real, so nationalism is real, and would still be real even if they were without sight, taste, touch, smell, sound. Reality – and the stage on which we project it – is the product of both external devices and internal interpretations. When Brunelleschi created his device for viewing the Baptisterium, he only created the device and the conditions for looking at his artwork. Each viewer would then come to make their own interpretations based on what they were given (Feyerabend, 1999). Each of these has weight in the construction of reality. In my opinion, even things that we take to be 'objective' are nothing but elaborate projections on a stage fashioned by the structures of the society we live in. These people in the States, they project a reality manipulated by the all-powerful Trump, on a stage built by nationalism.

Anyway, science is staged too …

CM: Science? Staged? How is it possible to stage science? I can accept your point that something can be staged. When access to information is uneven, manipulation can be done under an imbalance of power. Trump is using people's divided opinion of what's good for the country to his advantage, and to serve his own agenda, but this only happens where subjectivity comes into play. Objective facts such as science are different. Science cannot be staged! Science is proven through theories and experiments and endless studies.

PF: Scientists are unavoidably located within cultures and societies, which impact on the theories they choose to focus on, the experiments they carry out and the studies they endlessly pursue. Subjectivity therefore cannot be separated from objectivity. It influences the instruments they choose and the observations they make. A stage is set when a scientist sets up the conditions for their experiment; the resulting data, the so-called 'facts', is the reality projected onto the stage of the experiment. It cannot be separated from the social, cultural, and political context of the scientist. How can the 'reality' of science be anything other than projected on an ideological stage?

HA: And they use the language of science to share their reality, which, in itself, alienates common people from both the experience and the rigour of thought.

CM: I understand there are human elements even in science, but surely subjectivity can be set aside when the aim is the accumulation of objective fact over anything else? If all the mathematical proofs and calculations about the appearance of the black hole match with the actual photo of the black hole, does that not prove science reveals reality as an objective fact? Further, surely a person – a scientist, maybe – can trust their own sense and judgement to distinguish reality and fiction at least at a very basic level, in their own living environment, for example? It may be a cliché, but we do have to 'see it to believe it'!

HA: If only one could trust their sense of seeing. If I were to ask you for a universal reality – an 'a priori' truth – you would probably say $1 + 1 = 2$. However, what if it is one spoon of sugar plus one spoon of salt mixed in water, could there still be two spoons that could be counted in the mixture? $1 + 1$ here still equals 1. So, reality would always need some background against which it is a reality; in this case mathematically $1+1$ is always 2, but in a recipe, it changes shape and form to become a completely new substance.

PF: Yes – the background you refer to is what I might call the stage. In your case it is built on a mathematical ideology.

HA: This stage then presents a dominant way of thinking and ideology, and those less initiated in the dominant ideology can only become observers, while retaining a sense of trust that this is 'true' because they have been instructed that this is the case. The language, though, is inaccessible. We communicate through a language – a shared language that everyone can understand – but when the scientists, for example, communicate their work, they use a language that most non-scientists cannot understand, thereby slowly alienating understanding of the reality they seek to present.

CM: How is that the case? The language of science and math is taught in our schools, colleges, and universities. It is not like there is no initiation at all. The scientific language is accessible by the general public. Also, these discoveries and calculations are challengeable. They can be proven or refuted countless times by others. So, science is completely open. Besides, we have many more tools these days to help make sense of scientific fact, or even verify falsehoods. More technology and gadgets have been made available to the public, not least the omnipotent internet and ubiquitous smart phones. They help to give out information about all scientific debate and they do not choose a side.

HA: Today we do use many technologies, gadgets, etc., but we are mere front-end users. Most of us have very little understanding of what goes on inside the technologies or the gadgets. Do you not think this has created a total decoupling of thinking and knowledge?

PF: I can see how, in these kinds of cases, 'user interfaces' might be representative of a reductive process. Complexity becomes simplified – perhaps for ease of use, or perhaps to manipulate ...

HA: It is an avenue for possible manipulation. Such so-called modern realities, which can only be expressed in the language of math, science, codes, or algorithms, no longer lend themselves to normal expressions in speech and thought. Reality, then, could become what the algorithms believe you must know or sense and not what is sensory or commonly established. Gadgets that start predicting are starting to think for you, and slowly create a staged reality, in which you are a mere viewer.

CM: So basically, nothing is real, including language, science, and reality? Since nothing is without human intervention, and if everything we know is cultural and historical, are you saying there is no objective truth?

PF: That moves from the question of reality to the problem of truth. You have conflated them while one (truth) is only a linguistic relation to the other. We are just pointing out reality is subjectively based, and not reliant on objective facts. Even the definition of objectivity is subjective. *(Incredulously)* Of course, if you can point to a single universal truth that no one here could argue against, I will give you one million pounds. You would go down in the annals of philosophical greatness. Plato would be calling on you – the Philosopher Queen – to lead his venerated Republic ...

CM: *(Rolls eyes)* Ok – no need for flippancy! I guess I understand what you are trying to say. Neither of you seem to agree with me that reality is something fully external, constant, and unchanging. I see you believe it is dynamic, subjective, and ideological. Could it be somewhere in between?

PF: *(Sarcastic)* Ever the diplomat ...

CM: Maybe it is more likely this: reality is probably neither entirely fixed, nor entirely subjective – thus reality draws from the intersubjective? This suggests malleable interpretations of shared elements of reality. Your stage, Pauline, would be something constructed of a certain stability to withstand intersubjective projections of reality – the stage is not a thing that exists for one person only.

PF: *(Wryly)* That seems realistic ...

HA: That also presumes that the stage exists external to oneself. And, therefore, are you saying that everything on the stage is unreal? Is the stage set for a projected experience designed by the stage master for a collective and not an individual?

PF: By virtue of their appearances on the stage, the projections would be real by association.

CM: Ok, Ok, although now I have more questions! Reality feels to me like something we should be certain about – do you agree?

PF: I sense a shift from our ontological discussion to an epistemological one! We will indulge you, although I do not understand this imperative for certainty about reality, or about anything.

CM: I see, but let me explain what I mean. If we are saying reality is constructed in part by (inter)subjective interpretations, there cannot be any notable distinction between fiction and reality. We cannot lay claim to knowing anything about reality if there is no such distinction to be made.

PF: Why is this important?

CM: If we cannot know anything about reality, then everything we have discussed until now is, in fact, a futile speculation on a concept that has no bearing on how we live or exist. If we *can* know things about reality – such as the means of making distinctions between it and fiction – then *how* could we know it? Is there a way that we can learn to differentiate between reality and fiction? Who teaches us this and how? Is this the realm of education?

PF: You really do have questions! What do *you* think the role of education is in this?

CM: Education should dispense knowledge about what is true and real so I would suggest it has some kind of role.

HA: I agree with you, but only in part. Education is one of the primary activities of our human society. It should be the process of gently introducing the children to the world they have been born into and to pass on the goods of collective learning so far, presenting them with a chance to identify truths and realities (Arendt, 1961).

PF: I also agree with you Hina, but again only in part. I say that education – the right kind of education – should be the most necessary aid to life. It should not be an attempt to carbon copy the contents of older minds onto the younger; yet this is what we see (Feyerabend, 1991). Education has become a disabling factor in our ability to live fully because in it one reality is presented as the only one with no exit clause.

CM: It sounds like you are describing indoctrination.

PF: *(shrug)* Perhaps. I see little distinction between the wrong kind of education and indoctrination.

CM: But there must be a distinction, right? There is something malevolent about indoctrination. As I understand it, indoctrination deals in falsehoods, but the educator could be teaching the very true and real epithets of medicine, for example. How could that be like indoctrination?

PF: But where do we expect that they get these 'real' and 'true' epithets? Are not theories and observations on biology limited to what has been framed as the discipline of 'Medicine' in this particular time and culture, ignoring other theories and observations from other times and cultures? All of this is presented to the student without an exit clause. This is what I mean by wrong education.

This is almost indistinguishable from an indoctrination that seeks to instil an unshakable worldview in a student who is not simultaneously provided with the faculty to evaluate it critically (White, 1970), or indeed to identify that this is not the only available means of looking at the world. That unshakable worldview could be, for example, that the universe was formed by the Big Bang, or by a God in seven days. The indoctrinator in either case may find these explanations to be true. Indoctrination certainly has a common, pejorative connotation but it is an unfair generalisation to assume that it deals only in untruths.

HA: I agree, I think it is not that simple. The child is constantly being educated to become a part of the world and to ensure the continuity of the world. We hang on to the potentiality of young people because they are our hope for the future. But in this hope also exists a need to control, we – the old – want to prescribe what the world should look like and what the world needs to be. We want to dictate a vision for the future and use education as the stage to make that happen.

PF: Education as dictatorship?

CM: You might be right. Certain agendas in education are being promoted to ensure some of our cultural ways continue, but what you described does not sound like education in our life, in a free society.

PF: So you say. Tell me, then, what *does* education look like in a free society?

HA: Well, philosophically there are many answers but no common agreement. We wish to educate for a free society, but, just like our conceptualisations of education, our concept of free society is varied.

CM: If we have any hope of reaching a consensus, we need to first discuss our views on education and on a free society.

PF: OK, since we have discussed education somewhat already, let us agree on one conceptualisation that it should aid us in life, to identify and navigate co-existing realities. Agreed?

CM & HA: *(sounds of reluctant assent).*

PF: With this in mind then, I ask you again, what is a free society?

CM: Mine is simple, it is where all individuals have the freedom to choose their lives, their careers, their friends, their government. They can do what they want. Free will and free choices – that is what our modern world is! At least, that is what we are aiming for, perhaps?

HA: Perhaps not, given that the world of people is not individual but collective. Do you not think this emphasis on individual freedom has led to a 'loss of the collective world' (Passerin, 2006) that has restricted, or sometimes even eliminated, the public sphere of action and speech in favour of the private world of introspection and the private pursuit of economic interests?

As a society we have slowly focused on homogeneity and conformity to replace plurality and freedom. Our society is one where isolation and loneliness have eroded all spontaneous forms of living together. Yet, it is precisely this isolation which unites us psychologically and leaves us predisposed to influences (Ellul, 1973) which may be pernicious, or may not. This illusion of free society is just that, an Illusion .... *(sighs with derision)* And it is in this background of individual freedom, we are educating in the hopes of creating new generations of free citizens of the world.

PF: Sadly, with the education we espouse, what we actually get are the children of tomorrow imitating the leading idiots of today. A 'free society' is not necessarily only about the free will detailed by Carmen, it is about giving equal weight to traditions and understanding that, while we are rooted to a particular perspective or ideology by virtue of socialisation, this is not necessarily the 'right' one (if there is even such a thing). A society, which accepts this is one that is much more open to possibilities, as is the student educated in such a society.

HA: When society is collective, whose freedom must we consider? The freedom of the society or that of the individual? Is it every individual who believes in their personal freedom, or collective freedom of all the individuals that make a society, such that the freedom of the society transcends that of the aggregate individual freedoms?

CM: I am confused now. Are these concepts discrete, or contradictory, or enmeshed? If the society is a collective one, would not education for individual freedom eventually lead to collective freedom so surely this is what should be prioritised?

HA: Freedom is hardly linear, as you have skilfully described, there is more relativity to it. If we take a step back into the idea of freedom, you will find there is no inner freedom unless one experiences freedom in the outer world. Freedom needs a common recognition by, and in, others to uphold that freedom. 'Freedom need[s], in addition to mere liberation, the company of other men who [are] in the same state, and ... a common public space to meet them' (Arendt, 1961, p. 148).

To be clear, I am not talking about the freedom to choose between alternatives, or even the 'liberum arbitrium' said to be given to us by God, but the freedom to actualise new beginnings or to do something unexpected, which is not so easy to attain. This conceptualisation of freedom factors in human behaviour and thinking; therefore, the question of freedom is laid bare to interpretations, influences, and conditioning.

Just as a performance needs an audience, the actions of new beginnings need the presence and acknowledgement of others for it to be meaningful and real.

PF: I cannot disagree that there is unity in the inner, individual freedom of a person and the outer recognition of such freedom. And you are right to talk about interpretations – from these, there is no escape since all that we understand to be 'true' is formed by interpretation. But there is a logical anomaly in your argument: if one 'needs' others to recognise their freedom, as you say, then one's freedom becomes reliant on others. Those others, therefore, hold the power to exert or rescind freedoms, and it is entirely justifiable for them to grant freedom to one person at the cost of others, based on whatever they find fair or just. This certainly would result in an illusion, or mirage, of freedom but in a more sinister fashion than what you have described.

CM: I am still unclear on the conceptualisation of 'Freedom' to which you both allude. If I believe Pauline, it is the acknowledgement of heterogeneous realities. If I listen to Hina, individual freedom is a mirage, but collective freedom – resting on these illusory individual freedoms – can exist among people. So, if it isn't simply the ability to choose and do as we wish that I suggested, what are the essential criteria for identifying a 'free society'?

PF: In a free society, traditions that give substance to the lives of people must be given equal rights and equal access to key positions in society no matter what other traditions think about them. We should demand this as aspiring members of such a society (Feyerabend, 1978). In a free society, a shaman would have equal standing with a surgeon, and we – in the West – would not so openly indoctrinate into the primacy of science and all that this entails, to give an example. 'Education' if we consider it now as the system, pushes one view at the expense of all others – perhaps inadvertently, perhaps deliberately.

HA: Education further is being used to create a divide. Society decides who gets educated (Eligibility); the content of their education (Curriculum); and how they get evaluated (Assessment). Society also comes to decide what the rewards of education are (if any). Whether you were a woman in ancient Greece, or a child in today's time, what is right for you and your future is determined by policies and people who are seeking ways of determining what is normal and what is not. Opening up alternatives would mean giving the freedom to individuals to make these decisions.

PF: Indeed, societies do make these decisions. In my version of education in a free society, all members of such a society would be free to look at alternate views of eligibility (or abolish it), look at alternate views of assessment (or abolish it), and the curriculum would be wide open to ensure that no one subject discipline, and its associated ideology, is encouraged more than any other.

CM: What happens if the members of the society choose to abolish education entirely? Might know education at all be just as wrong as an education without an exit clause? From your own description this is a valid outcome.

PF: You have correctly exposed a curious conundrum, indeed. The possibility of no education must have the opportunity to arise from the freedom I have described. On the other hand, the exit clause can also only arise from the freedom I have described – the two situations are analogous.

CM: But doesn't the freedom of the older generation of the society to abolish education simultaneously take away the freedom of the younger generation to be educated? How can that be justified?

HA: As I said earlier, the older generation have a responsibility towards the world, and therefore towards the younger generation. Therein lies the justification.

PF: And as I said earlier, this is just a reflection of power from one group to the other, thus, inherently unfree.

(A short awkward pause ensues as each speaker reflects on this outcome)

CM: So, I am keen to know, is education still a *good* thing? We are always encouraged to seek an education with a view to some kind of freedom: intellectual freedom, or economic freedom. Some even believe they can get it through education. Surely, we cannot now be suggesting that it might impede freedom!

HA: Education can impede freedom if we do not recognise the possibility of freedom to act. The fact that someone is born and has the potential to do something completely new cannot be emphasised enough. It is our responsibility to nurture that potential, as it is only in action that a potential for a different outcome exists. Education is our responsibility as an older generation to pass the goods of our collective learning and understanding, but it's also a chance to allow the younger generation to scrutinise and decide whether it works for them still. Education is the point at which we decide whether we love the world enough to assume responsibility for it and by the same token save it from that ruin which, except for renewal, except for the coming of the new and the young, would be inevitable (Arendt, 1961).

It is in this acknowledgement that freedom is letting go of our assumptions of what is right, what is good and most importantly what is necessary for their survival. It is an understanding that what is valuable for the older generation may not be considered valuable by the younger. It is providing not a stage where actors come in and do the part, but a blank book where they use the learnings and the beliefs and write their own plays, their own destinies.

PF: *(with mock authority)* Come on now! Even in those empty pages imbued with hopeful potentiality we find ourselves locked into a cultural framework from which escape seems distant. Consider – in whose language do the young write their plays if it is not somehow evolved from the language of the old? I assume that if the young are to write their own plays, they also intend to perform them? If the play and the stage are analogous, then (a free) life and education/reality might also be considered analogous. Which becomes, in turn, paradoxical since 'education' at least as we understand it today works against the potential for a 'free society'.

If I suggest that education, within its stage setting and stage projecting role regarding reality, has the potential to either create or diminish freedom (depending on the educator's intention), my question to you is, how can we educate for freedom? Or should we?

CM: Maybe we should not? Assuming the purpose and the destination of education is freedom, would it not be problematic to assume the education for freedom would lead to a free society given that education itself can make no guarantee of any outcome?

PF: It is problematic to assume anything.

CM: So true! Although, as Hina mentioned, education is predetermined by culture and context. It sets the stage for projections of reality and influences the projections themselves. This surely strips education from the notion of individual freedom. So long as education is controlled, so long as there is human interference behind it, then the notion of education itself can only be set for a relativity of freedom.

Also, prejudgment and intention are already embedded in education regardless of the intention itself. Even if the intention is to create freedom, it probably ends up diminishing it. At the risk of offering another well-worn cliché: the road to hell is paved with good intentions! Therefore, the freedom education creates, if it can create, can only be perpetuated under a contained environment. Can that still be considered as freedom?

HA: This paradox is further emphasised when one stops to really seek evidence of reality and begins to blindly believe the perspectives given, almost becoming a consumer of said words, rather than a thinker letting the stage influence him; thereby slowly becoming caged into those beliefs and realities while believing oneself to be free.

CM: Are they not free? They make the choice to consume rather than critique.

PF: Is that an entirely *free* choice, in the most accurate sense of the word? A choice that has been directed, openly or surreptitiously, must at least lose some element of its free-ness.

HA: My point, indeed. Some individuals fail to realise that their choices and actions are influenced by the agenda of the society, or of agents within the society, and cannot really be attributed to free choice in the strictest sense. As much as decisions to act can be driven by rationality (and this we might confuse for a free will) they can be as influenced by appeals to irrationality (Ellul, 1973). The people storming the Capitol truly believe they are free to storm the building and stop the certification and they are doing so for a greater good – a rational decision borne from an irrational passion (patriotism). They fail to recognise the manipulation of their thinking process, which has been systemically encouraged through a staged propaganda by agents with a vested interest in directing the thoughts and behaviours of people in particular ways.

CM: *(Incredulous)* Propaganda! Indoctrination! I cannot believe we are still discussing these words alongside education! It now sounds like educators, at least those in places like schools, colleges, and universities, could be those kinds of manipulative agents. They want students to think and behave in particular ways too.

PF: *(Impatiently)* Of course! And if they engage in the wrong kind of education, they might even be successful! Perhaps the freest way to educate is not to educate at all, or – as in the case of the ignorant schoolmaster (Rancière, 1991) – do nothing, assume all men have equal intelligence, and watch as they educate themselves. Still, the self-educated man will use their education, or lack of, in the building, and projecting of, their own realities. It is likely that the prevailing social structure and culture will also have a hand in this. On the other hand, in his education at least he will not be pushed in a particular direction by people with ulterior motives – people with particular ideological goals, such as those esteemed politicians inciting riots in the Capitol, for example.

CM: I guess there's no such a thing as total freedom, especially when thinking about education. We are always trying to strengthen the future from our current position of understanding the present and predicting what could be, so we are always chained to the past while simultaneously tethered to the future. There are probably always going to be some sort of set forms to follow, that is somewhat unshakable at times. Just as the controllers of the education system somewhere benefit by this tethering and try to avoid revolutions of thought and action, so too does the future miss out on an opportunity for a new way of thinking and being ....

HA: You could almost say we are locked in a cage ....

PF: A staged cage!

CM: (exasperated) It sounds so pessimistic! Now I remember why I avoid talking to you ... It falls to me, I suppose, to look at the bright side (if we deign to admit there is one). Bear in mind that all cages have escape mechanisms. While these cages may seem unbreakable, there are always some people strong enough to free themselves, at least in part, and prepare the stage for a new production or a new action It may be that education's back door, which you mentioned earlier Pauline, offers one such potential escape mechanism.

(The idea that education has the potential to be a hopeful notion inspires nods of agreement all round. While our interlocutors seem to have reached a consensus the discussion, of course, never really ends – it is one that continues not only among our three speakers, but widely across education discourse for years to come, or so we envisage.)

References

Arendt, H. (1958). *The origins of totalitarianism*. Meridian Books.
Arendt, H. (1961). *Between past and future: Six exercises in political thought*. The Viking Press.
Arendt, H. (1978). *Between past and future: Eight exercises in political thought*. Penguin.
Buchler, J. (1942). The philosopher, the common man and William James. *The American Scholar*, 4(11), 416–426.
Ellul, J. (1973). *Propaganda*. Random House.
Erler, M. (2004). Socrates in the cave: Platonic epistemology and the common man. *Plato Journal [Online]*, 4.
Ewegen, S. M. (2019). What is philosophical dialogue? In B. Stocker & M. Mack (Eds.), *The Palgrave handbook of philosophy and literature* (pp. 41–59). Palgrave Macmillan.

Feitosa, C. (2020). Borders between performing arts and philosophy. *Brazilian Journal on Presence Studies, 10*(1), 1–25. https://doi.org/10.1590/2237-266092410

Feyerabend, P. (1978). *Science in a free society*. NLB.

Feyerabend, P. (1991). *Three dialogues on knowledge*. Blackwell.

Feyerabend, P. (1995). *Killing time*. University of Chicago Press.

Feyerabend, P. (1999). *Conquest of abundance: A tale of abstraction versus the richness of being*. University of Chicago Press.

Lewin, W. (2021, 27 July). *Video of capitol riot shown during First Jan. 6 committee hearing*. https://www.youtube.com/watch?v=DXnHIJkZZAs

McIntyre, L. (2018). *Post-truth*. The MIT Press.

Passerin M. (2006). *Hannah Arendt*. https://plato.stanford.edu/archives/fall2019/entries/arendt/

Ranciere, J. (1991). *The ignorant schoolmaster: Five lessons in intellectual emancipation* (K. Ross, Trans.). Stanford University Press.

White, J. P. (1970). Indoctrination. *Journal of Philosophy of Education, 4*(1), 107–120.

Notes on Contributors

YUELING CHEN is a current PhD student at the University of Strathclyde, Scotland, Glasgow. She is working in the field of linguistics and early childhood education. Adopting the mixed-method approach, she explores children's understanding, experience, and perception of foreign language study. She is interested in and publishes broadly in the fields of philosophy, pedagogy, literature, and popular culture. She tutors several modules for the School of Education. Alongside her teaching, she assists on an ongoing leadership research project as Research Assistant. Before her PhD journey, she completed her MSc in Education Studies in 2019 at the University of Strathclyde.

SEBASTIAN ENGELMANN, Dr. phil., is Junior Professor for History and Theory of Education at the University of Education in Karlsruhe. He studied Social Sciences and English at the University of Oldenburg and completed his Bachelor's degree there with distinction. He then studied Educational Science in the Master's program and Applied Ethics in the Master's program at the University of Jena. He also completed these courses with distinction. He completed his doctoral dissertation at the University of Jena on the socialist educator Minna Specht, making a relevant contribution to research on the history of socialist pedagogy in the interwar period. After a time of employment as a prae-doc in Jena, Sebastian Engelmann moved to the University of Tübingen as a post-doc, where he was able to expand his expertise in the field of history and theory of education at the renowned Institute of Educational Science there. This was followed by a call to a junior professorship in Theory and History of Education at the University of Education in Karlsruhe, where he teaches in both the bachelor's and master's programs in teacher training. Sebastian Engelmann conducts research on the history and theory of education, on alternative education, and on democratic education. He has published numerous monographs, articles, book chapters and edited volumes on these topics. His current book *Lebensformen des Demokratischen: Pädagogische Impulse* is currently being critically discussed in Germany. He is co-editor of the journal *Museum und Bildung* and a member of numerous funded networks.

JANE ESSEX is a Reader at the University of Strathclyde, Glasgow, UK. Her main work is in the field of Initial Teacher Education. Her research focus is inclusion in STEAM (science, technology, engineering, arts and mathematics) and her research focuses on how STEM can be made accessible to all learners. She is an active member of the Royal Society of Chemistry and was awarded their Inclusion and Diversity Award in 2019. She has recently written her first book: *Inclusive and Accessible Secondary Science: How to Teach Science Effectively to Students with Additional or Special Needs* (2023).

KATJA FRIMBERGER (PhD) holds a Master of Arts in Theatre Studies from University College Cork in Ireland and a Master in Education (with English and German) from Universität Hildesheim in Germany, Lower Saxony – where she also trained as a secondary school teacher. Katja was awarded a full three-year PhD research scholarship from the University of Glasgow's School of Education (in Scotland) in the area of Applied Drama and Theatre. Her project explored international students' lived experiences of interculturality through a performance-based research pedagogy, drawing on German theatre maker Bertolt Brecht's theatre and actor training theory and practice. Katja subsequently worked at her Alma Mater as Research Associate for the three-year UK's Arts and Humanities Research Council's (AHRC) funded £2mill. Grant project 'Researching Multilingually at the Borders of the Body, Language, Law & the State', where she theorised the role of arts-based research methods in multilingual settings. She was a lecturer in Theatre at Brunel University London and, now back in Glasgow, she is a lecturer in Education at the University of Strathclyde. Katja's research focuses on the philosophy of theatre/film/intercultural education. She has published on German theatre maker/theorist Bertolt Brecht's and Latvian director Asja Lācis' theatre pedagogy; arts-based research and intercultural communication pedagogy. She regularly collaborates (as actor, producer, educator) on narrative-based film-making projects with filmmaker Simon Bishopp and was project lead on a range of film and digital animation education research/ knowledge exchange projects, collaborating with stakeholders in the charity/ education sector. Her projects received funding through Creative Scotland, the Paul Hamlyn Foundation and the School for Social Entrepreneurs.

BERNHARD HEMETSBERGER, Dr. phil., graduated in Education at the University of Vienna, Austria. Furthermore, he passed a teacher's degree for History, Psychology and Philosophy for secondary schools (Gymnasien) there. Tertiary employments led him from the University of Vienna, Austria, as PraeDoc for Historical and Comparative Research on Education and Schooling, to the University of Federal Armed Forces Munich, Germany, as PostDoc for General Educational Science, to the University of Klagenfurt, Austria, as PostDoc for History and Theory of Education and Schooling. Bernhard Hemetsberger's research focuses on social perceptions of crises and their educationalisations, by combining general, historical and comparative educational approaches. In this vein, he also explores how scholars present (educational) concepts and answers to their contemporary problems. In doing so, further topics as politics and governance in educational systems, grading, (school) achievement, examination practices and assessment cultures are investigated. Notably, this is found in *Schooling in Crisis. Rise and Fall of a German-American Success Story* (2022) and *#Schule am Ende? Kritik und Probleme öffentlicher Bildung* (2023).

KARSTEN KENKLIES, Dr. phil., studied History of Science & Technology & Art, Philosophy, and Education Studies at University of Jena/ Germany and St. Andrews/ Scotland. Dr. phil. (2007) in History of Pedagogy, Professor in University Duisburg-Essen (Chair History of Pedagogy), & University of Jena (Chair Comparative Pedagogy); now Senior Lecturer University of Strathclyde/ Glasgow. Research Fellow at Tamagawa University, Tokyo, Japan; co-founder of ExET (www.exet.org). Research: Systematic structures of theories and practices of education in the context of the History of Ideas, of Science, Philosophy and Art (from antiquity to the present, along exoteric & esoteric lines of tradition); intercultural pedagogical dialogue, especially with East Asia. Monographs (selection): *Science as an Ethical Endeavour: Robert Fludd and the Reform of Education in the 17th Century* (2005); *Social Pedagogy and the Ethos of Reason: The Foundation of Education in the Platonic Dialogue Nomoi* (2007), (with R. Koerrenz et al.) *History of Pedagogy* (2017). Co-editor (e.g.): (with A. Blichmann) *Jewish Pedagogical Culture as Modern Tradition* (2015); (with M. Waldmann) *Queer Pedagogy* (2016); (with K. Imanishi) *Enlightenments: Modernisation in Europe and East Asia* (2016); (with D. Lewin) *East Asian Pedagogies* (2020); (with N. Friesen) *F. D. E. Schleiermacher's Outlines of the Art of Education. A Translation and Discussion* (2023).

DEIVIDE GARCIA DA SILVA OLIVEIRA has completed his Master's and PhD in Teaching, Philosophy and History of Sciences at the Federal University of Bahia-UFBA. He had a Post-doctorate position at the York University-Canada, and spent a period as Visiting fellow at the University of Pittsburgh-USA. He also holds a Master's degree in Logic and Philosophy of Science at the Universidad de Valladolid-Spain. Deivide's research focuses on scientific pluralism, Feyerabend's philosophy, Feyerabend's philosophy of education, history and philosophy of evolutionary theory, Galileo's methodology, Philosophy of Artificial Intelligence, and Science education. Deivide's PhD and Master degrees focused on Paul Feyerabend and his philosophy of science and education. He is also founder of the research group G-Efficientia at the Federal University of Recôncavo of Bahia, member of the Brazilian Association of Philosophy (ANPOF) with direct membership of the research group Philosophy, History and Sociology of Science and Technology, and member of the Brazilian Research group of Philosophy of Science, both hosted by ANPOF. Member of the Canadian Association of Philosophy of Science-CSHPS. Deivide is the author of many papers about Feyerabend; the most recent one is titled: 'The cosmological divergent proliferation in Feyerabend's pluralism' (2021). He acts as referee of many important national and international journals of philosophy and education, and as editor of the Brazilian edition of a book with translations from the *Stanford Encyclopedia of Philosophy* concerning the entries of Feyerabend, Popper, Kuhn and Lakatos.

VIJAYITA PRAJAPATI is a PhD candidate and tutor in the School of Education at the University of Strathclyde, Glasgow, UK. She tutors across the postgraduate and undergraduate programs and leads the MSc module in Alternative Education. Her doctoral thesis will examine the concepts of education and inner listening as they are understood in intentional communities, using Findhorn (Scotland) as a specific example. Her forthcoming work will see her contribute to the Handbook of Adult Education. Before undertaking her PhD, Vijayita earned an MEd in Adult Education, Community Development and Youth Work and has a postgraduate diploma in Adult Education from Indira Gandhi National Open University in New Delhi. Her interest in adult education stems from a long career as an adult educator, career developer and training and development specialist.

LÍLIA FERREIRA SOUZA QUEIROZ is a PhD Candidate at the Federal University of Bahia-UFBA in the program of Philosophy of Science & History of Science & Teaching of Science. She has been studying Feyerabend and education since her undergraduate studies and continues to engage with this topic under Deivide Garcia's supervision. She is also high school teacher of Biology (2017). Her master thesis is titled 'The Teaching of Scientific Errors Throughout a Historically Approach That Is Sensible to Context: Contributions from a Pluralist Epistemology' (2019). The PhD project is titled 'Erros Científicos: Perspectiva pluralista e as contribuições para a Educação Científica'. Among her papers are 'Epistemologically Progressivist and Traditionalist Analyses of Scientific Error in Rescher's, Allchin's and Feyerabend's Philosophies' (2021) (co-authored with Deivide Garcia), and 'The Relationship Between the History of Sciences and the Image of Science: The Case of Puerperal Fever in the 19th Century' (2018).

NICOLA ROBERTSON, PhD, is a Teaching Fellow in Education Studies at the University of Strathclyde Glasgow, UK where she teaches across the post-graduate and undergraduate programs. She earned her PhD in 2022 and her doctoral thesis asks the question of whether propaganda can be considered pedagogical. In 2019, she earned an MSc in Education Studies, also from Strathclyde, and she holds a BSc in Information Technology from the University of the West of Scotland. Her current and forthcoming published works focus on the disparate yet interlinking research areas of education, technology, philosophy, and popular culture.

JAMIE SHAW is a philosopher of science, currently employed as a Postdoctoral Researcher at Leibniz Universität in Hannover. Before this, he was a SSHRC Postdoctoral Researcher at the University of Toronto after completing his dissertation, entitled *A Pluralism Worth Having: Feyerabend's Well-Ordered Science*, at the University of Western Ontario in 2018. He is the co-editor of *Interpreting Feyerabend: Critical Essays* published with Cambridge University Press in 2021. His primary research interests are the methodological and political dimensions of science funding policy, twentieth-century philosophy of science (especially the work of Paul Feyerabend), and environmental philosophy. He has been involved in many organisations including the Paul K. Feyerabend Centenary Foundation, the Forum for Advancing Science and Education Through Philosophy, and Philosophy of Science, India.

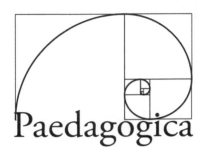

Paedagogica

Sebastian Engelmann, Norm Friesen and Karsten Kenklies
General Editors

Paedagogica publishes original monographs, translations, and collections reflecting the thought and practice long known, for example, as *le pédagogie* in French, *pedagogía* in Spanish, and *Pädagogik* in German. Pedagogy in this sense starts with the influence of one person or group on another—often an older generation on a younger. Pedagogy is not just about school or college, but interpenetrates many spheres of human activity, forming a domain of practice and study in its own right—one that is ethical in its implications and relational in its substance. This pedagogical tradition has been developed over hundreds of years, for example, by John Amos Comenius (Komenský), Jean-Jacques Rousseau, Johann Friedrich Herbart, Maria Montessori, and Janusz Korczak.

For additional information about this series or for the submission of manuscripts, please contact:

sebastian.engelmann@ph-karlsruhe.de
normfriesen@boisestate.edu
karsten.kenklies@strath.ac.uk

To order books, please contact our Customer Service Department:

peterlang@presswarehouse.com (within the U.S.)
orders@peterlang.com (outside the U.S.)

Or browse online by series:

www.peterlang.com

Printed by
CPI books GmbH, Leck